Leave No Child Behind

Leave No Child Behind

Behind

Preparing Today's Youth
for Tomorrow's World

JAMES P. COMER, M.D.

Foreword by Henry Louis Gates, Jr.

Yale University Press   New Haven and London

Set in Postscript Minion type by Integrated Publishing Solutions.
Printed in the United States of America.

Library of Congress Control Number: 2004304784

ISBN: 978-0-300-10391-5 (cloth)
ISBN: 0-300-10391-3 (cloth)

ISBN: 978-0-300-10967-2 (pbk.)
ISBN: 0-300-10967-9 (pbk.)

A catalogue record for this book is available from the Library of
Congress and the British Library.

The paper in this book meets the guidelines for permanence
and durability of the Committee on Production Guidelines
for Book Longevity of the Council on Library Resources.

10   9   8   7   6   5   4   3   2

Contents

Foreword

James Comer was born in 1934 in East Chicago, Indiana, one of five children born to Maggie and Hugh Comer, a house-keeper and a steel mill worker (one child died in infancy; the eldest child in the family was Louise, the daughter of Hugh Comer and his first wife). Maggie has become something of a celebrity in her own right on school curricula. In *Maggie's American Dream: The Life and Times of a Black Family,* Dr. Comer brought his mother's philosophy on life and learning to a broad public. Since its publication in 1988, the book has helped hundreds, perhaps thousands, of students understand the sacrifices and motivations of an earlier generation, the importance of education, and the crucial role played by family and community in achieving that education. The first part of the book is a transcription of Maggie's words, and they explain as clearly as anything else he has written Dr. Comer's fundamental principles of education, community, and leadership.

While everyone these days seems to talk about the need for school reform (some even talk about the children who have been left behind in our current public schooling crisis), Dr. Comer has devoted his career to facilitating the necessary reforms, to providing a uniform set of tools and opportuni-

fit as we try to figure out how schools can better serve the societies that house them.

Dr. Comer is the author or editor of eight books in which he has laid out, either individually or with his colleagues, a remedy for our schools that has proven time and again to have the desired results. They are *Beyond Black and White* (1972); *Black Child Care* (with Alvin F. Pouissant, 1975; revised as *Raising Black Children*, 1992); *School Power: Implications of an Intervention Project* (1980); *Maggie's American Dream: The Life and Times of a Black Family* (1988); *Rallying the Whole Village* (edited with Michael Ben-Avie, Norris M. Haynes, and Edward T. Joyner, 1996); *Waiting for a Miracle: Why Schools Can't Solve Our Problems, and How We Can* (1998); and *Child by Child* (edited with Ben-Avie, Haynes, and Joyner, 1999). Dr. Comer was a monthly and trusted contributor to *Parents* magazine between 1978 and 1994, and he has written hundreds of syndicated articles on children's health and development for numerous publications. He has also served as a consultant to the Children's Television Workshop, which produced *Sesame Street*, and to the Public Committee on Mental Health chaired by Rosalynn Carter.

A member of the boards of several colleges and universities, foundations, and corporations, Dr. Comer has also received forty-one honorary degrees as well as accolades and awards from many organizations, including, in 1996, the Heinz Award in the Human Condition from the Heinz Foundation in recognition of his tireless work with disadvantaged children. The American Psychiatric Association presented him with a Special Presidential Commendation in 1990, and he has received several other awards recognizing his contributions to psychiatric medicine and childhood development. Robert Coles and Marian Wright Edelman, two of our nation's most admired thinkers on children and what our society must do for them, and what they can do for themselves and for their society, have cited Dr. Comer's work as thoughtful and necessary. It is not going too far to say that our schools, and our children, would be lost without him.

When I was growing up in the 1950s, becoming an educated woman or man was just about the "blackest" thing an African-American could do. Although we cherished sports figures like Willie Mays, Hank Aaron, Althea Gibson, and of course Jackie Robinson and entertainers like Duke Ellington, Nat "King" Cole, Harry Belafonte, or Ella Fitzgerald, it would never have occurred to anyone to equate their importance to "the race" and the urgent quest for civil rights with the accomplishments of Ralph Bunche, Mary McLeod Bethune, Adam Clayton Powell, Thurgood Marshall, or the young southern minister, the Reverend Dr. Martin Luther King, Jr. No, education was the private face of the civil rights movement, and becoming an educated black person was commonly thought to be the most effective way to fight antiblack racism; pursuing academic excellence, in school and in college, was a sort of bullet fired squarely into the heart of racial discrimination.

Since 1968, when Dr. King was so brutally assassinated, a paradoxical effect has unfolded within the African-American community. The size of the black middle class has almost quadrupled, but at the same time the percentage of black children living at or beneath the poverty line is about 40 percent, almost precisely what it was when Dr. King died in 1968. While explanations for this curious class divide are legion, no single theory is sufficient to explain the disastrous statistic result in an era of a vastly expanding economy and equally expanding professional opportunities for black people because of desegregation and affirmative action programs.

Just as shocking, and depressing, to many of us has been the deconstruction of our public schools. Our schools have lost their effectiveness as conduits up the class ladder in American society, especially for poor minorities for whom the American public education system was an economic and social lifeline, a class escalator. Today, however, far too many of our public schools, especially in the inner cities, are sites of miseducation, chaos, violence, and disorder. Perhaps even more troubling, for far too many of our people, education has been coded as "white," surely a perversion of traditional black values honed out of the cauldron of slavery and Jim Crow segregation for two centuries by determined, aspiring African American slaves, former slaves, and citizens.

How did this attitudinal change to the value of education occur within the African American community? And, just as important, what in the world can we do about this, a veritable nightmare for all of us who both love education and recognize the inescapable necessity of education to racial justice and economic mobility?

Many educators, philanthropists, and reformers have theorized about solutions to the crisis of public education in our country, and many have launched programs designed to address aspects of this crisis, often with remarkably successful results, such as Daniel Rose's use of chess in the middle school curriculum to revolutionize attitudes toward learning, sharpened analytical skills, and civilized behavior in a school in Harlem, or Lenora Fulani's extraordinarily creative entrepreneurial after-school program in Brooklyn. Bob Moses's Algebra Project is another outstanding program, and Anthony Appiah and I have begun a series of Martin Luther King After-School Programs in Boston, Baltimore, and Cleveland, based on the teaching of computer skills and African American history, and these

have had some positive results. But few theorists or practitioners of educational reform have embarked upon a systematic,
holistic approach to the variety of causes of dysfunction in the
American educational system. A major exception is Dr. James
Comer.

Comer's theory is backed by decades of practice, experimentation, and implementation. It has been so very effective
in reversing decaying in our schools that many of us believe
that the greatest tragedy of the Clinton administration was its
failure to name Comer the secretary of education. No single
program has proven to be more effective in transforming the
system of instruction, learning, and development—in other
words, the web or network of relationships necessary, a priori,
for education to occur. In the Comer Process, the school, the
family, and the neighborhood are united in a seamless web of
reinforcement and constructive reaffirmation, literally day to
day, unobtrusively yet decidedly ever-present in the very fabric
of a continuous education process, one not relegated merely to
the classroom.

Comer's theory of healthy educational reform is based
on one principle, and one principle alone: "relationships, relationships, relationships," as he puts it, relationships of the sort,
at home and in the community, that nurtured Comer (and
me!) and all of us in his generation and my own who were able
to move from a socioeconomic status best described as the
working-but-stable-poor squarely into the broader American
educated middle class.

The Comer Process is elegant in its simplicity and stun-
ningly effective in its implementation. As he puts it so well,
"Good relationships among and between people in the institutions that influence the quality of child life, largely home and
school, make good child and adolescent rearing and develop-

ment possible. Good relationships make student, adult, and organizational development possible, which, in turn, makes a strong academic focus possible." Indeed, he continues, "development and learning are inextricably linked."

This is Comer's great achievement: to realize that the public school is just another aspect of child development and that the learning process is infinitely more complex than amassing a body of facts outside of this self-reinforcing network of nurture, psychological support, concern, care, affection, ego gratification, and mentorship. Schools are an extension of the family structure; family, in turn, must be an extension, and a reflection, of the learning environment fostered by our schools. In other words, as he concludes, "a preventive mental health approach, an aspect of public health" is central to the educational process that ideally should unfold in our schools as well as in our homes. School is just one more aspect of a child's "social environment," as Comer puts it, and it is in our social environment that "constructive attitudes, values, and ways of living—work, family life or relationships, child rearing, citizenship contributions"—are created and perpetuated . . . or they are not. And if they are not, disastrous consequences can ensue. Elevated test scores alone, Comer argues, "cannot produce the outcomes we want and need for our children or our nation." Rather, "good child and youth rearing and development can do so, and they can simultaneously produce good test scores." Reforming the traditional links among family, neighborhood, and school "creates a context or culture" that nurtures good behavior and the passion to learn, to excel, to defer gratification, to aspire.

In this marvelously straightforward book, replete with anecdotes and examples from actual practice and experimentation, Comer shows how he and his colleagues took two elementary schools in New Haven, ranked thirty-second and thirty-third in the city on standardized tests, and transformed them into schools whose students achieved the third and fourth highest level in mathematics and language arts test performances along with the best attendance in that city. This engagingly written book, a summary of a lifetime of learning and thinking about public education, shows not only how Comer did this, but also how the Comer Process, if properly implemented, bears the greatest hope of achieving a genuine, lasting revolution in public education in this country. Every school-teacher and administrator, every legislator, every parent— anyone who deeply cares about educational reform in the twenty-first century—should be compelled to read this book. Comer is convinced that the seemingly unsolvable problem facing our schools can be overcome, and here he shows us how.

HENRY LOUIS GATES, JR.
Cambridge, Massachusetts

I
Right Church, Wrong Pew

At the Zion Baptist Church of my youth it was not rare for the "sisters" to have visions. One Sunday afternoon before the Baptist Young People's Training Union meeting, when I was about eight or nine years old, Mrs. Johnson told me that she had had a vision about me. She saw me as a little minister (I was very small) traveling all over the country to spread the gospel. She was delighted. That was not my vision of my future, but I responded with respectful appreciation of her revelation.

After thirty-five years of work in schools—hundreds of trips, speeches, and articles later—I am forced to revisit her prophecy. When I travel to speak about how schools can change to promote development and learning, I think, "Mrs. Johnson was in the right church, but the wrong pew." I am a preventive child psychiatrist, not a minister. One definition of "gospel" in the *Britannica* dictionary is: Any doctrine concerning human welfare which is considered of great importance. Desirable child rearing, development, behavior, and learning could qualify.

Our modern knowledge about child rearing, development, and learning is more than a doctrine. It is based on a vast
body of scientific findings.[1] Because of this, and my own life
experience and work, I argue that changes in public school education over the last decade are moving in the right direction
(right church)—toward standards, high expectation for all,
accountability. But the almost exclusive focus on curriculum,
instruction, and high-stakes accountability based on test scores
alone is the wrong pew.

The direction to the right pew in education—like the
real estate mantra of location, location, location—is relationships, relationships, relationships. Good relationships among
and between the people in the institutions that influence the
quality of child life, largely home and school, make good child
and adolescent rearing and development possible. Good relationships make student, adult, and organizational development possible, which, in turn, makes a strong academic focus
possible. Indeed, development and learning are inextricably
linked. Both are needed to adequately prepare young people to
be successful in school and in modern life.[2]

The right church and right pew scenario would be the
creation of a very large educator workforce that is capable of
creating a relationship context in all schools, which would enable all children to both develop well and learn well.[3] In such a
context or culture, high expectations and accountability can
come from within the learners and the teachers. Students
would meet high standards. And staff, parents, and students
would hold themselves accountable.

Educators, policymakers, and business leaders agree that
these are the outcomes they seek. But they generally use the
models of their respective disciplines in trying to understand
and overcome the obstacles to achieving them. Thus, reform

approaches over the last quarter century or more have generally been based on principles and practices in business and
manufacturing, and in the biological and the physical sciences,
and are of limited value in primary and secondary education,
sometimes even harmful.

Even principles of social and behavioral science, which
are important relative to relationships, when applied in education relate primarily to individuals rather than to systems. But
the education enterprise—schools; districts; staff preparatory
institutions; local, state, and federal government; business; and
others who influence policy—is made up of highly interactive
systems, both internal and external. Their operations create
multiple, changing variables, many of them intangible but
very powerful, that can affect each other in limiting and harmful ways when not well managed. The way these systems interact must be taken into account as much as or even more than
individual or group (teachers, students, parents) behavior.

Our traditional model of teaching and learning, while
drawn from ancient practices, was reinforced by the success of
manufacturing at about the time universal public education
was being established. As a result, many, if not most, practitioners and the public think of academic learning as a mechanical process governed solely by genetically determined intelligence and individual will. The assumption is that those
with the best brains or "machines" will get it and others will
not. Pouring in or tacking on information, as one would attach
a part to an inanimate machine, was not illogical in a manufacturing age with often compliant students who had limited
opportunities to gain information from other sources.

Even so, many students, for many reasons, sometimes because they were animate and reactive, did not succeed under
the mechanical approach. Today even fewer will sit and take in

what they often consider to be irrelevant information when
there are so many exciting opportunities for learning outside
of school. Also, we send a double and confusing message. We
praise children for being active learners and expressive people
outside of school yet expect them to be docile learners inside.

In the past, those who did not do well in school could
leave and still earn a living that would enable them to take care
of adult tasks and responsibilities. Many young people, if not
most, will not be able to do so today or in the future.[4]

Most recent school reform approaches have not been very
helpful. Some, as noted above, were based on principles drawn
from business, often tinged with political ideology, and were
not really applicable to public schools. In the early 1990s there
was much talk about competition and choice. Public schools
were viewed as inefficient government bureaucracies. Many
argued that private and public schools of choice, such as charter schools, could do a better job for less. Some believed that
such schools would be particularly valuable for poor, often minority children in dysfunctional public schools. It was believed
that success in these schools would help all schools improve.
The findings are mixed and sobering. There is no evidence that
choice and competition can *routinely and widely* improve our
system of public education. Traditional schools with similar
students probably produce similar good outcomes.

Some notions about school improvement are drawn
from business and our justice system, mixed injudiciously.
These perspectives have given us merit pay and high-stakes accountability or "reward and punishment" to solve education
problems. Both are supposed to promote motivation. Whereas
educators want, need, and deserve salaries that will allow them
to live in dignity, or in the style of others who provide essential

services, no practitioners enter the profession to become rich. The reward educators seek most is to help young people develop, learn, and be successful in life. Much teacher frustration, dissatisfaction, and even some acting-out behavior is due to the fact that our system(s) of education do not support them in doing so.

If they do not succeed under difficult circumstances, they are punished in the name of accountability. We point them out, write them up in the local newspaper, stigmatize them, run for public office on their backs, and send them away in embarrassment and shame. Some will cheat to survive. Many who could be successful become dissatisfied and leave the profession. One of the unintended consequences of teachers and administrators who, in frustration, change careers is that it discourages interested and able young people from entering the profession. I have heard many educators say that they would never encourage relatives or friends to go into education.

While there is some recognition of the need to help schools and staff under stress, little to no financial support has been made available to do so at the state or federal levels. Even if funds were made available, the infrastructure and knowledge base needed to help is rarely in place at the local or state level.

Efforts to reduce school and class size are a movement in the right direction, but such efforts often miss the point. Putting a warm body in a classroom with fewer students rather than making certain that educators are capable of promoting good relationships, development, and learning reflects the mechanical and infrastructure mentalities that are all too prevalent.

A young teacher insisted that she would be able to control the sixteen children in her third-grade classroom if the administration would put up a partition to cut her room in half.

The size of the room was not the problem, nor was the number of students. The teacher had been a top student in college, but she did not know how to create a climate for learning in her classroom. Although small class size can help, there is evidence that a good relationship climate and good instruction are more important. How to establish such a climate is an important teacher competency.

Even evaluation and research in education are adversely affected by the use of models that are not sufficiently applicable. Evaluation tools in education are designed to be as rigorous as those used in the physical and biomedical sciences. Measurability is characteristic of "hard data." But because such factors as beliefs, feelings, attitudes, climate, trust, and values are powerful determinants of human behavior—but difficult to measure, particularly in complex interactive systems—the assessment methods used in the physical and biological sciences are less useful in school settings.

Also, traditional research models often provide numerical outcome markers without context and process explanations. Thus, outcome measurements can reflect dysfunctional conditions in and outside of schools as much as or more than the curriculum or program, or the performance of students or teachers being assessed. Without observation and description of the complex interactions taking place, it is often impossible to know what the numbers mean or how to use the information to bring about useful change. Many believe that the use of "hard data" is more scientific. But using such data in instances where skillful clinical observation is more helpful is comparable to attempting to place a round ball through a square hole. Hard data and clinical observation should be complementary. Because of our overreliance on numerical indicators, we can miss or greatly undervalue the importance and great power of teaching and learning precursors or facilitating conditions.[5]

Furthermore, the troublesome achievement numbers that have caught the nation's attention are largely from schools in communities that are dysfunctional for a variety of economic and resultant social and psychological reasons. American students in more affluent communities are now achieving as well as the highest academic achievers in the world. But there is evidence that children from difficult economic and social environments can also perform at much higher levels. To help students in greatest need, and schools and parents working with them, we must understand the way economic and social stress factors create dysfunctional institutions and interfere with preparation, motivation, and learning.[6]

In schools where a sense of community can be created, regardless of socioeconomic backgrounds, students, staff, and parents can be engaged in a process of continuous growth and learning—learning communities. Such communities can lead to improved student development and academic achievement, as well as to improved staff and parent performance.[7] But the relentless focus on low test scores alone and promises of quick, easy, and inexpensive fixes make it difficult to adequately focus on how such communities can be created school by school and district by district across the nation.

The inappropriate models and emphases now used to shape education practice, evaluation and policies, and the mentalities and behaviors they generate are themselves a big part of our education crisis. There are more useful ways to understand the needs and obstacles and to shape education policy and practice.

The mission of public health is to prevent problem health conditions and to promote effective functioning, both human and environmental. Epidemiology is the study of the distribution and determinants of health-related events or states in the

human population. Ecology is the study of human popula-
tions and their interactions within their physical and cultural
environments. These are better but rarely used models for
helping us understand how people perform in such powerful
interactive institutions as schools.[8] And yet these disciplines
are almost foreign notions in the education enterprise—an
enterprise whose mission it is to promote desirable functioning. A preventive and interactive perspective is more useful in
designing and sustaining systems that work for students, parents, staff, and the society.

What is the public health connection? The purpose of
the public school is greater than preparing students to achieve
high test scores. The purpose is to prepare students to be successful in school and in life. Life success requires skills that will
enable individuals to be good family and group members,
learners and problem solvers, workers, and citizens of their
respective communities. When most people can function in
these ways, open, democratic societies can be promoted and
sustained.

Indeed, then, one purpose of public education is to promote the common good. In fact, federal involvement in education was rationalized under the "common good" clause in
the Preamble of the U.S. Constitution. There was and still is a
presumption that education will help prevent problem behaviors and create conditions that will promote our democracy
and general welfare.

An education that promotes good development can enhance a student's chance of avoiding problem behaviors of all
kinds—drug and alcohol abuse, violence, vandalism, bullying,
early sex and teen pregnancy, dependency, and criminal behaviors.[9] These are public health issues. Thus schools, in preparing students for a successful adult life, should be intention-

ally involved in the promotion of positive mental health. To do so, an understanding of how to turn normal but potentially harmful human responses into growth-producing responses is needed. A preventive mental health approach, an aspect of public health, is needed in all aspects of schooling.

The failure of schools to support families in preparing their children for adult life is costly in human and financial terms, particularly for those living under social and economic stress. Such families become marginalized, and this makes it difficult for them to carry out tasks required for mainstream participation. The concept of "mainstream" here is more than socioeconomic status. It is a reference to constructive attitudes, values, and ways of living— work, family life or relationships, child rearing, citizenship contributions—that are held by most of the people and contribute to the well-being of a society.

Our society is paying a high cost for the control, containment, and support of adults who, if they had been helped in school, and in the home and community, could have been productive, contributing citizens. The inability to function, manage families, and rear children well in one generation very often leads to the same inability in subsequent generations. Increasingly repressive controls will be needed to manage the growing number of young people who are not being adequately prepared for mainstream adult life. This will weaken our ability to remain an economically competitive, open, democratic society.

A focus on higher test scores alone cannot produce the outcomes we want and need for our children or our nation. But good child and youth rearing and development can do so, and they can simultaneously produce good test scores.

The flawed models from which we are drawing policy and practice initiatives run the risk of fragmenting and creat-

ing greater discontinuity and instability in our education sys-
tem(s). Children need more continuity and stability in the institutions where they live and work than do mature adults.
Also, public schools have the responsibility of protecting our
democratic system. Religious schools, some schools of choice,
private schools, and other programs do not, and it is more difficult to hold them accountable.

All but the elite private schools and some special programs are organized so that most incentives for learning must
come from outside the learners and the learning situation; we
know that learning and preparation for adult life takes place
best and most when the motivation is from within. This internal motivation is a product of good child rearing and development. School improvement approaches, even with good curricular programs and good instruction, that are not based on
good child-rearing and development principles, and do not facilitate reasonably harmonious systems interaction, cannot be
any more effective than the present system.

A concern about the loss of productive lives among too many
able young people at a time when a higher level of development was needed led me away from my plans to become a general practice physician in my tough steel mill hometown of
East Chicago, Indiana. My journey to and work as a preventive
psychiatrist at the Yale University Child Study Center led to
many insights. This led my colleagues and me to create a
model, the School Development Program, that helped parents,
staff, students, and the community to establish conditions in
schools that would help students develop and achieve in a way
that could prepare more of them for successful adult lives.

My concern about education and about the future of
America probably began during my internship at St. Cather-

ine's Hospital in my hometown. Three friends from my neighborhood, African-American boys with whom I went to kindergarten, had started on a downhill course, eventually leading to an alcohol-related early death for one, a long jail sentence for the second, and a life in and out of mental institutions for the third. These outcomes occurred despite the fact that they were just as intelligent as me and my four siblings and any of the other students in our predominantly white, working- to middle- and professional-class school.

Their situation called my attention to the challenges of other African-Americans. The attractive, promising senior-class woman who made certain I was safe as a little seventh grader on a school trip to the state capitol in Indianapolis was a broken woman at thirty. A very intelligent, creative student leader became a bellhop in Washington, D.C. I treated patients in the emergency room who were disfigured for life as a result of petty arguments. I moonlighted with the physician I had planned to work with after my internship. It appeared to me that many in his huge practice were clinically depressed because they could not cope with their social environment.

All around me I saw an ugly picture of defeat and despair. Race and poverty were contributing factors, but not the root causes. The steel mills paying good wages were still belching smoke; soot fell on my car as I washed and dried it. And the racial incidents I experienced in high school and college were mild and were balanced by white people who went out of their way to support fairness. Racial attitudes were improving in the society. What was going on?

The question became an obsession. That year I read as much about slavery and its aftermath as I did about medicine. What I read did not explain what I was observing. Many African-Americans were making significant progress, but a disproportionate number were not. My mind was ablaze with questions. I had to know more. I had to give myself time to think. I changed my original plan to do my military service time in the reserves and decided to serve the two years in the United States Public Health Service. (I admit that making a house call at 3:00 A.M. to tend a drug addict who faked an overdose to prevent her sister from throwing her out did not weigh in favor of future general practice.)

While in the service in Washington, D.C., I observed more of the same—even worse in a big city with fewer industrial jobs. I got involved with an all-volunteer "bootstrap" community agency, Hospitality House, trying to help families that had been thrown off the public welfare rolls for minor violations. Most were mothers and children without other income or extended family support. Their spare belongings were often piled on the street in front of the volunteer agency.

On one occasion when I stopped by the House a youngster about eight years old was crying quietly in the corner. It was the Easter season. His teacher had told him that if he could not bring a dime to school for the Easter egg hunt, then he should not come back himself. His mother was distraught but could not help him. She literally did not have a dime. I gave him a dime and he went back to school. The powerlessness and deep appreciation displayed by the mother are still etched in my brain. The children at the house—transients in the schools they attended—were outcasts and experienced one indignity after another. And yet they were great kids.

I would sometimes sit on the backstairs and read to or play with them. They were bright and eager for my attention. One stern look, like the one my father once gave me, would end misbehavior. They reminded me of my childhood friends.

Around the corner from Hospitality House young men

gathered for day labor jobs. The scene was like a picture out of slavery. The employer's agent stood elevated at the back of a truck and picked a load of workers from a large group of husky black males calling out to be selected for a day of work. It was clear to me that, without a good education, my young friends were going to be in that roundup in a few years. And it appeared that the schools they attended could not prepare them for the mainstream economy of the 1960s and the future. To buy more time to decide about my career future, and to try to understand why schools, welfare, health, and other systems were hurting potentially able children and families rather than helping them, I decided to study public health at the University of Michigan.

I did not know enough about the field to be sure that it would be helpful. But I remember my Howard University Medical School professor, Dr. Paul Cornely, a distinguished leader in the field, pointing out that public health and prevention were more responsible for improved health than the entire medical profession. I think I resented that remark as a soon-to-be physician, but I remembered his claim. If the children and families I observed were to have a chance, then some form of prevention of the problem conditions I was observing would be necessary.

At the University of Michigan School of Public Health, I was introduced to the disciplines of epidemiology and ecology. My major was administration. This discipline provided me with a brief introduction to how and why organizations work the way they do. Human ecology was in its infancy. Although the focus was on environmental ecology, it was not much of a stretch to see the parallels to human interactions and the impact of institutional policies and practices on them. I also studied children and youth programs. During that year, 1963–64, I wrote a term paper arguing that schools were the only organizations strategically located to help all children grow and to compensate for the difficult conditions that interfered with the growth of many.

I needed to know more about people, and by then my desire to do general practice medicine was all but gone. I trained in adult psychiatry at the Yale University School of Medicine Department of Psychiatry. A year of work on a milieu therapy ward provided me with a powerful insight. The ward was a community of patients, therapists, and other helpers. I was struck, sometimes startled and worried, sometimes relieved, by the impact the social environment could have on behavior. The possibility of helping and hurting people through group pressure was all too apparent.

It occurred to me that the social environment must have an even greater impact on children. I was also struck by the fact that many of the problem behaviors, even neurotic and psychotic conditions of adults, had some of their roots in childhood. (A person's biological makeup made a contribution as well.) These impressions led me to the Yale Child Study Center. Several incidents during my training there made me deeply aware of the pain of children who experience difficult conditions at home, as well as the support teachers need, but generally do not receive, to help such children in school. Such incidents made me aware that much of the public, as well as too many educators, do not understand the conditions that support or serve as obstacles to learning.

People in and out of education speak of learning as if all students are empty vessels eagerly waiting to be filled, or just bad and unmotivated. Because of the many factors involved in one's biological, social, and psychological makeup and the interactions of a child with his or her environment, even children who have had good support, at home and at school, can have difficulties in school. The challenge is even greater for those with the burdens of dysfunctional families and communities on their shoulders. Such children come from every socio-economic, racial, and religious background. With limited skills, they often respond in inappropriate and troublesome ways. Educators must be able to help them function in ways that will enable them to become eager learners.[10]

I am reminded of my experience with a four-year-old from an affluent, well-educated family whose behavior at home put him at risk for school problems. His mother suggested that I might want to have his ears tested because he did not appear to hear anything she said to him. Hearing was not the problem. He was an only child and his parents were not getting along well. He was afraid of losing them—abandonment. He had become quite good at throwing tantrums to draw their attention away from their conflict.

On his first visit he threw a mighty fit on the stairway and refused to go into the treatment room, as several senior psychiatrists passed by and observed my work. My supervisor explained that my patient was trying to show me his problem. He suggested that I help him look at himself, which might cause him to look for a better way to communicate. The next time he threw a tantrum, I got down on the floor beside him and pretended to have one myself. He looked at me, stopped, and we went into the therapy room together. He then used wild "daddy" and "mommy" fighting play in the dollhouse to tell me his problem. We were able to help the family and the child.

On another occasion, I was called to the emergency room to see a nine-year-old who was said to be catatonic—rigid and speechless. But his facial expression, more often seen among African-Americans, told me that he was very angry about something and would not talk to anybody. I bantered, "Who hurt my man? Who made him so mad?" Finally he grudgingly explained. He had been acting up at school and was difficult at home in uncharacteristic ways. He had also been asking his mother and "stepfather" to buy him a bicycle. On his parents' pretense of taking him to look for a bike, he found himself in the emergency room.

The acute problem was easily resolved, but I did follow-up therapy with him to get at the underlying issues. As it turned out, he was the oldest child of five and had the name of the father he never knew. After I had established an adequate relationship with him, I pointed out that "the only child who didn't belong situation" must be difficult for him. He angrily stormed out of the treatment room and walked through the tunnels of the hospital, with me walking a few steps behind him. When he calmed down, I agreed to help him talk to his parents about his feelings. He was adopted by the man who was rearing him and his sibs, given the same last name, and his school and home behavior was no longer a problem. This experience made me greatly aware of the importance of having a sense of belonging in a family or meaningful group as well as the anguish of feeling like an outsider.

On another occasion I was working with an eight-year-old boy referred for school problems. During therapy, he told me that he lived with his mother and siblings, but his father was around the neighborhood. The father was an alcohol abuser and was neglectful and undependable in his relationships with the family. He would promise "I'll come by next Tuesday" and not show up, maybe for weeks. On other occasions, he might unexpectedly come with toys, promise to stay, be around a few days, and then he was gone again. One day, just before our play therapy session, my patient, with his friends,

saw his father on the street corner, drunk. As we tossed a Wiffle
ball, I said that it must be embarrassing for him to see his father like that. He turned and fired the ball at me as hard as he
could and began to cry. I walked over and embraced him. He
held on, quivering, shaking, angry, and hurt. If one has had a
reasonably supportive childhood experience, it is difficult to
get a strong sense of the deep level of pain felt by children living in environments that are not supportive. The anger and
pain can go inward and hurt the child, and outward and hurt
those around him or her and the society. And this boy's situation was mild compared to that of many others.

Once I began working in schools and observed children
speaking through behavior rather than words, I began to understand what a difficult position we have put teachers in. We do
not prepare them to "read" child behavior, but we expect them
to respond to it in ways that can be helpful. We do not do that
to other professionals.

My "paint can case" reflects the great difference in preparation and support. I was working at an easel with a very anxious, active girl of eight when she threatened to throw a can of
paint at me. After the session, as soon as I could I sought help
from my supervisor. He listened to what went on in the session
and smiled. He told me that she liked me. "What? Certainly a
strange way of showing it!" I thought to myself. He explained
that she did not know how to engage appropriately. He suggested that if she threatened again, I might say to her that if she
threw that paint at me, I would be so angry that I would not
want to play with her. I could not imagine that this would stop
a patient that my colleagues and I had privately dubbed "the
wild child," but when she threatened again, I used his suggestion. She slowly lowered the can, and with the confidence from
understanding, I was able to help her find better ways to inter-

act. Through this incident, my appreciation of the power of relationships was deepened. The value of an experienced supervisor—unavailable to most teachers—was apparent.

I am not suggesting that teachers need exactly the same kind or level of support or training as child psychiatrists. And the adults in school need not be professional therapists to be able to work with special needs children. But we can provide school people with more and much better preparation and support than is now the case. Nor am I suggesting that most students are ill. In fact, many being labeled as ill or deficient are not and would not present as such if school staff were better prepared to create a context or culture that would help them function well. Indeed, some children who are now on medication would not need it in schools capable of promoting positive mental health.

My point here is that the experience of many children at home and in the community, and their reactions to it, often make it difficult for them to develop well and be open, eager, and able to learn. I will return to this point when we explore child and adolescent development and behavior below.

When I finished my training I did not think about working in schools. Even if I had, there were no school programs for people with my interests and training. Not sure what to do, I returned to the Public Health Service, assigned to the National Institute of Mental Health.

It was 1967 and race-based discontent and rebellion was flaring in many parts of the country. The research being done struck me as more useful to the researchers than to the cities and people being studied. I was frustrated, unhappy, and looking for an opportunity to address race relations, child development, and education issues in a hands-on research and problem-solving way—through action research.

The late Dr. Albert Solnit, then the director of the Child Study Center at Yale, contacted me. He asked me to direct a Ford Foundation–supported program in two elementary schools in the inner city of New Haven, Connecticut. This opportunity allowed me to address the three issues I had long been concerned about: child rearing and development, education, and race. With my wife and two young children, I headed back to New Haven and Yale, like a rabbit to a briar patch.

Schools and education turned out to be more a thicket, perhaps a jungle, than a briar patch. But we survived, learned, and flourished. Throughout the balance of this book I will explore why education problems are so complex and difficult to address, and what can be done about them.

Discussions about schools and education call to mind the biblical Tower of Babel. One of the major reasons for this is the fact that although we can agree that the purpose of education is to help prepare students for success in school and in life, there is no easy way to measure whether a school is achieving this. So there are many theories, demonstration programs, and research and outcome claims. In this mishmash, the only thing that *appears* to be "hard evidence" is test scores. But human behavior or performance, and its meaning, are too complex to be captured by numbers alone.

I am not arguing against the value or use of science-based data in education. I am reminding us that such data can be misinterpreted and misused. Indeed, despite the fact that test scores tell us only part of the story, and probably a small part, powerful policymakers at the national, state, and local levels have locked the entire education enterprise into improving them. This has slowed our search for complementary evidence and more useful benchmarks and measures. It has taken the focus away from the need to provide all practitioners with the skills necessary for understanding child development and behavior and promoting the kind of student development and learning essential for school and life success; indeed, needed to raise test scores.[11]

Taking massive and decisive action without deep understanding can be harmful. The story of the harm being done to a significant number of children and school staff by high-stakes testing is slowly emerging. Educators and policymakers, like physicians, should be held to the ancient Hippocratic charge, "Do no harm," and should be held accountable. Yet because of my work in schools, I understand the need of policymakers to "do something" in the face of poor school conditions and performance in many places, and to act on what *appears* to be the best thing to do—raise the test scores.

When I began my work in two elementary schools in New Haven, Connecticut, in 1968, I was shocked by what we found. The schools were thirty-second and thirty-third out of thirty-three in the city on standardized achievement tests. They had the worst attendance. The student behavior problems were overwhelming. Parents were angry, alienated from the schools, and unhappy with me, our project, Yale University, and everybody else they felt could help their children but were not doing so.

The almost completely new staff brought in for the project was in disarray from the first day; almost all were gone by the end of the year. My first reaction was that we had to change the environment; children could not develop and learn in that chaotic situation. After stumbling through the first year, we recovered. After five years, we discontinued working in one of the original schools and added another school with a similar profile. Eventually the two schools in our project achieved the third and fourth highest level mathematics and language arts test scores and the best attendance in the city. There were no serious behavior problems, and one school had no teacher turnover for thirteen years, and then only for personal reasons.

These schools were almost all African-American and poor. There was no change in the social and economic makeup of the community. After the first year, the teachers were drawn from the regular pool of practicing and new applicants. The staff was 70 to 90 percent white. The schools used the same curriculum and instructional program as the district.

Our speculation was that the climate, context, or culture of the school was the major culprit. In a dysfunctional culture, the kind of interaction and bonding needed to promote development and learning cannot take place. Thus, our focus was on creating a school context in which the adults could support the development of children and not focus only on raising test scores. But test scores went up significantly. And equally important, student-staff-parent behavior and participation improved greatly.

Eventually, the framework (School Development Program [SDP]) we created was used in as many as one thousand schools across the country. Most were lower-income, elementary schools, but we worked with schools across the socioeconomic spectrum and with all racial groups from pre-kindergarten through twelfth grade. When the framework was implemented well, student test scores and behavior— student, staff and parental—usually improved.

The results of a meta-analysis of comprehensive school reform models done by Geoffrey Borman, University of Wisconsin–Madison, and his associates in 2002 shows the effectiveness of our approach. Of the twenty-nine most widely implemented models studied by Borman, only three, using the highest standard of evidence across varying contexts and varying study designs, could be expected to raise students' test scores. One of the three was our School Development Program.[12] The point of importance here is that SDP was not designed to raise test scores, although we knew that had to happen if we were to survive. This finding, and others, support the position we took from the beginning.[13] When we create conditions that support the development of children, they will learn.

Today, in discussions about school there is much finger-pointing and blame without much listening. Almost everyone who has anything to do with schools is blamed for his or her shortcomings. The least powerful—students, parents, and school staff—are blamed most and heard from least. While the adults go around in face-saving blame circles, the needs of students are not being met. Situations like this often create denial, conflict, distrust, guilt, shame, and other feelings that do not help matters.

Many of the most vocal leaders and policymakers with passionate negative opinions about schools have not been in the average school since they were students—and the more affluent and powerful the speaker, the less likely it was that they had attended an average school. Most would not know what to look for even if they went in, including too many researchers.

One of the reasons for the blind eyes is the fact that most policymakers, opinion leaders, professionals, and the general public disconnect their own success from their own developmental experience. This is a cultural affect. One of our most cherished beliefs is that we make it on our own. This is a flattering myth that we can no longer afford. It is part of the reason we expect similar outcomes among all students without providing adequate support in school for the underdeveloped and appropriate learning opportunities for all.

Also, because of the disconnect, social and behavioral scientists often make child care and rearing sound unimportant and make child development sound autonomous and complicated. As a result, development is seen as some mysterious "scientific-thing," the purview of mind and body doctors and social workers. Educators do not want to be seen as child rearers—"not professional enough," "the task of parents," "teachers teach." And too many parents do not understand that the way they rear their children greatly influences development and learning. The way each simultaneously serves the other—care and rearing, development, teaching, learning, parents, teachers, other support professionals—is not fully appreciated or missed.

Listening to the voices of the people on the frontline can be a reality check. Doing so was very helpful to our Yale Child Study Center team when we went into schools thirty-five years ago. We lived in two schools, *listened* to all the players, and experienced their challenges. What we learned was sobering, useful, and different from what too many are still saying today about the nature of problems in school and how to address them. I want the reader to hear, as our team did, from staff and parents who should be informing the school improvement movement but are not.

What we heard and observed made it clear that parents, school staff, and students all wanted to succeed. This observation led to a search for the underlying problems, which in turn led to the construction of a model that permitted school-based participants to engage in prevention, problem solving, and learning-promotion activities. A similar search and problem-solving approach is needed nationally.

II
Voices from the
School House

When our Yale Child Study Center team began its work in schools in 1968 we quickly realized that one of the greatest obstacles to progress was the amount of finger-pointing and blame among and between staff, parents, and students. This promoted strong negative emotions, defensive behavior, and problem-solving paralysis. One of the most useful components of the school improvement model we developed was a no-fault policy, coupled with a focus on problem solving. This component will be described in detail in a later chapter. I mention it here because the same approach would be useful in the national debate about education.

Listening to all sides will enable us to search for the underlying problems that contribute to what we are too quick to label as bad behavior or inadequate knowledge and skills among all involved in education—educators, students, parents, politicians and policymakers, business and opinion leaders, and others. The perspective of educators is heard less often. When it is heard, they are often accused of giving excuses. But they are the key to positive change. We cannot make an objective and collaborative search for underlying problems or develop effective solutions without hearing their voices.

Because of my thirty-five years of work in schools I know that most educators are doing the best they can to address problems they did not create and are not adequately prepared to tackle. Some are miracle workers. Noneducators may be more open to explanations beyond what appear to be shortcomings after listening to talented, committed educators who are making their best effort.

To gather data for this chapter, in 2003 I interviewed more than two dozen people, mostly teachers and administrators who had been using the School Development Program (SDP) for at least three years or, as in the case of the retired superintendent and school board member, were very familiar with it. I did so because I am very familiar with their skills and effort; they have all been very successful in very difficult school settings. Their observations and concerns cannot be discounted as rationalizations for failure. The interviewees are from Long Island, New York City, Detroit, and the Chicago area.

I asked these people to help me give you, the reader, a realistic vision of their challenges, what kind of public behavior they found to be harmful, and what kind of public behavior would enable them to do a better job. In one case I used a principal's report on her school to illustrate how students' personal and academic growth could be promoted under difficult circumstances. We also have student and parent data, but I will not present them here because my experiences suggest that the best chance for nationwide school change will come from a better public appreciation of the challenges educators face and what they will need to do their jobs well.

Here is what they had to say.

Interview with a White Elementary School Teacher, Detroit

Every time we turn around we hear so much that is negative about inner-city schools when there is so much that is positive to be told, at least in our school and a lot of Detroit schools. It's ridiculous.

The newspapers focus on the schools that are doing poorly. They don't report on the ones that are doing well. They don't look at the high level of parental involvement in school. They'd much rather do a story on a few parents picketing downtown. They do stories where you can blame somebody, especially the teachers, or find somebody abusing a child. The media really tries to serve their own interest. Anything negative about Detroit sells.

The governor and politicians are pushing charter schools and private schools. They don't focus on the whole child. And if you don't focus on the whole child, then all that you do instructionally falls apart. If they would spend as much money on supporting the work of good public schools as they spend on charter schools and research, they'd get better outcomes. I don't think the media or politicians want to see success in the inner city, and it's endemic in the society.

The suburban schools are no better. I live in a suburban town, and I see it. They do not give good emotional support to the children. They are not welcoming to the parents. I know they have a drug problem out there just as here in Detroit. But it's hidden. Nobody wants to talk about it. It just makes me mad. But when people learn that I'm working in Detroit they look at me as though I am odd, or worse. Why would you teach there? Or, they say something like, "You are brave." They are so wrong. Many of our schools are very good places … good people, good outcomes.

You know, sometimes churches will send groups from the suburbs into our school as part of an outreach program. The children they send are so afraid because they've been given the wrong notion from television and newspapers about what to expect in Detroit.

It's not that we don't give them a chance to learn about us. We've contacted the media whenever there's a program that is unusual or outstanding. We've had cultural programs that were really outstanding, and they wouldn't attend. We've had interns from Japan that would have made a good story. They were not interested. They are never interested when there is an opportunity to tell the public good things about us. One day we saw them outside taking pictures, but they didn't come in. And then the story came out with our school as the backdrop. It was about how schools in the suburbs were doing better than those in Detroit.

They were at our elementary school, which has some of the best test scores in the state and is one of the best schools in the state. Since they're interested in test scores you would think they might want to know how we got them in a school with many low-income students. They used us to tell a negative story, when we are one of the best positive stories around. We have clean, safe halls. They won't show the poster we made of all of our children gathered smiling. Instead they show the dilapidated building across the street. Nothing positive.

This situation is bad for the children and their parents. It makes them feel like second-class citizens. I've had parents who said to me that their kids wouldn't go here if they had the money to send them somewhere else. They're made to feel that it's a bad situation by the press.

Things are not right when you can't get praise in good schools. It's bad for the morale of teachers in schools serving poor children. It's because of the media that so few teachers want to come to Detroit. It is one of the reasons there is so much teacher turnover in many schools.

I don't know what they're trying to do. It looks like an excuse for not investing in our children. The charter school, the private schools, they're not going to solve the problem. They have yet to figure out how to help the children. They quietly let the children they can't manage out of those schools, and they have to come back to the city.

Interview with Administrators, School Board Member, Parent, and Three Teachers, Westbury, New York

ADMINISTRATOR: One of the greatest difficulties that we're dealing with right now is multiple families in what used to be single-family homes. Some of the houses are like a bus stop. There's one property tax base there, and many of the children who come into the schools from those homes need special services, most of them. The district is obligated to educate them. People don't understand how much money it costs. It's a real drain on the system. There are many social needs. So a social worker may be involved, a psychologist is involved. For example, the children are here with mom, but dad couldn't come, they couldn't afford to bring

him, his papers weren't right. As a result, there's anxiety, which also interferes with learning and test
taking. To compound the unfairness, there is a rich
housing area across the street and our district has
to bus the children who live there to schools of
choice elsewhere.

We have a lot of immigrants as well as other
poor people who are working, and their children
are being cared for in these houses. One of the families in the home is supposed to provide supervision, but it doesn't. There is no one there to give
them a routine: Come home, have dinner, do your
homework. "You sit here to do your homework.
Your books are here, you keep everything here."
Sometimes the children tell their parents that they
did their homework but they didn't. Or they tell
them that they forget it. There is no follow-up because there is a lack of order in the home.

TEACHER ONE: Immigration takes its orders
from somebody. What many employers want, and
immigration policy provides, is low-cost workers.
But then the government doesn't want to pay for
the services that the families and their children
need to be able to function—health care needs and
so on. It just takes those people and dumps them on
the schools without taking responsibility for them.

TEACHER TWO: Don't let the taxpayer off the
hook. We benefit from low-cost workers, but we
don't want to pay to educate their children.

TEACHER ONE: To me it's an overall social problem. It's institutionalized racism—in our politics,

in the news media, in the corporate world. The spiritual content is missing—"Do unto others"— so the challenges that we're talking about, even though we can do these reforms in the schools, will be with us until there is some kind of overall change in the direction of the country.

TEACHER THREE: Part of the problem is that the parents are so busy that they are dependent on the school system to provide for their children— character development, homework help, child care. The school is supposed to do all the things that they can't get to because both parents are working; many of them have more than one job. And so the expectation is that the school will answer all these needs.

PRINCIPAL ONE: And we also have domestic violence. I know every community has it. But you compound that with the fact that the mother is here, and her entire support group is in another country. The only person she knows here is the person who is abusing her. And this is the person who brings the children to school. As a result, we've had cases where the children are worried about mom and they can't make it through the school day. For the most part, the wealthiest children have resources to address these issues. Sometimes our children are in those homes with domestic violence, and there is no help. It's a tragedy for all, but our children have so many things against them. It makes it very hard for them.

TEACHER TWO: I once had a student whose family lived in one of those homes. There was only one room that had heat or electricity. That was how they monitored the billing. If you have electricity in only one room, we don't know how many things you're going to have plugged in there. It's a fire hazard. The kids used to sleep on a mattress on the floor, all of them. They slept in their clothes and jackets because it was so cold. And the youngest one would wet, and so everybody came to school in the clothes they had worn sleeping in the wet bed. That was what they could afford at that time.

PRINCIPAL TWO: I had a little child who had a terrible temper tantrum. He was kicking me—that poor little guy. I happened to be making rounds and I saw him throw something across the room. I spoke to him. He was getting very emotional so I asked him to step outside. And then he started screaming he wanted to go back to Georgia. The grandmother took six siblings from Georgia and she's trying to give them a better life here. But he misses his mother and he's not used to structure and grandma's trying to give him a lot of structure. She's working very hard. I have to commend her.

But when he has a bad day, he's not respectful to his teacher. When I tried to move him that day—because I didn't want to leave him screaming in the hall—I got kicked. The assistant principal ran to my aid and he got his head butted. The little child was really just acting out. Fortunately, grandma came to school. Every time we call grandma she comes. We made a plan for him, a mentor through our Costco Employee Tutorial Program. Part of it is mentoring and a part is to help him handle his feelings. Most of the children I see are acting out more than just being bad kids. But when I went to school no one ever did that. And now it's almost that you don't know what to expect from them, and at what level.

When you look at the students sent to my office for misbehavior you will notice that most are children who don't have a mommy living with them. They're in foster care. Sometimes they live with other relatives who don't love them. And they're in such turmoil. You can't pinpoint at what point during the day or during the class that they think about their missing mother. But then nothing you do helps them. And so my little guy was having a tough time in class.

TEACHER ONE: The high school has a 35 percent mobility rate where other communities are much more stable. New immigrants come to an area and maybe they'll stay a couple of years, but they're constantly trying to improve their livelihood. So they're moving around a bit.

I have first graders who are the first in the family to go to school. We have children of whom the parents are so proud because the second grader can read and reads the notices to the parents. Unfortunately, those same children aren't the ones whom we graduate. We are consistently educating groups of kids who then go somewhere else. So we meet many of their needs and then they move. Also, many teachers come here and get amazing training, staff development, and then they're lured away by districts that pay more money.

- Lack of stability due to immigration and "non-structured, chaotic homes"

Also, we have children at every level who are newly arrived and they're non-English speakers. It's a very challenging situation. In a stable situation, your children come in September and they leave in June. And perhaps the family will move over the summer. But I'm taking in children now. It's March, and I'll take in children until we have the official cutoff in June. And so if the test is given in May and the children are eligible, the children who have been in maybe three schools or no other school are presented with an assessment.

TEACHER TWO: Also, many of the immigrants have to return to their country at certain points, which they usually like to do when it is summer in their country, which is the middle of our school year. So they will leave for six to eight weeks and never speak English within that period of time. Then they come back and here we are again. It's almost like our summer vacation when the children always lose a little ground. Upon their return, we start all over learning the language that the child has lost. Quite a challenge.

How can you compare our scores with Jericho (Long Island) where there are many professional families? Maybe every household has a college degree. Many of their children are in the same system for twelve years.

TEACHER ONE: Just as societal changes impact children, they impact adults. We're dealing with a different set of professionals. The commitment, in some cases, and the behavior, and what gets modeled by the teachers sometimes supports the negative behaviors that we're trying to work on in the kids.

TEACHER TWO: I can't say it's just the younger teachers, but some people have gone into this profession over the last ten years for the wrong reasons and also with a certain sense of entitlement. "I have this job and I'm going to have it forever and you can't make me do anything."

There's another area that I think needs to be addressed. Sometimes just the way the adults speak to the kids makes me shudder. Most of the time they're good teachers, but the first reaction is a raised voice or a harsh voice, and I'm thinking maybe they're used to that at home. I don't know if a child likes that. It's degrading. What you want to do is to build up the ego so that these kids have confidence. They've got enough beating them down.

I know people get frustrated because there is so much overcrowding in the classroom and other problems. I think there needs to be some way that teachers can find more aides or help in dealing with the kids, other ways of speaking and other ways of dealing with them, or other ways of handling situations that happen. I've seen good things. But then the effects of the good things are diffused by somebody else doing just the opposite. Then you wind up with kids who speak terribly to the teachers. It goes around and around, when relationships could be better.

PRINCIPAL ONE: Going back to the teachers, I think sometimes every now and then the teachers forget that the conditions of the children are very different from [those of] their own children. And sometimes they take things personally when a child is late. I know once we had a donation of Kleenex and I thought, the teachers can give it out at parent-teacher conference. And one teacher at SPMT [School Planning and Management Team] said, oh I feel like social services. I said, well we are, and the children need it, and that's why we're giving it out. But I think sometimes you forget because your child may have their own handkerchief in the top drawer of the bureau whereas our children don't even have a bureau.

I know that the teachers are under stress because of the emphasis on making test scores go up regardless of all the other things they're doing, and must do.

TEACHER THREE: I have some 70 students. A quarter of those students failed when I sent out the report cards. And I looked at the relationship between those who failed and their attendance and their tardiness. And it's hand in hand.

PARENT ONE: I'd be willing to celebrate homework everyday. When you think about your child, your toddler who is learning how to go to the bathroom. You celebrate every trip.

TEACHER ONE: My son is eight years old and he still wants me to celebrate every success!

TEACHER TWO: It's so related to developing self-esteem. And I just don't have a problem with saying, Wow you did all that homework by yourself?

there are fewer books in the public library, there are fewer books in the home, there are fewer books in the classroom. But the school is in a position to make a difference.

We should have the money to fill our classrooms with resources that the children need. We could allow the children to take these resources home. We can invite families in to share them. But I feel that we're being attacked on all sides, and we're expected to perform at a standard that is almost an impossible dream. And what frustrates the staff is that they feel that no matter what we do, it's not enough.

We're waiting for the budget. You have a reading aide because we have so many children who are in need of Title I services, and then the budget is cut. Now you don't have a reading aide, and you don't have a classroom aide. It's not fair because the children need a lot of support, and the government is not set up to give the children what they need to be successful. And then people are writing books about schools that are failing. And paid well for it.

Interview with a Retired African-American Superintendent and Current School Board Member, Midwestern City

I have become very cynical over the years. Either the powers that be in education don't want to give poor kids a good education, or they just don't know what they are doing. Or maybe they know what they are doing. The real problem is the way we finance education in this country. I've watched the tax base in our district deteriorate drastically over the years. The educated middle-class children of former immigrants now live in the suburbs. Their children need fewer services. Poor blacks and Latinos, whose children need more and expensive services, are trapped in the city.

Instead of facing up to these real problems, they dazzle us with tests. I am not against testing, although we are testing the kids to death without paying for what they really need in order to pass the tests. They are saying that we are not trying to do our job, so they will force us to do so with standards and tests. We want to do our job, and we have some successes, but it is a big job. And we need more help than the powers that be are willing to fund.

Our kids come to school two years behind the professional-class kids, a year behind the working-class kids. And they move often—across town and in and out of the country. We need programs and people who are going to go all out for them. And many do, but the best are recruited away after we train them. We can't compete with the salaries in the suburbs. And the state and federal government funds and the private foundation funds for the programs we need are here today and gone tomorrow; just like the kids.

The result is that we get a lot of white teachers who couldn't get into suburban schools. Don't get me wrong, some are special. But some have problems they don't know they have. This is really the first generation of post-civil-rights-era young people. Many genuinely think they are not prejudiced. But they did not grow up around black or brown people. They don't have firsthand knowledge of the problems. And some have a feeling of superiority that they have hidden from themselves, which makes it difficult for them to take advice from minority colleagues, even when they are experienced teachers.

As a result, they do and say things that get them into trouble with the parents, and then they run for help, literally in some cases, or they leave. One teacher harshly scolded a parent and then hid when she saw her returning to the building. A school in one of the poorest areas had six permanent subs as a result of such incidents, all black and brown without full teacher training, and all managed their classrooms better. We also have poor attitude, low-performing minority teachers. It is not about race. It is about comfort level, attitude, and skill. Our salary schedule means that we get too many who can't do the job, or who need a lot of help.

I think some of that same "we know everything attitude" has led to the test craze. I had hoped for more from the people in charge. But they are just like our young teachers. They are not and have never been in a position to understand what our children need. Show me the evidence that "test them and they will learn" will work. I can show them the evidence of programs right here in this district which improve learning and overcome low self-esteem, the effects of lean learning environments, and poor teacher attitudes. But we can't keep such programs going. Why not fund our successful programs rather than dictate?

Some of the "help" that is provided is good for the consultants but has very little to do with how to overcome the baggage our children carry. Whatever happened to the idea that local public servants know their communities and can do the best job? It would be okay if what they were doing made sense. But they just don't get it!!! This same standards, same test, get everybody ready to go to Harvard as social justice mentality makes no sense. Kids don't start out at the same place or receive the same help along the way.

I agree that talent is everywhere. Most blacks and Hispanics who have finished college can tell you about ten to twenty kids that were just as intelligent who didn't make it. But school learning has to be nurtured, just like golf and tennis were nurtured for Tiger, Serena, and Venus. And nurturing costs money. That's what they don't get, or don't want to get.

Education is a big boondoggle for a lot of people. Many people don't have that determination to give the kids what they need regardless of what it takes. They don't have a special stake in what happens to our kids. For them, it is a job and an income, and for some of these consultants, a very good income. I worry a lot about what is going to happen because so many of our teachers who go the extra mile, black and white, are now retiring. They have a special concern because their students are often the grand- and great-grandchildren of people they grew up with. Also some are so disgusted with the test mess that they are leaving early.

I can only hope that somehow, some group will get the country to change the way we finance local education and use testing to help us teach rather than dictate how we teach. It bothers me that minority leadership has fallen asleep on this one. We have the most to lose.

Interview with Carmen Gonzalez, Principal, P.S. 46, Brooklyn, New York

Our school is a prekindergarten through sixth grade elementary school with 600 children. We're located in a tough Brooklyn neighborhood: the poverty rate of our school population is 94 percent. In the 2000–2001 school year, we had 56 children with asthma, 13 of whom were in the American Lung Association's Open Airways program. We also had children medicated for ADHD and anemia—in some cases caused by sickle cell disease and in some cases caused by malnutrition.

In one case, the child had to be rushed to the hospital. He had come from a refugee camp in Guyana. Sitting in the back of the classroom, he had passed out. The teacher sent down the emergency pass, so I knew I had to get upstairs immediately. I ran. The child wouldn't wake up. We called for the nurse. She came up. We called 911. They came. The child's sickle cell anemia was so bad that he needed a transfusion. He had no doctor. He had no health plan. We were able to help him both in time and in an ongoing way before anything else really serious happened to him.

Other illnesses over the past five years have included high blood pressure, cardiac conditions, digestive disorders, juvenile arthritis, lead poisoning, obesity, physical impairments, skin disorders, rheumatic fever, diabetes, muscle disorder, scoliosis, and renal disorder. Also, almost one-third of the children (176 children) had vision impairments.

Now, how do I know all this? These cases went through our Child Study team, which is more popularly known throughout the School Development Program as the Student and Staff Support Team (SSST). The SSST is an integral part of the structure of SDP (it's not a separate entity, but rather a contributing factor to everything that happens in the school). Our Child Study team handled 1,428 cases in the 2000–2001 school year.

All the teachers, parents, and kids know the way in which the Child Study team does things. If the teachers have concerns, they can either write them and send a referral form, they can tell us verbally, or they can just call us on the phone and say they have a crisis right now in the classroom and can we intervene? And the parents, through the parent newsletter and the calendar, know that team meetings are scheduled every Monday morning from 9:00 to 11:00 A.M. They can walk in at other times as well.

We see the cases one by one and give them some priority as they come in. We do interventions or present classroom lessons for teachers who have consistent issues with children or classroom management or very sensitive topics, such as the 9/11 crisis. Basically this system has made the school community understand that there are people who care about kids and parents and staff. The children know they can tell us if they're having problems with a particular adult or someone has disrespected them or they just are very depressed and need to talk. The parents are our biggest clientele.

Thirty-six percent of our students are "fostered" (that is, living under the care of someone other than their parent). These children connect us strongly with community organizations, and several of their social workers are based in the school two or more days a week in order to serve the children and their adult caregivers. These people are also part of the team. (Originally we got grants to support these services, but the results were so good that now the school district is running similar programs in five schools.)

It is our school policy that no child is referred to special education or to any kind of program outside the school without having gone through the process of child study. It is the main system of our school.

Some cases are very difficult. In one case, the parent came in because she wanted help with her child. She started by presenting an extremely negative picture of the child, who was then in the second grade: "The child doesn't do this, doesn't do that, doesn't listen to me." We sent someone up to get the child. The child came and sat next to the parent. He crossed his arms and just looked down. He wouldn't look up. We tried to talk to him. He wouldn't talk.

Finally I said, "Well, we can't help you if you don't let us in and let us understand what your problems are."

He looked at his mother and said, "She hates me." It was as simple as that.

At that point, the social worker turned around and said to the mother, "We need to talk, and we need to talk at length because your child is feeling very strongly about how you are interacting with him."

The parent turned around and was ready to slap the living daylights out of him. We stopped her from doing that. We asked her to please step out of the room. We spoke to the child. We wanted to hear his version of what was going on.

The child just sat there and cried. He told us: Mom uses him and abuses him. If he doesn't cook her food right, she kicks him. If he doesn't iron right, she belts him. And it went on and on. The psychologist asked the little boy, "If there's one thing that we can get your mother to do, what would you want that to be?" He said, "I just want her to hug me once." We all broke down in tears. It was so hard to stop the emotion.

We brought the mother back in. We told her: "Your child needs an expression of love. Just for once, would you hug your child?" Do you know that she would not hug her child? She would not. I'm sharing this with you so you understand that some cases are very difficult.

We're still working with them. We told the boy that when he's good in school, we can call his mother for the good things instead of the bad things. We also gave the mother an ultimatum about the alleged physical abuse (we told her we would have to bring in the administration for Children's Services) and the physical abuse stopped.

We're no longer operating in crisis mode. Because the Child Study team is well trained and has trained the school community, everyone can say, "I know what I'm doing, and I can do it well." Teachers routinely intervene with parents who may be upset and acting out. Before, no one would take ownership. Everyone would watch a crisis and comment about it, but not do anything about it. How many schools do you go into where they just watch you in trouble and they don't come and pitch in and help? It's completely different now. Everyone is a stakeholder here.

When I first came to the school, my children were coming in at 10:00 A.M. thinking that there was no problem. "You're lucky I'm here, girl"—that's what they told me. The daily attendance rate was 74 percent at that time. We worked on it, and it inched up. We went up to 85 percent, but we could never get that 90 percent.

We analyzed the late logs and the absence logs. We realized that a lot of students are getting themselves up. They're dressing themselves. They're making their own breakfast. I had one child burned all the way down his body because the hot oatmeal spilled on him.

We thought about it and finally my attendance coordinator said, "These students need their own alarm clocks." We raised about $500 from businesses in the area. We bought one hundred alarm clocks. If children are chronically late or chronically absent, we don't give them late detention. We give them early detention. They have to show up at 8:00 A.M. for a week. The attendance coordinator meets with them. We feed them. They get their breakfast and we give them homework support. Then, the attendance coordinator teaches them how to set the clock. They use the clock in the morning to monitor their time. (In fact, at least one parent has used her son's clock in order to make sure she got to a job interview on time.) They keep journals. How long does it take you to get dressed? How long does it take you to eat? How long does it take you to walk from home to school? You can't change everything, but you can change that internal clock.

Joey (pseudonym) came to us from another country at the beginning of the 2000–2001 school year. He had received special education services all his life. This was the first time that he came to a system where he was integrated with his own age group. In his country, special education students are placed according to their cognitive level. He was twelve years old and learning with kindergarteners. So Joey had no concept on how to interact with his peers.

We did a whole medical review on him. We requested a psychological evaluation. During that case study we saw something in Joey that pointed to an additional problem that had not previously been identified: we discovered that he confused everything that he took in visually. The psychologist told us that it was a very rare kind of disability. His visual processing didn't match what was really there. We put him with a fourth-grade teacher who was very nurturing and caring.

What we hoped from Joey at the end was that he would learn to socialize with others his own age. We all worked continuously with him on sequencing issues. Guess what? In June, Joey was on the winning baseball team. The class held him up on their shoulders and rah-rah-ed him. The first time Joey smiled was when his team won the baseball competition. So we knew that at least we had made one breakthrough with Joey, and that was in his social skills. You should see him now: he's in our fifth-grade special education class, and he's getting outside occupational therapy, physical therapy, and psychological services. He's reading on a second-grade level, he comes to school every day, and he smiles all the time.

Well, how about behavior? We went from fifty-four suspensions in the 1999–2000 school year to just one suspension in the 2000–2001 school year. We piloted an in-house suspension program. We have a separate room. We have a social worker, a counselor, and a teacher. Students have to do all their class work. It is graded. They write a great deal and reflect on themselves. They reflect on what they could have done differently. How could they have avoided this? They are not allowed to socialize or play. They don't eat with their friends. We make it harsh because we don't want them to like it. We want them not to want to go back to the suspension room. They learn very quickly that it's easier to do an Act of Kindness than it is to do in-house suspension.

What is an Act of Kindness? I truly believe that it's not enough to say "I'm sorry." For instance, a girl is about to sit down and you pull the chair from under her and she falls on the floor. She's hurt—but more than this—she's embarrassed. You can't just say, "I'm sorry." Yes, you're sorry but you're going to do it again because the only consequence you had was saying "I'm sorry." So what we do is called Acts of Kindness. For two weeks, the child who pulled the girl's chair must pull the chair for her to sit on. In the cafeteria, he must bring her lunch to her table. He must clean up the lunch table for her. He must remove the tray. He carries her book bag throughout the school. He holds the door open for her. And let me tell you, after three days that boy is pleading with me: "Please, please— enough, enough!" I say, "Not until the little girl—who got her feelings hurt more than anything else—not until she says it's okay will it be okay." Usually the other child comes to me and says, "We're friends now." Then I accept the apology. I make them go through Acts of Kindness because I feel that they have civil and ethical responsibilities.

My school is spotless. If there's graffiti in the bathroom, I find out who did it. Not only do they go to in-house suspension, but they also spend a week with the janitor.

If students don't wear their uniform, guess what I do? They go around and collect uniforms for needy children. For other infractions, they have to read to younger children for ten hours. Let me tell you something: it works. I have very few children in in-house suspension. The ones in Acts of Kindness eventually come to me and say, "Ms. Gonzalez, you were right. That wasn't very nice what I did." So they stop that kind of behavior.

The Child Study team assesses itself three times a year. We see how we are doing because we want to get our bearings. Are we on the right track? What, specifically, are we doing? We ask ourselves these questions: Are we communicating our vision that all children can succeed? Do we encourage teachers to assess student learning styles? Do we constantly practice and apply the Comer principles? Do we fully and fairly participate in all child study conferences? Do we seek volunteers or tutors? Do we seek grants? Do we take care that our community partnerships are healthy? You need a good Child Study team because this is your right arm. If you're meeting the needs of all the children, you aren't going to have as many serious problems in your school. If you provide the social and emotional care and the psychological and physical care—if you get glasses for the kids and a serious reading program, and they're happy in school because they play an instrument or they're running on the track team—then you're not going to have problems with test scores. The students will be healthy and accomplishing all around.

On the very same day in which this summary was completed, the school district released the 2001–2002 summary of school performance which showed how well the students performed on the math and ELA standardized tests. Schools in the district were ranked based on the percentage of students who had moved from the lower levels of achievement to the highest level. P.S. 46 was ranked number one.

III
Change and Challenges

The voices from the school house acknowledge that there are problems from within but even many of those stem from something going on beyond the school house that is much bigger and more powerful. In the late 1960s and early 1970s, our Yale team came to realize that the problems in education were not just a matter of somebody or particular groups—parents, teachers, unions—behaving badly, not doing their jobs. Again, they all wanted to succeed. The problem defeating school staff, parents, and students was the massive and rapid societal change that had been taking place and was intensifying. It is still taking place. We had to understand the effects of these changes to better understand the nature of the challenges in schools and how to address them.

Around the middle of the nineteenth century, technological and scientific discoveries began to significantly change the conditions of community, family, and child life. The changes were slow and almost imperceptible at first, but eventually they became rapid, massive, and profoundly consequential.

Despite the many changes wrought by science and technology, including new expectations and desires, *the basic needs of children have not changed.*

All children need protection and sustained support to develop and prepare for successful participation in the life of their societies. The speed and magnitude of change in the nature of life in science and technology-based societies has created an enormous challenge. Our formative (family and school) and sustaining (economic and political) institutions have not adjusted fully or fast enough to be able to meet the needs of most children, but they must.

This gap between the support for development that children need and what society provides, more than anything else, lies at the root of most school problems. It is a challenge across the racial and socioeconomic spectra. Until we make necessary adjustments, we are not going to be able to prepare most young people to be successful in school and in life. Such issues as public or private operation and funding, physical design, and infrastructure concerns—class size, the curriculum, instruction, assessment approaches, and the like—are secondary, almost irrelevant. *Rarely, in school surveys, is the question of whether children are receiving adequate support for development even asked—and support for development is one of the most basic human needs.*

Because "being there" matters, I would like to reflect on my own experience. First, I was eleven years old and just beginning to observe the world around me when highly consequential technological, scientific, and social changes began to take place. I saw a television for the first time when I was about fourteen. Second, I had the kind of rearing and developmental experience all children deserve. Third, I grew up in three worlds—in a well-functioning, low-income, African-American family and its network; in close contact with struggling families; and as a minority in a school serving predominantly white students from working, professional, and executive class families.

Also, I made the journey from an uneducated and undereducated family to a high level of education and participation in complex mainstream institutions in one generation. Many children must do so today. Much of what is needed for them to succeed in this experience is not new and could be taught in school, much like putting vitamin D in milk.

Most important, I have spent thirty-five years demonstrating that *it is possible to create a framework that can make it possible to support child and adolescent development in schools;* that when the approach is implemented well, underdeveloped students can develop and learn at an improved level, often a much improved level, and they can behave in a way that increases their opportunity to succeed in mainstream systems. An education delivery framework that creates reasonable contextual conditions in previously difficult to dysfunctional schools is important. The dysfunctional school into which it is difficult to introduce good education practice is analogous to the impermeable cell membrane that blocks needed nutrients from the blood.

During my journey, I directly experienced the negative and positive effects of race and class, change and chance. And I often used protective mechanisms seldom considered by many mainstream researchers, policymakers, and decision makers. Our society is sensitive and defensive about our racial history to the point that we do not learn from it. We create education programs that do not consider how race issues can interfere with schooling. If we could consider these effects—from a "no-fault" perspective—we could limit, even prevent, related problem development and behavior among many students, staff, and parents.

I am hopeful that reflection on a few snippets of my own growing-up experiences will remind us "from whence cometh our strength." Powerful experiences in community, family, and school shape our development from birth to maturity. These experiences make the expression of our potential possible. Reflection on our own lives should suggest what is needed for all children and where we might look for human resources.

As I mentioned in chapter 1, I went off to kindergarten with three black friends who were as bright as anybody in my family and anyone in our school. They went on a downhill course in school and in life despite the fact that our parents had the same level of education and similar jobs and we were in the same good school. My siblings and I went on to earn a collective total of thirteen college degrees. Eventually I realized that the only difference between my sibs and me and our three friends was the quality of the child-rearing and developmental experience that we received at home and in our primary social network of friends, kin, and organizations in which our family felt a sense of belonging—namely, our church.

Good child care and rearing sparks and fuels an interaction that promotes child and adolescent development and growth. It begins with the parent or caretaker providing for the physical and emotional needs of the child—safety, food, clothing, emotional warmth, comfort. An emotional attachment and bond begins to develop between the child and the caretaker that is the prototype of all future relationships.

The best condition or context for growth is when children are very much wanted and valued, and when parents and caretakers have the skills and desire to help them grow and develop well. Good child rearing generally leads to good development, though a difficult environment can lead to troublesome outcomes despite good child-rearing techniques. Because of the unique capacity of human beings to construct their own understanding and reality, troublesome outcomes are possible even when rearing and the social environment appear good, and good outcomes sometimes occur in spite of difficult conditions.

My sibs and I were born into a family in which we were very much wanted and valued, and our parents were skillful child rearers. This was the case despite my mother's own difficult upbringing and the limited school time of both. My mother was born into extreme poverty in rural Mississippi. She was the third of five children, and her father had two children from a previous marriage. Her father was a good man who loved and provided for his family. But when she was six years of age, in 1910, he was killed by lightning. Because the children were too small to help with the work, a cruel stepfather came into their lives. There were two more children from this marriage, nine in all. They moved from place to place, living in one shack after another; and he unexpectedly abandoned the family from time to time. Also, he was abusive in many ways and would not let the children go to school.

When my mother was eight years of age, it occurred to her that the way to a better life was through education. When she was sixteen, she ran away to a sister in East Chicago, Indiana, with the hope of going to school. But her sister could see no benefit in a "colored girl getting an education" and was not supportive. After several months, she had to drop out of school. She began to do domestic work. When she left school she declared, "If I ever have children, I'm going to make certain that every one of them gets a good education!" Then she set out to very carefully find a like-minded husband.

He was twelve years older. They met in Sunday school—my father as teacher, my mother as student. He had been married once before and had a child, a reason for great caution given my mother's childhood experience. She only agreed to go out with him after his ex-mother-in-law wrote a letter of support. They were married two years later.

My father was from rural Alabama, the son of a minister. He had about a sixth-grade rural Alabama education. His family was poor but well functioning and in the process of buying their farm from the former slave master's heirs. To save the farm after boll weevils destroyed the crop in 1918, he left Alabama and worked in the steel mills in East Chicago. He, too, felt that the only way to a better life was through education. They set out to have a family and to provide us with what they had not been able to acquire for themselves.

But they were not in a hurry. It was twelve years before I was born. During that time my parents reared my older sister, Louise, my father's daughter. They were enmeshed in a church-based culture and community. And my mother continued to do domestic work for some of the most successful families in town. My father worked as a steel mill laborer, and they built their home with their own hands. Then we came, four of us almost one year apart over a five-year period.[1]

As I describe our childhood, keep in mind the fertile ground in which we sank our roots—an emotionally rich church culture, exposure to and participation in the mainstream culture, parental ambition and a belief in the American dream of better opportunity for all, and just enough income to keep hope alive. And our parents had an understanding that children had to be prepared for a better future, and they delighted in doing so. As a result we received a great deal of *nurturance* from the very beginning.

In the summer, after work or on weekends, my mother and father would take us to Lake Front Park where they would play with us, or sit and talk while we played. I still remember sitting on the front porch eating popcorn and drinking malted milks on warm summer evenings. Also, we were served Popsicles from the freezer. All of the snacks were homemade because it was less expensive, more fun, and more personal.

Every Sunday evening my mother would read us the "Sunday funnies." Two of us would sit on her lap and two down in front. We would squeeze in as close to her as we could get. Each of us had a favorite column that we would ask her to read again until she had read the paper two or three times. The funnies were not great literature, and my mother read at a second-grade level or less. But that was not important. The nurturance, emotional warmth, and closeness that we received provided us with the beginnings of a powerful sense of belonging and security; again, the most important of human needs. And in the process, reading was given a powerful positive emotional charge.

A reasonable sense of security and belonging fosters confidence and prepares children to take on the challenges of their environment and, with help and approval, gain competencies that enable them to successfully manage the challenges of their world. As they succeed they begin to feel, "I am somebody of worth, value, and competence." "I am. I can. I will." These conditions, combined with the need for self-expression, are the foundation of motivation. Caretaker guidance helps make the process constructive.

We received the *guidance, skills, and values* needed for appropriate social functioning and self-expression through many casual interactions, interactions that reflected our parents' attitudes, beliefs, and ways of approaching life. From my more philosophical father we often heard:

"If you can't be the best, be among the best"—be competitive, excellent.

"Nothing beats a failure but a try"—initiative, effort, chance taking.

"A man's word is his bond"—be responsible, show trustworthy behavior.

"The measure of a man is the way he treats his fellow man"—respectful relationships.

"Never let your race stop you from doing anything you want to do"—and much more.

And from my pragmatic mother:

"Be reasonable."

"A procrastinator's work is never done."

"Never mind the teacher, you get it upstairs. They can't take that away from you."

"If you are on time you are five minutes late."

"Recognize trouble, and stay away from it."

One of the places such mental and moral morsels were frequently served was at the dinner table. But dinnertime was more than messages. We ate at the same time every evening—regularity. We were expected to talk about the things that went on during the day that might be of interest to everyone—reflection and reporting. Through subtle clues, sometimes insistent suggestions, we were asked not to talk too long, to give others a chance to speak, to listen to what they had to say—

skills of conversation. Spontaneous discussions were encouraged, even strong emotions, but we were expected to keep emotions under reasonable control—free expression within limits and with self-control. Teasing was fine and fun, but you could not hurt anybody's feelings too much—a family value. Pretending you were hurt to get sympathy was frowned upon—no victims here.

My mother prepared everyone's favorite dish from time to time—collard greens, cherry pie, German chocolate cake, hot rolls, cube steak. Each child received special recognition on the day his or her favorite food was prepared and on birthdays—you are special and we celebrate each other. Sharing, cooperating, and enjoying the success of brothers and sisters was encouraged. These practices discouraged jealousy. The product of all of this was a family environment of warmth, trust, and mutual respect and appreciation.

What a far cry all of this is from what we heard in "Voices from the School House" in chapter 2.

My mother was not always sweetness and light. She would sometimes show irritation when we did dumb things that young people do because their brains are still developing and they are inexperienced, undisciplined, and still lack task commitment. She might say, "Use your head for something besides a hat rack!" And revealing her purpose, she sometimes said, "I ain't raising no dummies!" But most of the time both parents simply showed approval and disapproval through facial expressions.

My mother spanked, but my father never spanked us. She was irritated but not out of control when spanking, nor was she inconsistent. My father got the same results without spanking at all. I was more concerned about his disapproval than her spanking. Interestingly, she never spanked my second brother,

Charles, who was somewhat shy. I was shocked when he told me that he was never spanked. He laughed and pointed out that Norman and I provoked her more than he did. We did so to "get her goat," to get her to lose control. This is a child's way of getting a bit of power over all-powerful adults. It is important to note that here selective, situational judgment was being used to promote inner control, desirable behavior, and more assertive expression where needed.

Frequently the dinner table discussions would spill over into informal but intense after-dinner debates. Any issue was grist for the debate mill. But the rule was that no matter how badly you were losing the debate, you could not fight. We were very competitive and did not want to lose. So you had to listen, think, and express yourself quickly. I would find myself walking home from school thinking about a carryover debate issue and how I could more effectively address it. Thinking, expression, and personal control were practiced in these activities.

We were encouraged not to be dogmatic, but not to accept the viewpoint of anyone without question. This value was put to the test when as preadolescents we began to raise questions with my father about his religious beliefs. Both parents were very religious. From my mother's perspective, raising such questions bordered on disrespect for my father. But he encouraged us to do so, presenting his point of view and enjoying the fact that we challenged all things.

In one of the after-dinner debates, I expressed my opposition to public welfare. This was a position that my brother Norman was more likely to hold, but catching me in it, he began to decry my heartlessness, lack of concern for poor people, and the like. My mother would often rest on a cot just off the kitchen where the discussions took place, listening but rarely commenting. On this occasion she said, "But Jim, what would happen to poor people?" I suggested that when work was not available, government should provide a job of last resort. I explained that I felt that money without work created harmful dependency. She said, "Okay," and no more. Incidentally, that took the wind out of my brother's sails and brought joy to my heart.

My parents believed that exposure to successful people and participation in constructive mainstream activities was educational. Our family doctor's son, David, came to play with us when his parents went out for an evening, and we played at his house on numerous occasions. We also played at the homes of a couple of classmates whose parents my mother had worked for previously.

Our parents, and sometimes friends, took us to the museums in Chicago, the zoo, the circus, Marshall Field Department Store during the Christmas season, the Chicago Cubs Park, and on other trips. When President Franklin Delano Roosevelt's caravan came through town, we were there. There was much discussion about what was going on during these "field trips." And before all such occasions, my mother gave us social interaction "suggestions." "Talk enough to be interesting, but don't tell all of your business." And wisdom to reflect on, "If you talk too much, people will find out how big a fool you are."

On one occasion, my mother was working at the polling place during an election. When I went by at noon she invited me over and took me into the polling booth, which was probably against the rules. I actually pulled the lever, which *was* against the rules. (We were a community of trusting friends, not party officials worried about rules.) Both of my parents realized that it was *exposure and participation* that generated hopes and dreams and that helped young people see the connection between what they are doing and learning in school and participation in the real world. Making that connection promotes motivation for school success.

I learned effective ways of solving problems by listening to and watching my parents. Once I listened to my mother talking on the telephone with my principal, Ms. McFeely. A bully had knocked my brother Norman down and sat on him. Norman bit the bully, through his pants, on the butt. During the conversation my mother never raised her voice. Initially I could hear the sound of the principal's voice, but she gradually quieted down.

My mother's responses went something like this: "No, I don't approve of my children fighting." (Pause while listening.) "But you said that the boy was a bully, bigger, and that he started the fight." (Listening.) "While I don't expect them to fight, I do tell them that they are not to let anybody walk over them (or sit on them)! Fight back if necessary!" (Listening.) "Now, if there's a medical bill we will pay for it." (Listening.) "Thank you for calling, and please let me know whenever there's a problem."

Interestingly, Norman grew rapidly and eventually towered over the bully, and over me. He eventually played football, halfback and fullback for Northwestern University. But he was taught not to bully and not to fight his brothers ("Brothers and sisters don't fight"). But they do—brotherly love fights. My brother Charles and I sometimes had to gang up on Norman to help him contain his aggressiveness. Until the mental, social, and emotional development of young people is more complete, the expectations of parents are not always met in their absence.

More or less similar childhood experiences prepare most children for success in school and in life. But children who are

from families whose social environment directly and in-
directly transmits troublesome and negative messages need
special problem-solving training, self-esteem promotion, and
identity protection. This need is often not recognized, and as a
result too many students, even when they are capable, often do
not do well or perform beneath their potential. Children from
depreciated or marginalized groups—some minorities, majority children in certain areas, others—are vulnerable to negative environmental messages. Such messages can come from
many places; they can be unintended or intentional.

My mother provided us with the kind of child care she
was asked to provide for the upper-income children in the
families for whom she worked. Thus, she gave us a bath in the
morning before she sent us out to play and again in the evening.
She changed our clothes between daytime and evening activities. Our care and support sometimes drew criticism or just
dismay from neighbors. One was overheard saying, "Who does
she think she is? Them children ain't nothing but little pick-
aninnies." When I was about three or four years of age, our
family doctor was called to treat me. When he left I said, "I'm
going to be a doctor when I get to be a big man!" My parents
responded by buying me a doctor's kit and playing doctor with
me—reminding me that the candy pills were for the patient,
not the doctor.

Another neighbor asked, "Why are you encouraging him
to be a doctor? We're poor people. You know he will never be a
doctor!" My mother told her that if she said that again she would
have to leave. These neighbors were African-Americans. Their
comments reflect the high level of group and self-deprecation
and the low level of aspiration and hope that existed, and still
exist, among many.

Self-doubt-producing experiences were and are even more common outside the family network. In the middle of my fourth-grade year, a student transferred into our class. She told me that she knew my mother. The reason turned out to be that my mother had worked as a domestic for her mother years before. By ten or eleven, social status is an identity issue. Although children don't think "social status," they make observations and ask questions that help them place themselves in the scheme of things—how they are valued, where they stand as reflected by their house, car, race, religion, occupation of their parents, and so on. Their conclusions can influence their aspirations and effort. My mother noted that I was a little troubled by knowledge of that previous relationship. The knowledge was a threat to my quest for a sense of adequacy, belonging, and security.

She stopped what she was doing, looked me in the eye and said, "Don't let that bother you none. You're just as clean as she is. You're just as smart as she is. And you can do just as well in school." She paused and with a no-nonsense facial expression said, "And you had better!" Fortified by the positive sanction of one of the two most powerful people in my young world, I did well.

Note that my classmate's comments were a gesture of friendship and an effort to get acquainted. Many, if not most of the negative messages minority children receive are not intentional or even spoken. Social environment messages I had taken in at this very young age generated my concern. In fact, six or seven years later when I became the first African-American head of the student body, the same young woman wrote a letter to the local newspaper expressing pride in our school's accomplishment in race relations.

Intentional negative racial messages, whether subtle or direct and harsh, can be more damaging. I learned that race problems and obstacles are best addressed like all others—in ways that make matters better rather than in ways that would allow antagonists to justify their behavior. And when matters are beyond your control, you find ways to achieve what you want despite the obstacles.

I wanted to join the Boy Scouts because my school friends were doing interesting things at the meetings. My father took me to the Scout meeting, and while I was inside he had a long discussion with the leader outside the door. I did not go back, but my father got Mr. Watkins to form a Scout troop at our church. I do not remember his explanation. I learned later that racial integration was banned by the national organization at the time. Nonetheless, my father made it possible for my friends and me to enjoy the benefits of participating in a group experience.

All of these experiences helped me grow along all the developmental pathways. Growth in the social-interactive, psychological-emotional, and ethical areas or pathways is particularly important in complex social systems, but these are all but ignored by educators and policymakers. The often subtle, challenging social situation can have huge negative consequences for any student, and for minority students in particular because they face them more often. Without good preparation, such environments can become hurtful and limiting. With adequate preparation, young people can turn the negative to positive support, or at least not be harmed.

A problem I encountered in the eleventh grade comes to mind. Grades were given at the end of ten weeks and a final grade at the end of twenty. At the end of the first ten weeks, I was one and two points, respectively, behind the two white students who received As in our language arts course. I was almost thirty points ahead of the next closest student, but I received a B. After being told that a B was a good grade and other palliative things, my teacher eventually said kindly, "I just don't think you're capable of making an A." That was the end of the discussion. I knew exactly what that meant. The grade she gave me was an expression of her racial stereotyping.

I did not raise my voice. I did not even tell my parents. I worked very hard that next semester and earned all As, and the top score in her class. But I did not take a chance. Her class was my first in the morning. I told her that I had forgotten my grade book. I collected all my grades, all As, and went back to her at the end of the day. She gave me an A without comment.

During my senior year, when I was no longer in her class, she asked my advice about how she might help an African-American student whom she was concerned about. He was very smart but not working up to his potential. Perhaps our discussion the year before, and the way the incident was managed, helped her confront her bias. Let me hasten to add that almost all of my white teachers were just. Some went out of their way to make certain that I was treated fairly. I did not have a black teacher until I went to medical school.

Our family was enmeshed in a church culture that generated and reinforced the set of attitudes, values, and behaviors we lived by. Our church culture was in sync with the mainstream culture—personal excellence, hard work, a delayed reward, good relationships. The church-based culture affirmed our value when the society did not do so at the necessary level.

My experiences at home and in our primary social network prepared me for school. They enabled me to elicit a positive response from school people, to attach and bond with them and with the program of the school. Doing well academically and socially were our prime family and social network values. And being involved in sports, the arts, and student government could be expected because our family supported participation in any activities that were believed to be educational. In fact, at one point, all four of us were student council representatives from our respective classes.

As a result of the care that had been given to nurturing us in our early years, before we started school, and our resultant ability to elicit positive responses, our family, school staff, classmates, and community all supported our growth along all the developmental pathways. My three friends were not so well prepared for school, did not elicit positive responses, and began a downward course almost from the beginning.

Our fourth-grade teacher created a contest designed to encourage us to use the public library in town. The winner would be the person who obtained a library card and then took out and read the most books over a stated period of time. I read the most books. My three friends did not read any. My teacher was so frustrated and angry that she said to them, in front of the entire class, "If you three little colored boys don't want to be like the rest of us, you should not come to our school!"

She was not a die-hard racist. We often held hands from her house to school two blocks away. She did not understand. They very much wanted to belong and to be successful in school. But they were the children, grandchildren, or great-grandchildren of former sharecroppers and slaves. The adults in their lives were intimidated by mainstream institutions and had not been able to pass on the skills of participation to their young. Had my teacher understood this, she would have taken them to the library herself. But almost nobody understood the ill effects of marginalization back then, and not many more understand or address them now.

An incident many years later provided me with support for my notion that student-staff attachment and bonding is important. When my mother was a patient in the hospital in 1990, Ms. Walsh, my first-grade teacher, was then a spry eighty-plus-year-old hospital volunteer. When she saw me, she threw her arms around my neck and said, "Oh, my little James!" (I was fifty-five years old at the time, but you are always six years old to your first-grade teacher.) She then stepped back, looked me over, and said, "Oh we just loved the Comer children. You were so bright, so eager to learn, got along so well with other children," and on and on.

She was describing the outcome of dedicated, skilled, child-rearing interactions; good development; and a genetically determined potential that was at least at or above the modest threshold level necessary for school and life success. It was "all of the above," not intelligence alone, that made our academic success possible. Good development and a supportive family and church-based primary social network made it possible to manage the environment of the schools we attended and the world beyond.

How important and powerful is a positive family social network or community? In the transition from high school to college, I went from a supportive school social environment to a usually indifferent, sometimes hostile university community environment. In addition to less support, the open racism of 1950s southern Indiana was a new burden. The Indiana University campus environment was improving but unpredictable. Unintentional and intentional negative racial and class messages were everywhere. Segregated fraternities and sororities, dormitory roommate policies, the flashy new cars of the affluent students, and much more greatly threatened my sense of belonging, my right to be there. In one absurd situation, an attempt was made to separate two Puerto Rican sisters, and roommates, one black and one white, to comply with the segregation rule.

Most of the professors were fair, some extra supportive, and some were carriers of racial stereotypes. In my first-year English composition course, the professor was reading my paper as an example of the best work in the class; he had given me an A. He graded papers anonymously, so when he had a question halfway through, he asked for the author and I responded. From that point to the end, he ripped the paper apart with criticism of every line as if it were F work. I was the only black student in a large class. Instead of proof of my right to be there, I experienced self-doubt and rejection. I made average grades the first year, not good enough for a future career in medicine.

When I returned home that summer, I visited all the "sisters" from our church who believed in me and had helped me grow up. My parents reassured me, and again I heard, "Get it upstairs, they can't take that away from you." With my confidence restored, my intelligence could be expressed. I returned to school and made the kind of grades I needed to make my career possible.

Good academic achievement can open the doors to greater opportunity. But again, it often takes more than intelligence, hard work, and high test scores to walk through them. Young people need the development that will help them to elicit support that will enable them to acquire the competence and confidence needed to interact well in most environments and with most people. To do so, they need the kind of experiences, support, and guidance that we received.

Even with the best of care, all young people are at risk because of their physical, mental, social, and psychological immaturity. The emotions of still-maturing adolescents, in difficult situations, can override the brain centers responsible for impulse control, morality, and good judgment even when young people know what is harmful and likely to be problematic. Indeed, this can happen at all ages. The immature are more vulnerable. Three family experiences suggest that good child rearing and development along all the pathways can be preventive and protective—public health goals—over the short and long run, in and out of school.

When I was about thirteen years old, one of the prettiest upper-class women in our high school was being regularly sexually harassed by her male classmates. (We did not think of it as such back then, but it was.) During a chance opportunity, and probably on an impulse, she and a girlfriend decided to exploit me, to take the initiative, to be assertive with a male. I was rendered all but helpless by desire and emotions. I needed help. I noticed that it was past my curfew and thought to myself that my father would be out looking for me. I got up, against the strong urging of my body, and left before engaging in risky behavior. A half block from home I met my father—looking for me.

Several males brought a female student who was drunk into the dormitory at Indiana University and gang-raped her. One participant excitedly knocked on the door of my brother Charles's room, inviting him to join. His first impulse caused him to jump up from his desk. But he heard my mother's voice, even though she was not there, ask, "Where do you think you're going?" He sat down. All of the students who participated were either suspended or dropped from school.

My brother Norman was one of several fraternity pledges who rebelled against the almost sadistic behavior of the pledge-master. The anger of the pledges got out of control. They were about to throw the pledge-master out of a third-story window. Norman managed to ask them what they thought would be the charge if he died as a result of the fall. The answer, murder, stopped the attack.

My siblings and I were able to respond in ways that prevented problem behaviors in adolescence because of developmental capacities gained through caring guidance or rearing by meaningful caretakers during our early childhood. Recall that we had been told "Recognize trouble, and stay away from it." More important, we had relationships with our parents that encouraged us to avoid problem behaviors. There was another important contributing factor—a constructive goal orientation. My parents understood the importance of aspirations and goals.

Many years later, I asked my mother how she would have felt if she had known that we often hung out on the street corner in front of the Turf Grill and Bar, the summer gathering place of many of the college-age crowd, and others. She laughed and said, "I knew. You were growing up and you had to have fun. But I knew you would not get into trouble. We were a team and we had our goals. You had been taught to avoid anything that would stop you."

Today, young people see and experience many more models of problem behavior because of greatly increased information and exposure, with less support for development. Given the conditions that have weakened the impact of family and community, help from other venues in which they are growing up is very much needed. In recent years, character education in school has emerged as a way of helping young people acquire desirable behavior patterns. Service learning programs have similar purposes. These activities can help, but they are not nearly enough. These programs usually do not address context and relationship issues to the extent needed.

It is in a child's family and early social network of friends, kin, and important organizations that character is "caught" more than it can be "taught," where the capacities for and habit of being a good person are established. Parents and other people in the family network are powerful models and motivators because there is an emotional attachment that makes them meaningful. To be effective, schools and other organizations attempting to encourage young people to develop character must reasonably approximate the modeling and relationship contexts of the primary social network or family. But educators and other policymakers have been reluctant to adjust, and to create such conditions.

The resultant problems are apparent in most schools, but an incident in an urban high school early in my work drew it to my attention in an indelible way. The district superintendent walked into the school and ordered a teenage student to "take your hat off!" The youngster looked at him disdainfully and said, "You kiss my ass!" Outraged, the superintendent asked, "Do you know who I am?" The reply, "I don't give a fuck!" The response, "I'm the superintendent, and you're suspended!" "That's cool with me," the student said and he walked out the door.

Today that same school is a community in which there are generally respectful relationships. Certainly, such incidents can happen anywhere. But they are much less likely in school environments where respectful relationships are the norm; where students sense fairness and belonging; and where questionable behaviors are addressed as developmental challenges rather than simply bad behavior that must be squashed by authority figures.

The relationship conditions that make desirable outcomes possible must be created within the schools—as they are not produced by ordinary conditions in the community anymore. Schools can provide some of "the village" they need. Indeed, schools—with help from parents and community—could be the leading social organization in restoring a reasonable degree of parental and community support for youth development.

Stories like "the superintendent and the hat," and others, permit many to argue that "those kids" are just bad and dumb. And stories like that of my family help many to maintain the notion that anybody who works hard and behaves can make it. They fit our up-by-your-bootstraps mentality and myth. They fit our intelligence-and-will explanation for school and life success. They also permit us to blame children and families for not being prepared to do well in school rather than to focus on adjusting the formative and sustaining institutions so that they can better meet the basic needs of students. We do this at a time when it is much more difficult to do well in life without success in school.

There is, then, a gap between the skill and developmental level of many of our young people and the level they need to achieve to participate successfully in a national and global society that has changed very rapidly, and promises to continue to change. The myths and rationalizations often cited ignore the huge challenges presented in "Voices from the School House." Indeed, they delay our putting in place the kind of supportive program like the one implemented in the school briefly discussed in "Voices."

The nature of human life makes a reasonable degree of security our most important human need. Birth moves us from the extreme security of the womb to extreme vulnerability outside of it and, with awareness, insecurity. The newborn human cannot survive without help. Much of what happens after birth is a quest for the skills and knowledge needed to cope and, through self-actualization and self-expression, survive and thrive in a way that provides meaning and purpose in life. A reasonable sense of well-being and security grows out of the fulfillment of these quests.

All human beings face threats to their ability to cope and to achieve gratifying outcomes. Claude Steele's work is illustrative of the universal nature of this phenomenon. He demonstrated that the stereotype of racial inferiority contributed to the academic underperformance of a group of otherwise able African-American college students. A group of white students when told that Asian students generally did better on the kind of test they were taking underperformed on the test. But a group of experienced, successful African-American professionals were not negatively affected by such misinformation.[2] This work suggests that the degree of threat varies with conditions in the environment and on the status of individual competencies and confidence. Young children are highly vulnerable to threats of all kind. Thus, the force behind their quest for knowledge, skills, competence, and confidence is great.

A successful quest usually requires good development. Limited success or failure in meeting these quests can lead to a deep sense of insecurity, harmful social and psychological outcomes, and problem behaviors.[3] Some will eventually give up or simply accept whatever life brings, often leading to constant underperformance. (I will return to this point when I discuss a child's effort to cope, or to "make it," as he or she addresses the challenges of school.)

Children are born exploring their environment in the service of survival. They are also born with critical survival tools—aggressive energy that is potentially harmful to them and others, and the capacity to elicit empathy and form relationships with caretakers. These tools, and the fact that children are profoundly dependent, make it possible and necessary that caretakers help them channel their potentially harmful energy into constructive energy of learning, self-expression, work, and play.

This usually occurs as a child identifies with and begins to imitate and internalize the attitudes, values, and behaviors of, first, the primary caretaker and, then, emotionally meaningful others. Through multiple and emotionally powerful interactions, the caretaker and others promote growth. The impetus for these interactions begins before birth with the parent's preparation for a baby. As a child becomes more independent, gains wider exposure, and is able to think at a higher level, the impact of these early experiences can be widely modified. But often they are not.

Parents or caretakers help children grow along many pathways. In our School Development Program we consider six pathways critical: physical, social-interactive, psychological-emotional, ethical, linguistic, and cognitive-intellectual. Contemporary education addresses primarily the linguistic and cognitive pathways. But it is growth along *all* these pathways that prepares children for school and for life. They must gradually take primary responsibility for their own growth, development, and performance.

It is the need to manage human aggression and meet relationship needs in a way that sustains life and promotes civility that causes groups to create social organizations. Through governance of various forms, economic and social arrangements needed to protect and promote a group—community, family and kinship, societal—are established. The most relevant here are family and school, where through child rearing, teaching, learning, and development children are prepared for adult life.

Through care and rearing, families and others help the child gradually regulate all body functions, mental and physical. They must help the child modify the expression of undifferentiated, "raw," potentially harmful aggressive energy. It must be brought under the developing child's control so that it can be used selectively and appropriately in pursuit of life's tasks, for meaning, and to sense purpose. This is done as caretakers help the child learn to negotiate family and other social networks.

The biological potential children are born with is realized and elaborated through the interactions with the people and things around them. Again, the interactions in desirable social environments lead to growth toward maturity in the six areas, venues, or pathways just mentioned that many believe are essential for future academic achievement. The potential for full intellectual development and academic achievement can be lost when the interactions needed for developmental pathway growth do not take place or are insufficient or harmful.

Growth along the developmental pathways is simultaneous and more or less continuous, but not necessarily so. It often occurs at different rates, is interactive, and the pathways sometimes facilitate, sometimes limit the expression of each other. Whatever the pattern, much development has already occurred by the time a child reaches school. Attention to development along these pathways can and should continue in school.

The best outcomes occur when the caretakers have the capacity for sociable and constructive interactions with the child. The same is true in the teacher-student relationship. But whether parents and caretakers are constructive or not depends a great deal on how they themselves have managed the social environmental conditions in their own family networks and in society, and the nature of their resultant personal attributes. Parents and caretakers in reasonably well-functioning social networks are more likely to have experiences that produce positive personal attributes.

The social networks of middle- and upper-income families, which experience less stress, more often function better. This makes sociable and constructive interactions with their children more likely. Such families are more often a part of the societal mainstream. As a result they are exposed to the most prevalent and expected attitudes, values, and ways, and the most rewarding opportunities of the society. They generally have reasonable access to all levels of participation in the political, economic, educational, and social institutions of the society. Again, I refer to those who do not have exposure and access as marginal to the mainstream.

We must keep in mind that many marginal families function well and provide good support for child development, although sometimes that support is not sufficient to provide access to all levels of mainstream institutions. And many mainstream families do not function well and do not provide adequate support for their children.

Here comes the rub. Our society in particular values self-sufficiency. It is a powerful expectation felt by everyone. It is recognized as the more honorable state even in networks where

most people are not self-sufficient, for whatever reason. The
society reluctantly and begrudgingly steps in to provide food,
clothing, shelter, and other basic needs. Because of this disposition, when societal involvement takes place, it is disparaging
and therefore less helpful than could be the case.

Being able to provide basic material needs and good
child rearing are two of the powerful ways caretakers and
heads of household experience a psychological sense of adequacy, success, and well-being. Not being able to do so often
results in negative psychological feelings, from low self-regard
to depression and dysfunctional behavior. The negative attitudes that exist in society about those unable to carry out basic
tasks increase their negative feelings about themselves. This
often makes conditions and behavioral matters worse. We observe these outcomes even in well-educated, highly paid engineers who are laid off in economic downturns, even when they
have had the benefit of early and longtime constructive experiences. Child and spousal abuse and other problem behaviors
increase during such periods. The problem is more pervasive
and difficult to overcome among people who are frequently
unemployed, are unemployable, or are on public welfare, particularly when they themselves did not have good childhood
experiences.

*Thus, the ability to provide one's self and one's family with
basic human needs—food, clothing, shelter, and more—through
work or earned income is very important. Families able to do so
are more likely to have high regard for themselves and to be real-
istically hopeful for their children. They are best able to provide
child-rearing experiences that lead to good development.*

Caretaker and child interactions at an early age create
brain structures that facilitate critical "building block" competencies. And although the human brain responds to biological

and social environmental influences across a lifetime, and children are remarkably resilient, good early experiences are probably disproportionately powerful. They lead to habits of mind and patterns of interest and behavior that put children on success trajectories. Unless altered by later experiences, they often persist as helpful tools in a child's quest for well-being and security. The same dynamic but with the opposite outcome is true with inadequate or harmful experiences.

A study of language development and parental sanctions points to a problem for many families that poses a huge challenge to society. A recent study by Betty Hart and Todd R. Riley of forty-two children showed that by three years of age a like-size group of children from nonmainstream families were exposed to 30 million fewer words than children of college professors. Also, the nonmainstream children had received twice as many prohibitions to behavior than encouragements, whereas the mainstream children had received six times as many encouragements to prohibitions. The experience of working-class children was roughly in the middle on both measures.[4]

The nonmainstream children will not be prepared for school. In 1968 we began pointing out that such children are underdeveloped and can be expected to achieve at a lower level than children who have had experiences that lay the foundation for academic learning. But because our society is so firmly wedded to the notion that academic learning is a reflection of intelligence and will, it is very difficult to establish educational approaches that will promote development as the foundation for learning.

Fortunately, human beings and groups have a unique capacity to create a sense of well-being and security out of spiritual, social, and religious beliefs and mind-sets that are not based on income or wealth. This was the saving grace of many in family and communal networks closed out of living-wage jobs in the mainstream workforce of the past. Many families from these networks were able to provide their children with good developmental experiences and even the attitudes, values, and skills that made mainstream participation possible once social and other barriers were removed.[5]

Today, supportive belief systems can complement the effects of workforce participation, but they are insufficient for an adequate sense of security. Participating in the workforce or receiving earned income is necessary. And because work has psychological, social, and emotional consequences for individuals and families, and in time for communities and the society, participating in the workforce is a critical individual need, perhaps a right, and preparing all to do so is an important societal responsibility.

Expanded opportunities in recent years have made it possible for more groups and families to function reasonably well and to feel some degree of security. But participating in the workforce was easier before technology and science greatly changed human and societal functioning. Change threatens the last to receive opportunity first and most.

Before the era of advanced technology, it was possible for most heads of households to earn a living through hunting and gathering, fishing, subsistence farming, and industrial labor without a formal or school-based education or with a minimal amount of education. This was the case throughout human history right up until the last stage of the industrial economy era, or the 1970s. In addition, travel was difficult and communication was limited. Thus, work had to be close to one's home. As a result, and very importantly, children were raised in close proximity to parents, without significant outside knowledge and influences.

As late as 1940 more than 50 percent of all Americans lived in nonmetropolitan areas, small towns, and rural areas. Even most big cities were collections of small towns.[6] People from every income and social group often lived within walking distance of each other and often interacted with each other. Children observed family and friends walking to work; earlier in history, they often worked with them.

Preparation for adult life largely involved friends and kin. Until early in the twentieth century, family and friends taught children to hunt, fish, farm, and otherwise secure a living. During most of the first half of the twentieth century, teachers and children often walked to school together. The teacher was sometimes a member of the church choir a child attended. The policeman on the corner was a family friend or simply known to all. Children, with their parents, often encountered school staff members in the grocery store or the post office.

Because of the relatedness and sense of community that existed under these conditions, what children knew about the world came to them from parents and their primary social network of friends, kin, and institutions in which the family experienced belonging—from people who were meaningful to them. At least five or six people, as well as two storekeepers, between my home and the school seven blocks away, knew my parents well enough to tell them when they observed me acting in a way they thought was unacceptable.

Such adults were in a position to censor or prevent children from access to information they considered harmful, and to give positive and negative sanctions that powerfully shaped child and youth expectations and behavior. The adults were generally in agreement about what was right and wrong, good and bad. And most adults were positive models, represented reasonable life possibilities.

There was often an important continuity of relationships. The same sales lady at the Minas Department Store in Hammond, Indiana, who had helped my parents buy clothes for me when I was born helped us select clothes when I went off to college seventeen years later. She worked in that same store for almost fifty years. Most sales and service providers were familiar to many customers and clients to the point of almost being an extended family member. As a part of my childhood community, she helped me and many other young people grow up.

Change was slow. For generation after generation, children were prepared for adult life in communities that were very much like the one where they grew up. The people in their community and the organizations to which they belonged were meaningful because of the interactions and ties established first by their parents, and eventually by themselves.

This is not to say that the past or "the good old days" were better. We were not as good a democracy then as we are today. Poverty, disease, abuse, and exploitation of the least powerful were the norm, and these are still significant problems. Contrary to popular belief, education is better and more available today than a century ago. Health care, education, and other services were limited and primitive, but uncomplicated—not tied to insurance, jobs, and the like. The sense that "the good old days" were better flows from the past opportunity for employment or self-sufficiency with little formal education; from little need to obtain services beyond the family social network; and from the ability to meet emotional and social needs through religion or spirituality and communality. Also, most of the people who romanticize "the good old days" did not experience the worst of them.

IV
The New World

As late as the turn of the twentieth century we were still at a horse and buggy level of science and technology (not far removed from that of the wheel) and its related lifestyle. And then there was change, rapid change. We raced from there to a world that included automobiles, jet planes, and an interplanetary rocket level of technology in just eighty years—within the life time of many senior citizens, yet a blink of an eye in terms of human history.

Until about the middle of the twentieth century it was possible for people to meet their basic human needs with low levels of academic achievement and without much systematic societal effort. Since then, scientific and technological advances have changed the nature of the economy and the way most people earn a living. This increased the need for a higher level of academic achievement. Such achievement requires a higher level of overall personal development in families and communities than was necessary previously. But the application of science and technology to most aspects of life simultaneously created forces that make it much more difficult for

families and communities to adequately support the development of children.

High mobility; rapid, visual, and now virtual mass communication; and workforce turnover have been especially challenging. These conditions reduce the birth-to-maturity continuity of close relationships with meaningful, protective, and
supportive caretakers that most children once received in their
primary family network environment.

Many things necessary for family functioning that were
once available mostly in the local community and through the
primary family network—food, clothing, shelter, health care,
education, entertainment—eventually had to be met in a more
impersonal secondary service network, often outside the community. Work beyond the family network became routinely
necessary to purchase services, making work a critical need.[1]
The car became part of daily life, people traveled farther for
work and on errands, and as a result, today few adults can be
seen walking through their neighborhood on their way to
work or while going about their daily business.

Teachers drive to school, which are sometimes considerable distances from their homes. Fewer teachers sing in the
same church choir or walk hand-in-hand to school with their
students as I did. For their part, young people often work and
play beyond the supervision of adults who are known or
meaningful to them and their families. And unlike the situation of the store clerk who sold my parents clothes when I was
born and again when I went off to college, we now purchase
goods and services from an uninterested (in the job or in the
customer) teenage salesperson, who changes every six months.
Also, for the first time in the history of the world, information
and entertainment from sources outside their primary family
network can go directly to young people. Children often hear

and see attitudes, values, and ways of behaving that would not receive their parents' approval and that are sometimes harmful. Responsible adults have little chance to limit or prevent their exposure, or to help them respond appropriately to what they receive. As a result, even when children are reared in close proximity to their parents, powerful outside and impersonal influences affect their lives. Today, children are often targeted for exploitation of one kind or another. This is not to say that children were not victimized in the past, but because families were more often embedded in networks that provided a sense of community, the task of protection and support was more under their control.

Leaders at local, regional, and national levels form a _tertiary or policy network_ around and among families and make decisions that influence the availability and quality of important services. But in part because it had always been possible for people to meet their basic needs without much systematic societal effort, and with low levels of academic achievement, the need to systematically enable communities and families to promote the quality of child and adolescent development needed to make it possible for most to get an education and to manage the more complex social environment was not given adequate attention.

The sense of community slipped away gradually, often in the name of progress—a house in the suburbs, a television set, and such—and the downside of its loss was not fully appreciated. Communities are important in supporting the development and preparation of children for adult life.[2] Because of the application of scientific and technological knowledge to all aspects of life, good family functioning, child rearing, and development are more essential today than ever before. But in the

importance of community

absence of a sense of community, such outcomes are more difficult to bring about. These convergent factors have contributed greatly to our crisis in education.

While all leaders had a responsibility to push for the necessary adjustments to change, educators were in the best position to identify youth development as the critical need to address in a society that was becoming more complex. But most of the education enterprise—institutions that prepare school staff, practitioners in schools and systems, and relevant policy and decision makers at every level—did not recognize that underdevelopment would make it difficult for the young to meet the challenges of change. Instead, most educators proceeded as if no significant change had taken place; or even if it had, as though no significant program adjustment was necessary. This continues to be the case.

A mechanical approach to teaching and learning remains the rule in most public schools. It is still generally believed that a child's ability to learn academic material is due to a genetically determined level of intelligence and simple desire or will. The understanding that development and learning are inextricably linked is still not accepted by many, if not most. Class and racial attitudes and beliefs rooted deep in our cultural and social history made and make it difficult for us to think otherwise and to appreciate the powerful way that a good developmental experience creates a sense of adequacy and security and positively impacts learning.

The intelligence-and-will notion contributes heavily to an expectation of a deficiency among some students—more often poor and minority, but often rural and marginalized whites. It supports the ability of some to claim superiority over others. It leads to schools never opening the gates of opportunity to many students while widening the door for those already prepared to pass through.

Families from groups that were, or could become, a part of the political, economic, and social mainstream at the turn of the century were best positioned to undergo the three to four generations of change or social development that paralleled rapid changes in the economy. Their limitations were personal and through chance—bad decisions or life management, illness, job loss due to new technology, geographic isolation, and so on.[3] Some groups faced early efforts to exclude them from the economic, political, and social mainstream. But wealth, or access to wealth, and the knowledge and skills of some among them, combined with the organizing, direction-giving, facilitating power of their more or less intact and cohesive cultures of origin, made it possible for them to overcome exclusionary efforts and extend reasonable opportunities to their masses. Also, almost immediate access to the mainstream American political structures helped. This phenomenon is still operating with many new immigrants today, black, white, and brown.

In such families, uneducated heads of households earned a living in an agricultural and industrial economy before the 1930s. They were able to give their children the acculturation and modest level of education needed to participate in the largely industrial economy between the 1930s and 1960s. Many children of that generation received the higher level of development and education needed to participate in the last stages of the industrial economy from the 1960s to the 1980s and 1990s and into the postindustrial age beyond.

African-American families, some Hispanic groups, Native Americans, and some isolated whites were often not able to undergo a similar three generations of acculturation and social development. Although the historical experience of each of these groups was different, the effect was similar—cultural discontinuity and trauma, limited to no access to wealth or the political structures, social exclusion and abuse, marginality, and resultant psychological and social damage. The degree of damage done varied with the ability of each group—and of subgroups within each group—to limit the damage and to promote good outcomes.

The church and community-based culture of African-Americans, while still marginal to the mainstream, served important protective and promotive functions. It provided many with a sense of adequacy and belonging. This softened the effects of mainstream abuse and exclusion. The church- and community-based culture provided belief and behavior systems that made desirable social and family functioning and achievement possible. This outcome, coupled with the demands of the industrial and postindustrial economies, the effects of television, the support of other Americans, and other factors led to an intensified civil rights movement that broke the legal barriers to mainstream participation in the late 1950s and 1960s.

The movement began to open opportunity to Americans from all previously excluded groups, and to both sexes. But by the time significant social and political progress was made, around the 1970s, the last stage of the industrial economy that required little or no education was all but gone. Also, although the law changed, significant racism persisted within key political, economic, and social structures. This greatly slowed progress and consumed group leadership energy that should have been available for African-American community development, both individual and organizational.

Around the 1960s, before many were prepared to benefit

from new opportunities, the effects of high mobility and mass communication began to greatly contribute to a breakdown in community and family life across the racial, ethnic, and income spectra. Groups that had been excluded from participation in mainstream political, economic, and social institutions were more vulnerable. I will limit this discussion to African-Americans.

A disproportionate number of African-American families were closed out of the political, economic, and social mainstream during the three-generation change. Many that functioned reasonably well in a low-tech economy began to undergo a downward spiral. Indeed, some have experienced a more-than-three-generation downward spiral away from opportunity and participation in mainstream institutions.

Before the weakening of protective and promotive cultural structures within the group, many families used these structures to create beliefs and values, and to gain direction in their own lives; that, in turn, enabled their children to thrive. My family of origin is a good example. Such families are the ones now best able to take advantage of increased opportunities. As a result, one part of the black community is moving up and in, and one part down and out, with growing social and emotional distance between them. The decline of too many families and their networks, and continued exclusionary conditions in the larger society, make it difficult for African-American parents to send proportionate numbers of young people into the American mainstream.

Also, an enormous amount of national energy went into school integration efforts without addressing the ill effects of exclusion from the political, economic, and social structures. As a result, the most traumatized benefited least from improved educational and economic opportunities. While school integration was critically important in breaking down a symbol of inferiority that justified overall exclusion, it did not lead to the kind of support and experiences that many students needed to succeed at the levels of their ability

Finally, economic and social changes have greatly increased the number of two-parent working families and single-parent workers. Since the 1950s there has been an explosion in the number of working parents. The proportion of married women in the workforce has increased from 20 percent in 1950 to 61 percent in 1997. The proportion of children living with a single (workforce) parent has gone from 9 percent in 1950 to 27 percent in 1997.[4] Workforce participation at this level has put greater stress on already struggling families, contributing to further weakening of the positive forces of community. This is not an argument against women in the workforce. The challenge is to maintain adequate support for development whether mother, father, or both are working. Again, our society did not adequately meet this challenge and the most vulnerable—least well educated, lowest income—families are most negatively affected.

Many of today's students at greatest risk for underachievement or school failure are growing up in families that did not experience three generations of acculturation and upward mobility, or a psychological sense of doing so even if not real. Most often both parents, or the single parent, are in the workforce with low-paying jobs. The parents want their children to be successful in school and in life, but they themselves have not had the experiences they need to help their children do so. Some live under paralyzing economic, social, and psychological stress. They are unable to provide the necessary preparation even when they know what is needed and would like to provide it.

Such children, underdeveloped and thus unprepared for the school challenge, and for economic or other reasons, would have dropped out of school sixty, even twenty-five years ago. Perhaps 50 to 75 percent of the students in school today would not have continued after the sixth grade in the 1930s; they would have been absorbed into the economy. They would have still been in the position to meet their adult tasks and responsibilities. Particularly relevant here, they would have had a reasonable chance to rear their children well.

Educators rarely consider the implications of the change, that many of today's students enter school underdeveloped and will not catch up without adequate support for development in and outside of school. And many of these children must now move from undereducated and marginalized families to being well-educated adults with the high level of social sophistication needed to participate in the mainstream in just one generation. Living-wage employment requires it. Also, today's future worker will need the social, ethical, and psychological capacity to find, lose, or leave three to five jobs over a workforce participation lifetime.

In communities where too many are unable to do well in school and are unable to participate in the mainstream economy, too many begin to participate in the underground economies, now dominated by drugs. A large part of the mainstream economy, and its positive influences on communities, is outside the cities and rural areas, often in places where many minorities and poor people do not fully feel a sense of belonging. As a result, many young people who are well prepared to participate in the mainstream, ability and skill wise, must overcome transportation and relationship barriers to doing so. Thus, mainstream employment can be inaccessible even when students receive adequate schooling and good test scores.

The underground culture, and few societal efforts to make mainstream participation possible, have created conditions that make good community and family functioning more difficult and, in turn, good support for child and adolescent development more difficult. The underground, and related subcultures, is vibrant and populated by many bright and exciting people. Over the past generation, the music and style of the nonmainstream culture have become valued and valuable entertainment in the mainstream. For this reason it attracts many mainstream adolescents from all groups. It is an adolescent and young adult interlude for the young people who receive preparation and support for mainstream participation at home, in school, and in other activity networks. Such young people, in time, return to mainstream success habits and participation.

Some, however, are drawn into problem behaviors that change their life trajectories, sometimes temporarily, sometimes permanently. The risk is greatest for marginalized minority students. Even when such students do well in school, they will need a source of mainstream life skills not readily and emotionally available, as well as sustained social and emotional support in order to succeed in life. Recall the revitalization I received from my church-based primary social network after the race-based traumas I experienced during my first year in college. The once powerful positive effects of well-functioning and/or church-based cultures have been decreased by the breakdown in community and the powerful effects of mainstream media entertainment that glorifies often harmful nonmainstream habits and style.

Because they are not immersed in positive and protective family and community networks, many will embrace harmful nonmainstream habits and style as "our culture." And because the habits do not promote school and life success, their involvement is not just an adolescent interlude but often a one-way ticket to marginality for themselves and generations to come. There is enormous pressure on mainstream minority youngsters to "buy in." Many of them are being lost and will perform far below their potential in school and in life. Low-income minority young people are less likely to have the recovery resources needed and will receive fewer second chances to try for school and life success.

Regardless of the causes, science- and technology-driven change continues to move swiftly. Many young people across the social and economic spectrum are being left behind. Their families, for varied reasons, were not in a position to make it possible for them to have a reasonable chance to realize the American dream under the changed conditions of life. Many school people, past and present, wanted to give them a better chance, but they were not able to do so.

Shortly after we began our work in schools in 1968, we realized that many of the students were underdeveloped and school people were not prepared to help them grow. Because of my own developmental experience, and that of my friends, I knew what these young people had been denied. I suspected that if the school could approximate what I had received at home and at school, it would be possible for many more young people to be successful in school and in the new and changing world.

We knew we had to focus on youth development. But we found a resistance to doing so that I am still not completely able to explain. This resistance continues to exist. Recently I received an e-mail from a veteran teacher in the Midwest who encouraged me to continue writing about the importance of child development. Her principal had told her that her problem was that she was a developmentalist, and there is no room for developmentalists in education!

Child and youth development as a central and guiding focus is still an unacceptable notion to many, and yet recent brain research strongly suggests that a child's full intellectual capacity and expression are determined by the quality of rearing or interactive experiences with caretakers. Despite this, the "intelligence-and-will" over the "support for development" notion of learning prevails in many if not most schools. Our strategy was to demonstrate over and over and in as many places as possible that good support for development would make possible good academic learning and desirable behavior among *all* children. We had to live in schools to begin to understand how to do so.

V

Living In and Learning
About Schools

The team from the Yale Child Study Center that I directed in a joint intervention effort with the New Haven, Connecticut, public school system began its work in 1968 in two elementary schools, Baldwin and King. According to the design proposed by Dr. Al Solnit, then head of the Child Study Center (CSC), we were to live in schools for a year and experience their complexities, and with the input of all the stakeholders involved—teachers, administrators, parents, students, and others—create an effective intervention. Although the reason schools were failing so many children was not obvious, I estimated that we could understand and address the problems within five years. Thirty-five years later we are still working and learning.

There was not much research on school change available at the time we began our study. We had to draw on knowledge and clinical skills from the behavioral sciences and public health to make our way. We focused on solving the most pressing problems, and then on creating structures that would help prevent them in the future. Today this approach is called "action research." Working in this way led to the creation of a nine-element or component model that we eventually called the School Development Program (SDP).

Our team was deliberately chosen to reflect the helping professionals usually found in schools—a social worker, a psychologist, and a special education teacher. This make-up is cost-effective and, with supportive training, makes continuous organic or in-school change possible. The only cost to a district using this model is for training team members. Within three to five years of effective implementation, local people can gain and internalize the skills so that less intensive training is involved and at a lower cost. Because our pilot work was actually a research and development effort that benefited many beyond the first two schools, a per pupil cost-benefit analysis is not appropriate.

Our CSC team provided traditional school support services. Our real job, however, was to learn about the schools and to examine how everybody involved might work differently and more effectively, without added cost. Once the schools stabilized, I moved back from direct day-to-day involvement, in that psychiatrists are not regularly involved in schools. And most important, we believed that the problem was with the system and not due to student, staff, or parent illness.

Racial integration of schools through busing was a big issue at the time that we began our work in the late 1960s. Solnit and I discussed the possibility of arranging busing in at least one of our two project schools. My personal experience in a racially integrated school, and the experience of my three black friends who did not do well in the same school, suggested to me that the problem was more related to experience than to race alone.

When I was in the fifth grade, students from the only all-black school in town were moved to our neighborhood school. Most did not do well. But I knew their strength because my older sister had been a teacher in their previous school. In retrospect, the transfer students did not have a sense of belonging. Those who managed to do well had good family experiences to draw on.

The strong resistance to school integration led me to be wary of all political interests and issues. Education is a political issue, so politics cannot be avoided altogether. But our strategy from the beginning was to stay out of school and local politics and conflict and focus on what we believed students needed—vital environments and good experiences.

Solnit envisioned the creation of a portal model of intervention that could eventually be used in many places. But because of parental concern that the university might be using their children as research guinea pigs, we agreed not to write about our work—unless there were findings that might be helpful to similar children elsewhere. And because of administrator and teacher concerns about noneducators, we agreed that we would address only behavior and development issues. School people would be responsible for curriculum, instruction, assessment, and all else. We had no line authority in the schools, only permission to be there.

Our project was different from traditional research programs in schools and, frankly, not good for my academic career. It did not fit the more highly regarded experimental research design approach. Also, I was at risk of perishing because I could not publish. Solnit and I considered this problem with Bill Kessen, a highly regarded psychologist and Yale colleague.

Kessen encouraged us to proceed because the need to understand and improve schools was so very important. Also, I was more interested in trying to understand why my friends did not succeed than in moving up the ranks, and I did not think that academic life would necessarily be my future. Fortunately, my question was in sync with the research mission of the university.

Our program in the two elementary schools did not open. It exploded. On the first day of school, I walked down the hall at Baldwin School and was almost attacked by a teacher in trouble. She was anxious, wild-eyed. She grabbed my arm and saying, "Help me! Help me!" literally pulled me into her classroom. What I saw was unbelievable. Students were yelling and screaming, milling around, hitting each other, calling each other names, calling the teacher names. When the teacher called for order, she was ignored. When I called for order, I was ignored. That had never happened to me before. We headed to the hall, confused and in despair.

The parents were furious. The staff was angry, frightened, confused, divided, sometimes combative, but working as hard as they could. But almost everything anybody did to try to make things better, made things worse. The community that had been helpful and hopeful held its collective breath. A militant community leader stood at the top of the stairs and urged the staff and the parents to turn against this Yale experiment. He left when he discovered that I was the Yale program director. We were friends. One of the reasons I returned to New Haven was that I had friends and a track record of concern about the low-income community. I knew that the job would require trust.

The explosion occurred for several reasons. Funds were sent to the school system for a New Haven project director who was never hired. Some central office staff were very helpful. Some expected us to fail, and they may have even greased the skids. For reasons that remain unclear, many of the teachers were new and young. Several were still under the supervision of the project principal for instruction, a faculty member from a prestigious school of education. He was also in charge of curriculum and instruction. Another principal was in charge of administration.

Description of Open Classroom

The most inexperienced teachers were trying to use the popular innovation of the day, "open classrooms," when they still did not know how to teach. The rationale behind open classrooms, which were popular in the late 1960s and early 1970s, was that less structure would promote greater self-activation, exploration, and learning. The outcomes were best among successful, experienced teachers working with children who had good preschool developmental experiences in well-functioning school settings. These situations did not pertain to most in our pilot project, and the open classrooms in our project were a disaster.

Our CSC team had suggested that the summer before initiating the program be used primarily for organization, management, and relationship-building purposes. This would have allowed us to create the good relationships among parents, staff, and students that we believed would be needed to make change possible. We deferred to the Curriculum and Instruction group, who used the summer to focus on innovative curriculum and instruction and assessment matters. They tried to establish good relationships with the community by living in the neighborhood. But parents and other people in the neighborhood did not know them or trust their motives, and this tactic backfired.

Also, several nonproject schools encouraged parents of students with past school problems to attend our two schools, noting that there would be social workers and psychiatrists on the staff. And parents and staff were promised an opportunity to participate in school decision making, but there was no mechanism, guidelines, or experience for doing so. All of this created high hopes but a power vacuum and paralysis. These conditions contributed to the initial explosion.

Persistent tensions created by such differences as race, class, the status of the teacher preparation programs the various staff members had attended, professional and nonprofessional status, housing project versus private residence, the proclaimed difference in status of two different housing projects, and more fueled difficult relationships within the schools. These conditions precluded effective problem solving and led to chronic chaos and conflict.

Although racial feelings were raw and open in 1968, and our Yale team was largely black and the Curriculum and Instruction team largely white, the problem was trust and relationships more than race. Being African-American probably gave us a fifteen-minute grace period to turn things around, but that is all. It also created greater pressure. I still remember when, after a stormy meeting in which the parents agreed to give us time but made it clear that they wanted results, one mother pointed her finger at me and said, "I want my son to go to work with a shirt and tie just like you!"

Also, in the 1960s numerous helping professionals were poured into failing schools: civic organizations, community organizations providing recreation and other programs, university students and faculty doing research, and others trying to learn and help were in schools. Without an adequate management system, there was often confusion. Two groups might be assigned to the gymnasium at the same time. Who had permission to be there? From whom did they receive permission?

Lack of management = chaos

And who were these people? Did the students need what they had to offer? Was it useful under the difficult conditions of the school? Without a well-functioning management mechanism these questions and problems could not be resolved or prevented. The helpers were doing more to sink the ship than to right it.

Indeed, some of the same questions raised about the volunteers could have been asked about the tasks and relationship of staff and parents. The roles of the various stakeholders and the ways they were to operate were unclear. Experiences, education philosophies, and practice methods differed widely. Efforts to understand student needs and to establish coherent goals and practice were dismissed by some staff as authoritarian. Our CSC team felt that the absence of a well-thought-out education plan and process was harmful to the students and the project, but individual creativity and innovation in an open setting were the watchwords of the day.

As a result of these conditions, there was open staff and parent conflict as well as conflict among different staff cliques. Consequently, clear, desirable models of behavior and supportive adult guides were not available to the students. This left them without the structures they needed—appropriate rules, beliefs, attitudes, and ways of managing their world. Without adequate structure, the students were confused, anxious, and fearful.

Again, children act out and act up in such situations. Indeed, adults become confused, anxious, and fearful when there is insufficient structure, and they also act out and act up. Seeing adults behaving badly in their presence intensifies the children's insecurity and troublesome behavior, in turn bringing out even more troublesome adult behavior. The conditions in the school led some of the initial teachers to leave before the year ended.

The much more authoritarian teachers, who replaced those who left, used strong control measures, such as swift punishment and "back to basics" tactics, and had initial success. But this was 1968 with riots in the street and on television. After a month or so a second-grade class held a protest march against their strict teacher. This was the last straw as far as the parents were concerned. The explosion, faculty division and conflict, adult and student acting out, and parent discontent almost ended the project. As mentioned, we had to beg for time.

Given the situation, we could not, as originally planned, just be in the school for a year and learn; we had to act or lose the project. But we learned through our actions. As I mentioned, because our team members were African-American we had fifteen minutes of grace. About a month into the project, I used it to convince two of the most influential parents to give us time to improve conditions. I talked with one in the hallway for three hours. Because the other had to be home with younger children, I met with her at her home.

The house and neighborhood were much like my own childhood home. There, we talked about the conditions of the school. But we talked more about her hopes and dreams for her son, similar to the unrealized aspirations she had for herself. I shared my background, motives, and hopes for our project, her son, and children like her son. I suspect that we were not thrown out because we connected through our similar aspirations more than because we were of the same race.

To avoid having the project terminated, our CSC group suggested that we create a school management team representative of all the adult groups in the project. It enabled us to hang on and recover enough to survive that very difficult first year, and to regroup. This time we used the summer to build better relationships, plan, and prepare to get off to a much better start in the second year. The King School fared better during much of the first year, but not much better. And then it collapsed.

Although it was not intentional, the collapse of the Baldwin-King School program in such a short time—despite the fact that it started with high hopes, highly motivated staff, and good financial and personnel support—allowed us to experience in one year the powerful dynamics and negative effects of failure that one usually observes over several years. This enabled us to quickly identify and understand the causes and characteristics of chronic school failure. Our failing pilot project was a microcosm of dysfunctional schools everywhere.

Two years later, our third project year, the culture of the schools was dramatically different. In the second year, visitors to the schools marveled at the change, and by the third year, students, without supervision, walked down the halls holding hands. There was very little screaming or fighting. School assemblies, and even the lunch period, were orderly. The doors to classrooms that were once shut, with blinds drawn, were now open so that anybody could see and feel the pleasant and orderly conditions inside. Parents and staff talked with each other in friendly tones before, during, and after school. In the first year, a parent came to school to beat up a teacher; parents now came to understand and help. In the third year, more than four hundred parents, relatives, school staff, and friends attended the Christmas program that had drawn fifteen people in the first year. In the beginning any child who was vulnerable to attack in any way—size, performance in school, a physical challenge—would be attacked. Now students were helping the teacher help such students.

Eventually the choir from the church next door to King

gave a performance in the school. Adults planned social events in school, making it a welcoming place for students and adults. The students took highly successful field trips to institutions and were involved in events in the community.

The data collector who assisted our evaluator was only a high school graduate, but a keen observer and a caring person. When she left the program during our third year, she sent me a note describing the remarkable change in student skills, attitudes, and behaviors she had observed. When first asked to take tests some would cry, some were afraid to try, some scribbled with dark and angry marks—all reflecting their lack of competence, confidence, and high sense of insecurity. Although their scores had not gone up, for reasons we would discover later, they were no longer afraid. That was a critically important beginning.

At the end of the five years, we terminated our work in Baldwin School because the principal and several parents felt that it was now a good school, and they wanted to go back to a more authoritarian approach to keep it that way. The majority of parents and teachers opposed this decision, but true to our no conflict commitment, we left that school. We would rather switch than fight. It was a very difficult decision. But the battle would have sent a message that change is more painful than was the reality, and it would have consumed much energy and delayed our effort to develop an effective change framework.

We began working with another school with a similar profile, Brennan. At the end of the first project year, the initial school, King, was thirty-second in achievement by the fourth grade on nationally standardized tests, out of thirty-three elementary schools in New Haven. The school we began to work with at the end of the fifth year, Brennan, was thirty-third. In the eighth year, the schools were tied for third and fourth highest levels of achievement in the city; they had the best attendance record in the city; and they had no serious behavior problems.

What happened? How was such a dramatic change brought about? Was it possible to move the process to other places as Al Solnit envisioned? What was learned that could help society begin to close the gap between what children need to be successful in school and life and what we now provide? We used the management team that we had initially put in place simply to survive to create other structures that enabled staff and parents to begin to work together, experience small successes, and _gradually_ acquire mutual respect and trust. A positive sense of community began to be felt in the schools. The new culture became more and more supportive of student development and improved teaching and learning.

Also, we learned that we had to work with the building as a system rather than with individual students and their families. The traditional one-on-one or family social support and child treatment approaches—without change in the building as a system—did not work. Wendy Winters, our chief social worker, told me that during the first year 65 percent of the social work time went into efforts to help five of the most challenging children and their families, with almost no change. We did not have the relationship standing to influence their lives.

We abandoned a very common helping professional tendency to focus on individuals and families in greatest need. But by improving the overall functioning of school, we were first able to engage the best-functioning parents and develop a degree of trust with them. Their involvement motivated the next-best-functioning group, the next, and the next. Eventually, good relationships and trust between school staff and families was broadly based. At that point, some of the families having the most difficulty with school, health, and welfare services began to engage with the teachers and administrators and to seek advice and referrals from them. This approach enabled reasonably well-functioning people to help others.

A building or system focus was not a new idea, but it was a concept used more in organization and management and in ecology than in education. Even now, ours is one of very few school reform efforts that intentionally and strongly focuses on system improvement in the service of individual student development and learning. Most focus on curriculum, instruction, and assessment, and often incidentally and accidentally on development, usually not capitalizing on the powerful link between learning and development.

Ironically, while our strategy was to address the building as a system, the ability of our CSC team to help with individual student behavior problems made us valuable to the staff and led to a leadership edge over the Curriculum and Instruction group in the schools. In short, the first need of the teachers was an environment in which they could positively engage their students so that they could then teach and learning could follow. Being able to help staff meet this need opened discussions about how to create structures that would make the building a community and a supportive culture that could prevent problems.

In the second year, a very thoughtful visiting team of experts acknowledged our progress but suggested that I take a more active leadership role. I respectfully disagreed. It was my belief, and still is, that school improvement must grow from within, from organic growth. Systemic change is best carried out by school people regularly on site, with consultation as intensive as needed from people who can help them gain system change knowledge, tools, and skills. My role was the latter.

Working in this way leaves schools with the power to heal and grow after the help is gone. This is the only way to sustain improvement and to promote growth.

This approach is in line with the proverb: "Give a man a fish and you have fed him for a day. Teach him how to fish and you have fed him for a lifetime." Our SDP model is designed to help people help themselves, with decreasing support from outside trainers or others. They can then make systematic and continuing use of the model, and other knowledge and skills, as tools to systematically, efficiently, and effectively address the multiple, changing, and often confusing and overwhelming issues that confront schools.

Sometimes charismatic leaders and teachers can overcome enormous problems in a building and in a classroom. But just as in team sports, when there is a star the other players often do not fully accept their own leadership responsibility and do not grow as they could. A broad base of knowledge, skills, and leadership capacities does not develop in the organization. Such organizations collapse or slowly decline when the charismatic leader leaves.

We cannot create large-scale system(s) of good schools relying on stars or charisma. As in medicine and other human services, we must create systems where most people can provide good service most of the time while continuing to grow and get better. Our SDP design asks every participant to be a collaborator and a leader, including the students, and to learn and grow.

Currently school organization and management, teaching and learning, and development—when development is thought of at all—are usually considered separately. Our work suggests that because of the way children learn, these critical aspects of schooling must be addressed simultaneously and in an interactive way. The staff must be able to organize and manage all activities in a school in a way that creates a climate or culture that promotes emotional attachments among all the stakeholders. This provides support for good development, which, in turn, makes good teaching and learning possible.[1]

When we began to field-test the School Development Program model and ideas we ran into significant disbelief, even among those willing to try it in their schools. Indeed, a former neighbor of mine heard that I had indicated that spanking children was not necessary. She responded: "Oh no, I know that he did not say that. I knew his children. They were very good children!" The counterintuitive nature of many of our ideas about working with children prompted the facilitator in Prince George's County, Maryland, Jan Stocklinski, to request that our model be called the Comer School Development Program. She argued that attaching the ideas to a living source who was successfully implementing them would decrease resistance.

I was reluctant. As a twenty-two-year-old smart alec medical student I ridiculed "medical syndromes named after dead doctors." But I relented, and the name stuck. It has been applied to everything from our nine-element change process to our effort to promote child development thinking to teaching and learning in classrooms. Some refer to the model as simply "Comer." If this doesn't work for you, think "child and adolescent development" everywhere you see "Comer." The name is in the same spirit.

Finally, I elected not to discuss our work in middle and high schools in any detail in this book. We have worked in more than 250 such schools over the years. The model has helped school staffs turn around some very difficult situations and to improve academic achievement, significantly in some places. In a North Carolina middle school the confiscated weapons count went from more than forty in the first SDP year to zero in the second. The school was recognized for academic honors by the state in three years.

The model used is basically the same as the one for elementary schools, but the middle and high school students have greater input to implementation. They are involved in helping to visualize, plan, and implement the change process for their schools. A variety of approaches are used to promote greater positive student-staff and program attachment and bonding, in creating a culture that promotes student development and learning. But middle and high school students, parents, and staff are at very different developmental places than elementary school people. This makes the change process more difficult but still possible. But I cannot do justice to that framework in this book and will leave a fuller discussion of it to a future work.

VI
The Framework

The model or framework I will describe in this chapter rose, like a phoenix, out of the chaos of our first year. It emerged and evolved, as planned, through the input of all the stakeholders in the schools—staff, parents, and students, with our Child Study Center team facilitation.

What we learned and did in the pilot schools led to our *nine-element model* or framework that became and remains the core of our School Development Program. It consists of: three mechanisms—a governance and management team (now called the School Planning and Management Team [SPMT]), a parent team, and a mental health team (now called a Student and Staff Support Team); three operations—comprehensive school plan, staff development, and assessment and modification; and three guidelines—no-fault problem solving, consensus decision making, and collaboration or no paralysis.[1]

This framework enables the staff and parents to manage the three critical areas of work in schools—governance and management, student and adult development, and teaching and learning—in a way that channels energies into planning and problem solving and coordinates and integrates the multiple interactions that take place in schools. This promotes synchrony and synergy rather than the asynchronous and difficult conditions that often occur when there is no way to address these areas simultaneously.

Our framework first began to take shape at the height of parent, staff, and student discontent in our pilot schools. To avoid being thrown out of the schools, we created a *governance and management team*, which evolved into our School Planning and Management Team. This team, made up of twelve to fourteen members, was representative of all the stakeholders— administrators; parents; teachers; professional support staff, such as social workers and other helpers; and nonprofessional staff, such as custodians or clerks. When we moved our program to middle and high schools, students were included as well. The primary purpose of this team was to give all parties involved in the schools a chance to have their interests represented. It also served as the decision-making, problem-solving direction and the energy-giving engine of the program. Because it was a representative body, all the stakeholders had an opportunity to influence conditions in their schools.

When we began our work in 1968, most schools did not have such a decision-making and problem-solving mechanism. Even now many places do not. School-based management often focuses on efficiency and instruction, rather than on the creation of a school context or culture that will support development and prevent problems. A good school context is especially useful when student, staff, parent, and community needs and activities are beyond the ordinary. A principal alone cannot effectively address a school's problems, even if they are modest or even if she has the help of assistants. It requires col-

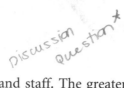

laboration with parents and staff. The greater the problems, the more this is true. Recent research shows that the leading cause of new teachers leaving the profession is dissatisfaction, largely because they feel unsupported by the administration* and/or have little influence on what goes on in their schools. Most of these dissatisfied teachers were or are not in schools where there is a mechanism for collaborative planning and problem solving.[2]

In the difficult early climate in our pilot schools, the adults in the school did not like or trust each other. There was much faultfinding, blame, and scapegoating. In self-defense, numerous cliques developed and rumors flew. Teachers went into their rooms, closed the door, pulled down the shades to the hallway, and attempted to survive. Parents either avoided the schools or came in to complain about the bad practices. Regardless of the quality of instruction or the curriculum, few students would be able to achieve at a high level under these conditions. The schools were going to fail without a change.

Because there was no mechanism for the staff to consider the challenges and opportunities they faced, both academic and social, they had no plan with clear goals, roles, and strategies for addressing them. Teachers came in and taught what they thought appropriate, or what a district manual dictated, and sometimes what a supervisor from the district thought they should teach.

Testing was not used to diagnose student needs in order to inform and improve teaching. In fact, state test outcomes from the past year did not reach the schools until well into the next academic year. Instead, state-sponsored and classroom tests and grades were often used to make ability judgments and placements in teaching groups, classes, and grade levels. Sometimes they were used to punish students who were acting up or giving the teacher a hard time. I observed a teacher give such a student a large red F at the top of the page. The student was bright but made a systematic error, adding columns on his multiplication test because he did not understand the underlying principle. The teacher either did not understand that he was supposed to help the student understand, or he was too angry to do so.

Goals for the students and the school were vague. The role of the principal was more administrative than in support of instruction. And I do not remember anyone talking about the development of students.

Without goals and strategies of their own, the schools were going in many different directions; indeed, around in circles. One of the reasons there were initially so many people in the buildings getting into each other's way was because there was no educational plan in place. For this reason, the schools were open to the offerings of every outside problem solver and helper who came along. The staff were not in a position to think about whether or not what was being offered would help them achieve their goals; if so, how would they use it, how much time would it take, who would supervise and help integrate what was being provided into their program, what was the staff time and energy required to do so, and so on. If they declined, they would not look progressive.

The task of the Governance and Management Team was to bring all the stakeholders together in a collaborative, problem-solving way. But this does not just happen among people who do not know, trust, or like each other, even though they are professionals. Effective training was needed to make it possible for team members to work in this way.

By serving as an initial member of the team I was able to carry out "embedded training." (An SDP staff member replaced me as soon as possible.) At first the team members were reluctant to express their views and looked to me or the principal to establish the work tasks and to make suggestions. In short order, however, the most assertive members dominated and expressed themselves in a way that was characteristic of the school culture—through faultfinding and blame, leading to denial and defensive behavior. The team members would sometimes attempt to make decisions that only the principal had the authority to make. The principals would sometimes ignore the input of the team or find questionable reasons to cancel meetings.

To address these obstacles we created the three guidelines that gradually helped the team work together effectively—*no-fault, consensus, collaboration or no paralysis*. No-fault problem solving was suggested to deal with the adverse effects of faultfinding and blame: intimidation, fear, conflict, an unwillingness to share concerns, and defensiveness. It put the emphasis on finding a solution to problems and on accepting personal responsibility and accountability.

This changed way of thinking and working had to be practiced, not just taught. It was easy to slip back to the previous pattern of interaction. The members of the team had to call on each other to remember to honor the guidelines. I am told by each new group using the framework that the no-fault guideline is the most difficult to live by, and that it is one of the most effective elements of the program—"liberating"— free from attack or blame. It decreases problematic attitudes, feelings, and behaviors and focuses group attention on the work task.

Importantly, the principle or guideline of "no-fault" does not mean there is no accountability. In a collaborative team, accountability is more likely to come from the responsible individual than from the insistence of the principal or person in charge. We adults retain some of our childhood reactions to authority, unconscious of course, and we can resent being called to task and can balk or act out in other ways. But when acting responsibly in the service of achieving a goal that is in the best interest of the students, we are more likely to do what we are supposed to do, especially when there is opportunity for peer review. In a culture of doing the right thing, and looking good, we do not want to look bad.

Our SDP facilitator, first myself and then the social worker who replaced me, met with the principals after every meeting to debrief. They began to realize that they gained power by sharing power and being open to input from others. This helped them move from a "command and control" to a "facilitator" mind-set. The former is more appropriate in the military. What previously had met with resistance got done because the group shared the responsibility for producing successful outcomes. When the principal provides leadership in all aspects of the school and is open to input from others, support and respect are increased, not lost, as too many believe.

Once "no-fault" became a part of the leadership culture, it was easier for everyone to participate in discussions and to find ways to make the other guidelines work. For example, through team member suggestions *consensus* was eventually carried out by trying an approach that most agreed on. But if that did not work, they would try what others had suggested previously, or an obviously better approach might become apparent during the problem-solving effort. The bottom line, again, was "solve the problem." Before there was a willingness to find and go with the best approach to a problem, building politics, winning and losing on an issue, and other factors unrelated to child needs influenced the decision-making process.

We raised "innocent" questions that brought our fellow members back to the school problems rather than to personal or power issues. Eventually, they did so without prompting, and we said less. When they shifted to a focus on meeting the needs of the school and the students, they gradually stopped using personal issues in a way that made problem solving difficult. As a result of this change, administrator, staff, and parent *collaboration* improved, and they became more effective problem solvers. As they successfully addressed school operations, and student and adult behavior problems, the confidence of team members grew. They began to believe that all problems had a solution and that working together they could find it. Their hopefulness, and the guidelines that helped them work together successfully, began to permeate most activities in the building, eventually changing the school culture.

The CSC social worker served a liaison role, helping parents on the team to work effectively. I sat in on a meeting after I was no longer on the team. A new parent at King, recently arrived from New York City, angrily called for a march on City Hall because a promise made to the school was slow in materializing. I looked at the social worker with some apprehension. She whispered, "Watch." Without prompting from her, experienced members of the team calmly explained the down side of the parent's suggestion: "Three minutes of notoriety on the evening television news, irritated central office officials, a reputation for making trouble, resistance, and a continued problem." Instead they decided to send a constructive letter to the superintendent, with copies to their alderman, inviting them to come in and discuss the problem. They did, and they were appreciative of the orderly process; the problem was resolved.

Teachers, administrators, support staff, parents, and our staff were learning side by side as they addressed real problems. When the several groups are trained separately, they miss an opportunity to learn the most important requirement: how to work well with team members with different roles, interests, and responsibilities. We found that mixed group, task-based training works best. I will say more about this when I discuss our current training program.

About fifteen years later, a small group of parents and staff were interviewed by a news reporter about the "early years." The interviewer asked what I did at the Governance and Management Team meetings. They could not remember. One parent finally said, "He just sat there and smiled most of the time." (I hope it was at appropriate times.) But my point is that the design and process enabled team members to gain the skills to do the work and to remember themselves as the achievers.

Well-educated parents address problems in effective ways regularly. But knowing how to do so is not enough when a solution to a problem is not expected. The latter situation sometimes contributes to continuous battles among people who feel marginalized and powerless. In the third year of our program, when things were going very well, I gave a "State of the Schools" report at the end of the year. All but one parent expressed enthusiastic approval. This parent asked angry questions reminiscent of the first year. I thought she was truly angry. The two of us were the last to finish cleaning up in the meeting room. As she left, she said, "Well, see you next year. I sure enjoy fighting with you!"

It occurred to me that when people do not expect "the system" to respond to their needs, they eventually begin to gain gratification from the fight rather than the outcome. The woman who argued with me passed away a year later. Aside from her personal history and family information, her entire obituary was about her work in the school. I was reminded of how important it is to help people belong and be effective in planning and achieving constructive goals, for their own sake and for the sake of the people, programs, and communities they interact in and with.

The four elements of our SDP described so far—the Governance and Management Team mechanism and the three guidelines—were most responsible for changing the organization and management and the feeling and relationship tone of the schools. As the Governance and Management Teams engineered the gradual reduction of major organization and behavior problems in the two schools, the interest of the participants turned to problem prevention and to promoting conditions that would make good teaching and learning possible. The name of the Governance and Management Teams was changed to the School Planning and Management Teams (SPMT) to better denote that they were doing preventive and promotive work and not just crisis problem solving as in the past, although they continued to address schoolwide problems. We were moving past the "firefighter" or crisis mentality. The SPMT carried out three operations—a *comprehensive school plan; staff development* geared to building needs and goals; and *assessment and modification* based on the findings.

The SPMT in each school created a *comprehensive school plan.* Eventually they created subcommittees that did the work and reported back. The management team reviewed, sometimes modified, eventually adopted, and implemented the finished plans. *The plan had both academic and social components;* this is the reason it was called comprehensive. Because of our agreement not to address curriculum and instruction, the CSC team focused on the social component of the plan.

We suggested that a systematic focus on creating an improved climate would support student development, teaching, and learning. This notion had not been a part of the university or college training of the staff. Their preservice programs generally did not emphasize or even discuss how these conditions might be related. This departure from the traditional was a cause for hesitancy, but because of the early difficult relationship conditions, the staff was willing to try.

The social program was based on observations we made during the first year. We had noted that many of the activities that go on in school, such as holiday programs, music, athletic contests, and so on, often took place without rhyme or reason, sometimes spontaneously or at the last minute. Little thought went into the purpose and possibilities of these events, other than that the students should have a good time. (I privately called it "doing nice.") The value to the children of these activities, as carried out, was questionable. Parents often did not feel any ownership or even feel welcome at the programs. At the same time, teachers and administrators felt that the parents did not appreciate the effort they were making to provide the children with good experiences.

Many first-year situations led us to consider how the environment either helps or interferes with relationships and, in turn, teaching, student development, and learning. Also, we noted that the rhythm of the school year was being ignored, and opportunities to create and maintain a positive school culture were being lost. For example, social activities at the beginning of the year that involved all the school stakeholders—parents, staff, students—were an opportunity to set direction and to get people off to a good start. After the Christmas holiday, students and the staff got the "blahs" in school. And the school year ended without reflection or celebration, missing a chance to celebrate the achievements of the students, parents, and staff, and a chance to set the tone and goal for the next year.

Our CSC team discussed these issues with the SPMT. The social program subcommittee considered the matter and decided to create a full-year school calendar and to strategically schedule all the nonacademic, or co-curricular, activities. The calendar served to decrease the sense of fragmented, unrelated activities and to create a sense of purposeful activities with goals that could be assessed and modified as indicated. The activities were to provide a sense of direction and to create a social climate that would support developmental growth opportunities for the students.

The result was a welcome-back-to-school potluck supper, a Halloween march, a Thanksgiving celebration that was part of a social science and history activity, a Christmas program, a spring fling dinner-dance held in late February, designed so that the planning excitement overcame the "blahs" of January and February. And there was a graduation program and activities that prepared students for the next year.

Each school had a similar calendar, based on its needs, interests, and energy. As the schools became more comfortable and creative, the social and academic programs were more often integrated. Book fairs, science fairs, a track and field event, and other activities all had academic components. With a schedule, the subcommittee could pace and space these events with academic objectives, energy, and personnel needs in mind. With its goals in place, a school was in a position to decide which outside resource or offering could help its plan and which to pass on or use at another time.

During the assessment of a calendar event, it was noted

that parents had gathered on one side of the room and the staff on the other. The interactions were not as full and comfortable as the planners desired. A parent-staff pairing arrangement was created for the next event. This made the purpose clear and the process less difficult.

Another time, while considering how to increase parent turnout at an event, several parents pointed out that they could not attend some events because they did not have babysitters. The Parent Team used money raised through some of their activities to provide sitters at school during the programs so parents could bring their young children with them. Also, it was noted that the best attendance occurred when food was served, especially when parents were involved in helping to plan the event and in preparing the food, and when their children performed in the program. The next logical step was to combine business meetings with social programs that included student performance and food.

Such thinking and planning was a big change, and the knowledge gained was used to make the next event more successful. As mentioned, during our first year about fifteen parents turned out for the Christmas program in a school of approximately three hundred and fifty students. This was owing more to a poor school relationship climate and poor planning than a lack of interest. Previously, at the last minute someone said, "Let's have a Christmas program." Others agreed, but the spirit was "You do it." Two years later, with essentially the same people, then able to work together and thoughtfully plan, more than four hundred parents and friends turned out to the Christmas program.

Breaking bread together breaks down barriers to good engagement created by race, class, income, occupation, language, style, and other differences. The situation we were in required such an effort. Stereotypes and misperceptions cut both ways. It was very important to undermine them.

During one social event, the parents were greatly surprised and pleased to learn that I could dance; indeed, I am a very good dancer. There was a feeling in the community that nobody at Yale could dance, not even the African-Americans. My tongue is only half in cheek. The Yale neighbor, and even the staff in the pilot schools, represented mainstream society. Without a feeling of connection, its people and values, particularly academic learning, could not provide strong motivation for people in the community.

The SDP structures and guidelines improved school governance and management and relationships among all the people in or with a stake in what happened in the schools. This made collaborative thinking, planning, and creative problem solving possible. Being a part of such a setting made parent and student engagement with school people, and the program of the school, more possible. And staff behaviors toward parents and students became more positive.

In schools implementing the model reasonably well, these social events have an enormous positive impact on the students, parents, and staff. They are usually joyous, exciting events. Recently I visited a school in Dayton, Ohio, that had just had a "father figure night," a social-academic activity. School staff were still glowing from the excitement of that evening, by then eight weeks past, when more than one hundred fathers turned out with their children in one of the worst snowstorms of the winter. The social climate positively affected academic outcomes. Their test scores were on the rise, and they were eagerly planning for next year.

I was struck by the fact that the same event had had the same effects twenty years earlier in a school in Prince George's County, Maryland. My point is that the events spring spontaneously from place to place, based on local needs, interests, thinking, and creativity. But they address the same need and provide the same reward everywhere—a sense of participation and belonging. Sometimes they are similar to events elsewhere, but often different. The SDP model promotes local expression while helping schools address essential and universal needs—the creation of a climate or culture in which all the adults can help the students develop and learn.

With barriers broken, students can attach and bond to the people and the programs of the school, with their parents involved. They can identify with, imitate, and internalize the values of the school, including academic learning. They can better accept the supportive guidance of the staff and their parents. They can feel safe and can take the chances needed to learn and grow along all the developmental pathways. This was not the case for my three childhood friends who could not elicit a positive response from the school and as a result, in part, began a downhill course in life. This was probably why the same children who did well in our summer Sunday school class did not do well in our racially integrated public school.

In focusing on both the academic and social areas, we were and still are different from most school improvement programs. Most programs called "comprehensive" often do not address relationship, context, interaction, and developmental issues. They are comprehensive with regard to the academic program, and sometimes not even fully comprehensive in this area. There is much discussion today about the need to create learning communities in schools. Given the relationship problems we found and continue to find in dysfunctional schools, we do not believe that a focus on instruction and assessment alone will make it possible to create effective learning communities, particularly in the schools most in need.[3]

The *social program* was one component of our comprehensive school plan. Putting it in place was challenging, but the powerful rewards of living and working in a rewarding environment allowed it to take root reasonably quickly. Our SDP team was given leadership responsibility in this area. The other component of the plan was our *academic program*. Establishing this program was a much more complicated process.

In spite of the fact that when the SDP is implemented adequately test scores rise, the claim that we do not have an instructional component is often cited as a negative. Ours was not an instructional program, and even now we are adding only instructional elements, not a full instructional program. The SDP was designed to create a school context that would facilitate any and all curriculum, instruction, and assessment programs. It provides the conditions that make instructional programs better or much more effective.

Very good instructional programs will fail in schools where adequate student-staff engagement cannot take place. We continue to believe that the context that sets the condition of engagement is the critical problem. When adequately presented, most instructional programs will work; and we acknowledge that some are better than others. But in our work, the decision about the instructional approach or program to use is made by the district.

Our peculiar problem in 1968 was that it was not possible to establish conditions that would support an effective academic program during that first year. Staff development could not be effective. None of the several academic leadership arrangements we tried worked. And before relationship conditions improved to the point that these efforts could be effective, people with the expertise left the program.

Teachers on the academic subcommittee took responsibility for recruiting curriculum specialists in the area who provided in-service training. Initiative taking was helpful and the sessions generally useful, but this was time-consuming and not as effective as a district-organized, building-level support arrangement might have been.

During the second year, a teacher autonomy instructional approach, with peer collaboration and review, was initiated. This was based on the notion that there was a need to respect the professionalism of teachers, to allow them to be responsible for developing curriculum and instructional responses based on the needs of their students. What we discovered was that most of the staff were not prepared to improve their curricular and instructional practice either independently or as a collaborative team. The outcomes among some were exciting, but on the whole they were not good. Even more troublesome, this approach greatly fragmented the instructional program.

This is not an argument for "teacher proofing" curriculum and instruction because teachers are not intelligent and able. Teachers, on the whole, are intelligent, able, and, equally important, as dedicated, maybe more, than most professionals. My observation was, and is, that their job is extraordinarily complex, often carried out under difficult circumstances without adequate preparation to teach, and without adequate support for teaching. When teachers cannot be successful they act out, burn out, or both. Public criticism stems from viewing the latter without paying attention to causal factors.

District-level staff development was not helpful. It was

not tied to what was going on in the classrooms, nor was it based on student performance data. It usually sprang from the mind of a central office staff member and was often based on some new instructional approach that had little to do with the needs of the students whom the teachers were trying to help. Even when potentially useful, or when presented in an entertaining or rewarding way, there was usually no process for introducing it back into their school or classroom.

The second operation of our emerging framework, *staff development* at the building level, and our third operation, *assessment and modification,* eventually helped us with our floundering academic component. Many of the teachers did not want to take a close look at academic outcomes. Thus, what they taught was not data driven. Their argument usually was that it was unfair to the students who had so many social challenges. Because most teachers were working hard and not making much progress, they doubted their own ability and that of their students.

Even today, with legislation that requires improvement, some caring school people doubt that their students can achieve at a higher level, and doubt that they can help them do so. I recently heard a well-meaning teacher say, "What do you want from these kids? I marvel at the fact that they even get here given the conditions in the community." There is still resistance to planning instructional programs based on academic outcome data.

Assessment of the social program outcomes gradually made the process a part of the building culture. This helped the staff become more comfortable and hopeful enough to begin to look at academic outcomes. They were beginning to believe in themselves as change agents and beginning to believe that the students could achieve at a higher level. In 1970 our pilot schools began to use data from nationally standard-ized achievement testing carried out by the city of New Haven.

Eventually a climate of trust and mutual respect devel-oped to the point that the teachers could begin to identify their own knowledge and skill limitations in areas where student performance was low and to call for staff development. Staff development activities were designed to help the staff achieve their goals in both the academic and social areas.

As they began to work on the academic needs of the stu-dents in their buildings, teachers resisted going to the district staff development meetings. We were able to work out an ar-rangement whereby half of the time allotted for district staff development meetings could be used for staff development in our schools. They could use this time to consider the needs of their own students. But sophisticated data analysis and pro-gramming did not take place until Edward Joyner, an educator and now the SDP executive director, upgraded our implemen-tation and training program.[4] An occasional problem, in the pilot schools and later, has been that some school staff want to enjoy the improved climate without pressing for academic im-provement. This is an implementation and a leadership prob-lem not a design absence of an academic focus.

We learned from our academic component experience, reinforced by many subsequent experiences, that it is very important to obtain district-level understanding and support in all aspects of the school improvement or reform process. Otherwise, there can be a notion that the project is the treat-ment and will lead to the cure without district-level adjust-ments. Projects can provide a framework, and even content, but improvement can take place only when school people use supportive tools and information effectively at the building and district levels. Also, because of the turnover and change in school systems, support must be broad based and not dependent on one or even a few leaders. The unavailability of support for staff growth can frustrate initiatives and dampen the hope created by good relationships and a more orderly environment. I will address this matter again when I discuss our districtwide or systemic work.

Despite the eventual attention given to the academic program, significant test score gains did not take place until the eighth year of our project. At this point, the staff and parents were functioning very well, and the social program had reached its highest level of effectiveness. Student behavior problems were at a minimum. Today, with more knowledge and skills, under average conditions, the model can help poorly functioning schools bring about improved social conditions in a year or two, and improved academic conditions in three to five years. Many schools have achieved both in one year.

I have now discussed seven of the nine components of our SDP school improvement framework. The mechanism most responsible for driving our change process was the School Planning and Management Team, or the *SPMT*, and the three guidelines or principles—*no-fault, consensus, collaboration*—that make it possible for the stakeholders to successfully work together. Next came the three operations that promote student development, teaching, and learning—*comprehensive school plan,* academic and social; *staff development;* and *assessment and modification.*

The final two components are the mental health team or the *Student and Staff Support Team* (SSST) and the *Parent Team.* The SSST is responsible for helping all the adults create a school context that is supportive of child and adolescent development and addresses the needs of individual children. The

Purpose of SSST

Parent Team helps to close the gap between the home and school and thereby provides a more seamless extension of support for child development from the family and community network to the network of the school.

The *Student and Staff Support Team* provides support for students, staff, and parents. This is the component used so effectively in P.S. 46 mentioned in chapter 2. The SSST is made up of all the helping professionals in a school—social workers, nurse, psychologist, special education teacher, and speech and hearing therapists, and other health professionals when present. As mentioned, our SDP team provided the ordinary school support services in the initial project. Because of the stigma associated with the mental health label, we eventually changed the name to the Student and Staff Support Team.

We learned early that school leaders could not mandate change. Also, our staff development sessions about how best to interact with children did not provide the staff with what they needed to "do it." Once we were walking out of a session in which we discussed the value of talking to children rather than yelling at them when we encountered several kids running down the hall. One of the teachers yelled sharply, but caught herself and said, "Oops." Learning to work differently takes what it takes to get to Carnegie Hall—practice, practice, practice.

As members of the SSST, our SDP staff members were able to infuse child development perspectives into practice by providing reminders, reinforcement, encouragement, and even empathy, through the authority that being helpful granted. Changing ideas and ways of working that go as far back as one's own upbringing and were reinforced in professional school and during years of practice, and which were never before questioned, even praised, is not easy. I sometimes expressed my understanding of how difficult it was to work differently by sharing one of my own experiences with change and to express the expectation that they would master the new way of working.

As a poor kid growing up on Lake Michigan, my desire was to someday own and enjoy a motorboat like the ones I saw on the lake. At fifty years of age, in the middle of the winter, I decided it was now or never, and I bought a boat. The first time out, I got stuck on a sandbar. That summer I bumped into the bridge twice, tore up three rudders, and encountered other problems. I found myself praying that it would rain so that I would not have to go out on the boat. I had read books on boating and taken courses, but I was not ready. Finally a neighbor took me out and gave me hands-on lessons. I learned and can now enjoy my new competencies and boating.

The staff appreciated the empathy. Also, they respected our opinions because we were in the trenches with them, experiencing just how tough it is to be a successful teacher or school administrator under all conditions, but particularly in difficult social and economic communities. I am sure they also appreciated the fact that the almost "silent hand" became more and more silent as they were able to manage the social and academic programs of the school with little more than the occasional observation or question.

The major problem with traditional school support services grew out of the way they were initially introduced. After World War II, and as the nation became more affluent, the need to help students with various kinds of challenges succeed became apparent. Operating from the prevalent mechanical and individual deficit model, these services were introduced in piecemeal fashion, sometimes from different and competing agencies. In the most dysfunctional schools helping professionals worked separately, using varied and haphazard referral systems.

Because our SDP team provided these services in the pilot schools, the problem was not initially apparent. When we began working in a similar profile third school, we discovered one student who was being "helped" by seven different service providers, none aware of what the other was doing. The requests for help were made in different ways in each case. The providers did not talk to or even see each other. Each helper came in and "helped" the child. The child could not benefit from this fragmented arrangement.

The helpers were brought together as the Mental Health Team and a standard referral system was worked out. This took considerable effort because some were part time and assigned to more than one building. They had schedules that made it difficult for them all to confer on the same day, in the same place. But once accomplished, the collaborative team proved much more efficient and effective. As a team, they could sometimes simply listen to a teacher's need and provide advice that solved a problem. When classroom observation was indicated, they decided on the appropriate helper based on the description of the problem. They were able to work out case management arrangements so that social services, treatment, and other actions could be carried out and monitored systematically.

Individual treatment turned out to be less needed than it at first appeared in most cases. During our first chaotic year, there were more than forty referrals to the Mental Health Team in one school during only the first semester. The helpers were swamped. But when the schools began to function well, the referrals dropped precipitously, and the small number of students with significant problems was apparent. No longer swamped, there was sufficient support staff available to help those in greater need. While the team continued to help individual children when indicated, there was a shift in focus to prevention.

Meeting time for the team was divided between individual case issues and what we called "global" or "schoolwide" issues. The latter amounted to exploring what it would take to make the schools child-friendly and supportive of development. The examination of individual incidents often pointed to policy and practice conditions that made the schools harmful to the health and development of students and interfered with desirable behavior, teaching, and learning.

One of the most dramatic incidents was that of an eight-year-old child from a warm, tight-knit community in North Carolina who was brought to New Haven over the weekend by an aunt. On her way to work on Monday morning, she dropped him off at the school. And because there were no orientation procedures, the child was taken directly to the classroom by the principal.

The teacher had had three transfers the week before. When the new student arrived, her facial and body language expressed frustration and, to the student, rejection. Alone in a strange place with unknown and rejecting adults, a relative he barely knew as his only support, and she was not there, he panicked. He kicked the teacher in the leg and ran out of the classroom. We thought this was a fairly healthy response for an eight-year-old in this situation, but of course the teacher did not.

This is the kind of situation where the child gets sent to the principal and receives a lecture or scolding. He is sent back to the classroom and someone might laugh or tease him. He might punch that person in the nose and be sent back to the principal. It would go around and around in aggressive, defensive, face-saving, and angry circles, with escalating acting-out behavior, until he is finally labeled disturbed and sent off to a helping professional like me to have his head fixed.

Instead of working on his head, our Mental Health Team met with and asked the teachers to think about what it must be like to be eight years of age and to find oneself in a strange place without support. They thought about their first trips abroad, the experience with strange money and a strange language, and the anxiety they felt. They identified with the student and began to give suggestions about how to make the classroom and the school a more welcoming place. Soon after, he was given an orientation to the school. The principal talked to him about what the school was like and what they were trying to do for their students. He gave him a tour and introduced him to various staff members. He also talked about the activities available and how to access them, where to go for help, and how to handle any problems that he had.

The child returned to a classroom prominently displaying a "Welcome Johnny" sign made by his future classmates. There were introductions. He was allowed to talk about where he was from and where he was living in New Haven. One of the most successful students in the class was assigned the task of helping him learn his way around. This process dramatically decreased the number of problems related to turnover. Turnover is very high in low-income communities; 50 percent in that school.

The students themselves became the carriers of the new school culture, as is reflected in another incident. Two years later, a nine-year-old who had been in three different schools during the first semester was transferred into one of our schools in the second. Somebody stepped on his foot during a classroom exercise and his "dukes" went up, ready to fight. In his previous transfers he had to fight to make certain that nobody would pick on him. Another student said, "Hey man we don't do that in this school." He looked around to be certain because he had not been in a school like this before. Sure enough the facial expression of his teacher and classmates confirmed that this was a "no fight" culture. He gradually dropped his "dukes" and became a carrier of this safe new culture along with his classmates.

As teachers received help in thinking about what was going on with their students, they began to come to the Mental Health Team meetings voluntarily, even when they were not presenting a problem from their classroom. It was an opportunity to learn about child development and behavior. In one such meeting, a teacher asked for help with a student in her classroom who was mute. During what had now become a case conference, another teacher, who had a sibling of the mute child in her class, reported that the family had been burned out of their home in a suburban town to which they had recently moved. It had been a socially upward move. There was some suspicion that it was a racial incident. On investigation, it was discovered that the two children, playing with matches, had started the fire that burned down their home. The family had inadequate insurance and had to move back into the city.

The incident occurred while the father was at the hospital visiting the mother, who had just had a new baby. Understandably the household was full of anger, hurt, frustration, disappointment, and loss at a time when there should have been joy. I suspect that guilt from the hostile side of their mixed feelings about the new baby got mixed up with their guilt about the fire. The children were afraid to tell what really happened. All of this was a heavy burden. The escape for the one child was to become mute. The Mental Health Team was able to call in help for the entire family. The child recovered.

On another occasion, an eight-year-old child did just enough work to be passed on to the next grade, but she did not look at her teacher, smile, or otherwise engage for the first seven months of school. She had had difficult relationships with adults and did not trust them. But her teacher had been caring, predictable, responsible, and kind. As a result, the child finally smiled at her. The teacher came into the teacher's lounge devastated because she knew that she would have to pass her on to the next teacher in two months and would not be able to build on the trust that had taken so long to establish.

Our Mental Health Team talked with the staff about the discontinuity in the lives of many children living under difficult social and economic circumstances. They often move from place to place, and some had people moving in and out of their lives even if they stayed in the same place. And too many have had abusive relationships. "Looping," or staying with the same teacher, was not a common practice in American schools thirty years ago. But out of the discussion about this incident, it was decided that first- and third-grade teachers would stay with their students for two years and then "loop" back after the second year. This approach proved to be very successful. Some children who made no academic gain in the first year made up to two years and more of academic gain in the second, with the same teacher.

Teachers can suggest summer activities that help children continue to learn because they will be reporting to the same teacher the next year. This is important in that children from home environments where learning is not supported lose gains made during the academic year over the summer. Transition discussions and activities, such as visits to the next year's class, minimized the ill effects of a move after two years, and the children were now older and a little less vulnerable. Teachers reported that there was no letdown or acting-out behavior at the end of the first year. Such behavior is common and usually related to feelings of withdrawal and detachment. And there was no getting-to-know-you testing behavior at the beginning of the second year.

After many such successful interventions, the trust grew and the relationships tightened between the staff and parents. As a result, one evening a mother called her son's teacher at home and told him that her son had run away. It was dark and cold and she was frightened. School had become a warm, friendly, supportive place and the teacher guessed where the youngster would go for comfort. He went to the school and there was the boy—in the dark and cold, huddled against the schoolhouse door. The youngster received help with his struggle for autonomy and authority: a common problem with ten-year-old males, particularly with single moms. The help of the male teacher and a supportive school climate served this family well.

As previously mentioned, in many schools handicapped children, or children with challenges of any kind, become the targets of teasing, bullying, and victimization. A parent who had moved from our pilot school to a suburban school district experienced this problem. She brought her child back to our school. The staff had helped the children in our school respect and take pride in helping the handicapped child function adequately.

Some of the problems the staff and Mental Health Team tackled together were less dramatic, but they provided important understanding about child development and behavior for the staff and served as effective ways to improve the school. For example, teachers expressed concern about the disruptive behavior of the kindergartners during the assemblies. Five-year-olds were being scolded and punished for their inability to sit still and pay attention to the program—"bad kids." The other teachers were wondering why their colleague could not control her class. And the kindergarten teacher was feeling put upon.

We supplied one crucial bit of child development knowledge. Children that age cannot sit still very long. Given that understanding, the staff devised a plan to bring the kindergarten students into the assembly last. They put them on the program first and had them sit to an intermission timed to their tolerance level. And then they had them leave in an orderly way. This worked for students and staff alike.

Also, our team and the staff created a Crisis Room for a very common problem that repeatedly disrupted classrooms and sometimes the entire school. Ordinary problems, managed without giving attention to what a child is struggling with, often got out of hand and created crises. A child might come to school in the morning upset about something that happened at home or on the way to school. Efforts to quiet or control him, or to get him to do his work, would often make matters worse and lead to teachers dragging angry, screaming students down to the principal's office for punishment.

I often point out that children cannot say, "Mr. Smith, I'm not functioning well today and I would greatly appreciate your special attention and support." They usually act out feelings they cannot put in words. We discussed with the teachers how such situations might be used to help children learn to manage feelings and develop better inner controls.

John enters upset and looking for trouble. "Look John, I can see that you're upset about something. Here is what I want you to do to try to pull yourself together." The teacher makes several suggestions but adds, "If you are not able to do so in

class I am going to ask you to go down to the Crisis Room" and
do so. Remember, loss of control is failure and management of
self is success in the minds of young children.

Most students were able to manage in the classroom once
the teacher provided attention and guidance. Some could not.
But now when asked, because what would happen next was
known and there was a structured or expected response, the
student got up and went down to the place where he or she,
usually he, could receive help without a fight. The teacher
would suggest the time it ought to take for them to do so. They
returned, recovered, every time at the suggested time.

The principal, the social worker, and eventually non-
professionals trained by the social worker managed the Crisis
Room. While at the Crisis Room, students were allowed to
talk about their problems and given suggestions about how to
handle them. They were asked to do their regular classroom
work during part of their time there, so they could not use the
room to escape class work.

We also had a Discovery Room for children who were
turned off or just did not know how to function in school. This
was often the case because of unpredictable relationships with
their adult caretakers. Sometimes they were harshly punished
for minor things, major problems were ignored, and the like.
These students were often put down and scolded. Some observed or were the victims of violence or sexual abuse. As a result, they lacked the confidence needed to explore and learn.
The Discovery Room teacher had exciting activities for them
and they often talked out some of the things bothering them
while they were doing their work and play.

Some teachers complained that the Discovery Room was
a reward for bad behavior, but they acknowledged that the
children appeared to benefit from it. In response, a visit to the

Discovery Room was arranged for teachers and students. The Discovery Room teacher helped them to understand what happened there, whom it was for, and why it worked, and she encouraged them to use it only if they needed to do so. The children who did not need it did not abuse the privilege, and the teachers were satisfied.

Many of the problems stemmed from inadequate in-school and out-of-school adult anticipation of problem situations, orientation, and explanations. As adults we get anxious when we do not know what to do, what to expect, or how to manage things. For example, an unexplained delay on an airplane made me a little apprehensive even before September 11, 2001. It helps when people explain what is going on around you and provide orientations, introductions, expectations, and the like. Yet we regularly expect children to manage all manner of complex, anxiety-provoking situations without providing them with much of anything in the way of background or support.

Even well-intended acts can be troublesome. They are worth considering to help us remember what children need. Several years ago, a child in the school where our project began was asked to be a part of a picture being taken for an award I was receiving. He was a well-mannered, cooperative kid, but the Halloween march was about to begin and he was afraid he would miss it. He could not put his concern into words. He was being asked to keep still but was too anxious to do so. I sensed the problem and told him I would make sure that he got to participate, and he was able to finish, just barely. My program was not his program. He did not want to miss out on what his peers were enjoying.

I understood. In fact, it brought to mind another incident from my childhood. I tell the story here to remind us of how lasting little childhood traumas can be; little stuff to adults, important to kids. One Easter Sunday Mrs. Johnson—the same lady who had the vision about my future—pulled me out of the line because they were running out of eggs. She knew my parents had an Easter egg hunt for us at home, and much more. Most of the other kids were not going to have that experience anywhere but in the church. She was right and she did the right thing, but I sure did want one of those eggs at church, like everybody else. I still remember the sense of denial and pain. I was not yet ready to be a missionary. I was about six.

Again, as adults we have had more experiences, and most of us have landed on our feet often enough to believe that we are going to be okay. Kids are still learning that the world is manageable, most of the time. They have a healthy self-serving perspective that is part of our human survival drive. Because they have had fewer experiences, they can be more easily and more greatly traumatized and frightened if they do not receive good support. With assurances from trusted others, they can learn to wait, to forgo immediate rewards, and even to tolerate missed pleasures. Indeed, this is very much needed to prepare for the realities of life.

Very early in our work, I became aware of the fact that teachers knew very little about child development and behavior. It struck me as odd and unfair that social and behavioral scientists were steeped in such knowledge but educators on the front line—the practitioners—had not been provided even the elementary concepts. When the child kicked the teacher and ran out of the room, I commented that it was a case of "fight and flight" rather than "fight or flight." The teachers looked at me as if I were speaking a foreign language. I was. This realization strongly supported our perception that the major reasons many schools were not working well was that the students were underdeveloped and the staff was under-prepared to support their development. But the teachers wanted to help their students: they came to Mental Health meetings voluntarily just to learn more about child behavior.

As a way of helping the teachers understand the causes of certain behaviors, we often talked about growth along developmental pathways—physical, social-interactive, psychological-emotional, ethical, linguistic, and cognitive-intellectual—and how developmental challenges sometimes led to unacceptable behavior. *A response that helped a student overcome a social or academic challenge not only prevented behavior problems, it promoted developmental growth.* In recent years, we have begun to discuss brain growth as an aspect of the physical pathway and see it in terms of how it affects behavior.

As we used these concepts to discuss the behaviors of students, the teachers began to use them to think in terms of development and underdevelopment rather than "bad" and "dumb." The teachers were delighted to understand how what appeared to be deliberate troublemaking was often related to developmental issues and social environment conditions. They were even more pleased to learn how to manage behavior problems in ways that helped the students grow. With this new perspective, the systematic creation of an environment to promote development made more sense. Today students, staff, and parents are learning about and using developmental pathways as a way to think about growth and behavior in order to achieve good outcomes.

Knowledge about the pathways is not new. Erikson, Vygotsky, Piaget, and many others have created a vast amount of theory and empirical and clinical evidence about these pathways, which are known to most social and behavioral scientists. But this knowledge was not being applied in education in a way that would enable the adults to create an environment that would promote the development of students. We made this knowledge available in ways that allowed it to be used to improve everyday education practice.

Through the *Parent Team* mechanism, the work of the parents in the school was structured in a way that both parents and staff gained more skills and knowledge about child development and growth along all the developmental pathways as well as ideas on how to promote it. In the schools of yesterday, few parents were directly involved, but those schools were a natural part of the community, with interactions that made home and school mutually supportive. As a result of the breakdown in a sense of community and the stress experienced by too many families, parents need more help in preparing children for schools. School staff need more help in supporting student growth in school. This is why we called for parent participation.

When we began our work in 1968 there was still much resistance to significant parent involvement in schools. I heard school people across the country say, "The parents should raise them, and we should teach them." In some cases resistance resulted from school improvement efforts that pitted parents against school staffs and districts. Much energy was expended in advocacy efforts and adversarial struggles for control without improving teaching and learning. These approaches are being rejected, and it is now generally recognized that constructive parental involvement is needed.

On the other hand, many schools complain that the parents will not get involved, and parents often complain that they are not wanted in the schools. The problem is the social network disconnect I described in chapter 3. Because the school is not a part of the child's and family's primary network as it once was, a relationship climate that makes good home-school interactions possible must be created.

Many parents in low-income communities did not have good experiences in school, and they often send their children to school hoping they will have a better experience but fearing they may not. Bad news confirms their fears. Thus no news is good news; avoidance and attack when there is a problem is defensive and protective. You cannot say simply, "you are welcome" or "y'all come." Our approach was to create a school climate that enabled doubting parents to experience respect and comfort, to be supported, to get involved and be supportive of the school, and to help create the conditions that enabled their children to succeed—reinforcing parental participation.

Our SDP has been given credit for being one of the first groups to deeply involve parents in the work of schools; even now we are sometimes called a parent program. But we encouraged collaboration rather than adversarial relationships, and eventually particular parental roles became one of the nine components of our framework. Our purpose, again, was to join the efforts of the first developers and teachers (the parents) with those of the second developers and teachers, school people, and extend the support for development beyond the family network.

Because of the way our SDP project began, parents first came out in anger, at one point determined to throw us out. We invited them to stay and help us. Initially they served on the existing PTO and PTA, and these groups evolved into the Parent Team in each school as the idea of interrelated teams emerged. The Parent Team elected four of its members to serve on the Governance and Management Team. Initially, to protect parental interests, there was an agreement that the parents could overrule a full-team vote, but as decision making by consensus became the practice, this procedure was not needed, and it was eventually dropped.

Some schools already have in place programs similar to our SDP components. On occasion, when the model has not been replicated correctly, similar or duplicate teams have been created, causing harmful competition and confusion. To avoid this, we have used the existing program as our SDP component.

Because we got off to a difficult start, our initial work with parents on the team was challenging. The least productive way to work was to ask them what they wanted. When asked, they demanded (it was 1968) a full-time doctor, a nurse, and other very expensive but wasteful services. These were really tests of commitment and expressions of anger at people and institutions that were more powerful than they were. Focusing on what would help the children learn best and gain the skills necessary to function in the mainstream of the society helped us move away from testing behavior to more useful discussions about how to best use resources to improve the schools.

The presence of the parents was protective and supportive in several important ways. They were community representatives rather than outsiders, who sometimes used the schools for their own social and political purposes. Recall my friend, the community activist who was trying to turn the parents against Yale before he knew anything about the project. The parents could be encouraged to act in the best interest of their children. And they brought the culture and interests of the community into all school activities, making activities culture sensitive.

The parents worked with the staff to carry out the comprehensive school plan, particularly the social program, and the academic when possible. Also, they created a set of activities, designed to help them learn more about how to help their children develop and prepare for school at home. Eventually their programs helped them gain the knowledge and skills needed to access various community services. They tapped our CSC staff, teachers, other school people, and relevant outsiders as presenters.

Three levels of parent participation evolved. Some parents only attended the calendar activities, the first level of involvement. At the second level were the half-time paid parent-assistants who worked in the classrooms and school. Most of these people also volunteered some of their time, often working full time at the school. They were paid minimum wage, and when the project no longer had funds, some served in the same roles as volunteers. Even today some schools have parent volunteers. The paid assistants were an important community-school connection. Most of the leaders eventually served on the Parent Team. Also, eight to ten parents involved in a building on a regular basis were enough to make any parent activity successful. The third and most involved level of parent participation was the group that served on the governance team and in support and sponsorship of social calendar activities described previously.

Parental involvement, anchored by a team and by parents working as paid assistants, enabled us to overcome serious parent-staff engagement and relationship problems. The paid assistants and the Parent Team were a critical mass. And because the Parent Team was involved in the comprehensive school plan, they had a large stake in program outcomes. Thus, they were very active in encouraging parent participation in and support of school activities, the first level of participation. The students observed their parents, or people like their parents, in important leadership roles in the schools. This sanctioned the staff and program of the school.

Again, in the first year or two there were difficult parent-staff incidents, including a physical threat against a teacher. But such incidents disappeared as good relationships were established, and good things were being said about the schools in the neighborhoods. When there were concerns, they were discussed and handled in a civil, problem-solving manner. Parents often helped their peers consider their own, or their children's, troublesome behavior that might have contributed to a problem situation and their responsibilities, as opposed to blaming it all on a staff person or the school.

The paid parent-assistant program should be given serious policy consideration. Not only did these assistants help the students, staff, and the school, but their work in the schools provided the scaffolding many needed to complete their own education or to obtain living-wage employment. By chance I was connected to a telephone operator supervisor who had been a parent in one of the pilot schools. She told me that through her work as a paid parent-assistant in our school, she gained the confidence and skills to obtain and hold her job and be promoted. She said that this would not have been possible without the school experience.

There are many such stories. The most impressive is that of a parent who was energized to the point that she went back and finished high school, college, graduate school, and is now a working professional. One of her two daughters is now a physician, the other a lawyer, and her two sons are engineers.

At the end of the five-year project, the schools were good places for children to live and grow. The parents and staff were functioning well. The social program had reached a high level of effectiveness. But the test scores had not gone up. The pressure for improved test scores was not as great then as it is now, but there was still a question about the value of the program. The Ford Foundation provided the financial support for our pilot project in New Haven. They explored the probable long-term feasibility of our approach by consulting with several psychiatrists. The consultants—my colleagues, trained to provide one-to-one clinical treatment and unfamiliar with a public health or ecological approach—felt that individual treatment would be needed. As a result a decision was made to discontinue financial support.

The foundation provided reduced funds during a phase-out year. New Haven school system personnel began to return to the school and began to work as they had done previously. They began to make treatment referrals for student problems that teachers now believed they could and should manage, with support from our SSST. The teachers believed it was important for them, as the continuous person in the life of the child, to address behavior problems in a way that would help the students grow. Finally, fed up, they staged a march on the principal and demanded that the school system social worker not be allowed back in the building. The parents charged the Child Study Center with abandonment. Al Solnit found money to keep us going until new grant support could be found.

VII

Development, Learning, and Democracy

Support for our work in the schools grew in part out of inspiration and in part out of desperation, as is often the case. The schools had been functioning well for two or three years, and the students were able, motivated, and learning. There were many indications that the students were as able and motivated as middle-income children. The staff was able and motivated. Parents were engaged and supportive. Why were the test scores not going up?

An incident in the fifth year brought to mind an experience from my childhood and provided a vital clue. The front hallway of the King School was being used as a polling place for elections. Because of this, one of the teachers was not able to hug and greet her students as usual, and she complained that the election activity interfered with her ability to connect with and inspire them. Her comment triggered my childhood memory of actually pulling the voting lever when I was with my mother and what a powerful, positive impact that had had on my development.

Our team had been speculating that the primary difference between the students in our low-income elementary schools and those in middle-income schools was that our students did not receive the kind of supervised preschool and out-of-school experiences needed to promote learning in schools. Many middle-income children receive such experiences from their family environment. We suspected that if we could engage our students and their families in activities in school that would adequately support their development, they would achieve as well as others. This would give them a better opportunity to be successful in life.[1]

Also, I had often thought of my previous work at Hospitality House in Washington, D.C. While working there, in 1961 and 1962, I first began to observe that the economy was changing rapidly; that life was becoming increasingly complex; and that the children there, and elsewhere, were not being adequately prepared. In 1974, thirteen years later, the children and families in our project schools were in the same situation or worse. Such children and families, without a good education, would continue to be marginalized in society.

During the 1960s, a period of great racial and social unrest in America, I had struggled to understand the complexities and contradictions of American life. I gradually came to appreciate the value of democracy as a political system, to understand it as an important counterweight to the harmful aspects of the human quest to survive and thrive. These concerns led me to reflect on Thomas Jefferson's argument for a public education system as protection for a democracy. In a 1787 letter to James Madison, Jefferson wrote: "Above all things I hope the education of the common people will be attended to, convinced that on their good sense we may rely with the most security for the preservation of a due degree of liberty."

He returned to this theme in an 1818 letter to Joseph C. Cabell: "If the children are untaught, their ignorance and vices will in future life cost us much dearer in their consequences than it would have done in their correction by a good education."[2]

Jefferson was calling for a kind of education that was more than knowledge of basic skills, the classics, or even science. He wanted a public education system that would enable the average person to understand political, economic, and social issues, their relevance to their own lives, and what was needed to improve and to sustain democracy. Very quickly, but consistent with human nature, education for personal gain became far more important than the principles of liberty and democracy. If you ask students today why they want to get an education, most will say, "To get a job."

Unfortunately, too many educators, business people, and celebrities pitching "stay in school" messages give the same answer. Education in the service of democracy has been lost as an important purpose, if it was ever established as such. *And yet, without a public education system that focuses both on the preparation of individuals to "get a job" and to be the underpinning of democratic beliefs and behaviors, we will kill the goose—democracy—that has laid the golden egg—a reasonable quality of life and income for most.*[3]

During the years that followed my Hospitality House experience I observed children in school not being prepared to get a living-wage job or to protect and promote our democracy. And yet my own experience suggested that this matter could be addressed in school if not at home, or in both places. Our Social Skills Curriculum for Inner-City Children (SSCICC) grew out of this mental ferment.

In 1976 I began holding almost daily sessions in my office with Carol Schraft, then our chief social worker. It was almost a therapy role reversal situation. I told her what my childhood experiences meant to me, how they promoted my development. She sketched out on paper how they addressed developmental pathway issues. We talked about the kind of experiences our students would need to help them grow, about whether and how the school program could be adjusted to make this possible. But we did not want to impose our values or interests on the parents.

Ms. Schraft conducted several focus groups with parents, exploring their ideas without revealing ours. Roughly, the parents were asked three questions: What do you want for your children as adults? What kind of experiences will they need to be able to achieve these goals? How can we begin to prepare them to achieve these goals while they are still young children in school? Contrary to the arguments about different cultural values that I often hear from professional educators and social science types, the parents wanted the same outcomes for their children as most mainstream parents—to become doctors, firemen, lawyers, teachers, business people, and simply good people. Their suggestions about the kind of exposure and experiences the children would need fell into four categories—politics and government, business and economics, health and nutrition, and spiritual and leisure time.

With the guidance of parents and school staff, we wrote a grant entitled "A Social Skills Curriculum for Inner-City Children." It was supported by the National Institute of Mental Health and put in place in our pilot elementary schools in 1977. This program enabled parents and school staff to support student growth along the six developmental pathways that facilitate academic learning (physical, social-interactive, psycho-emotional, ethical, linguistic, cognitive-intellectual). The goal was to better prepare the students to be successful in school by introducing them to activity areas where they could learn and begin to develop the skills needed to be successful in life.

The program helped us to secure the funds to live another day, to get the test scores up, and to fully appreciate that good development along all the pathways made school success more likely and had the potential for strengthening democracy. We had many more miles to go to make our point than we realized at the time, and we are still walking. But the Social Skills Curriculum was an important second step. It built on, as does all our work, lessons gained during the creation of our basic framework.

Some of the families in the schools had experiences much like my own. Many families were marginalized but caring, and they wanted their children to succeed in school and in life. Most were under economic and social stress and could not provide the children with what they needed to be successful. A few children were from antisocial families, but even these families wanted their children to do well in school.

The Social Skills Curriculum was embedded in the culture the SDP pilot project participants had created during the previous nine years. It was a culture that had overcome many of the obstacles to good development and learning often faced by such families. Thus, the nine-component framework that helped to create that culture also facilitated the Social Skills Curriculum.

Our Social Skills Curriculum for Inner-City Children integrated the teaching of basic academic skills and social skills with an appreciation of the arts, and athletics when possible. Reduced funding had all but eliminated the elementary school athletic program in New Haven. Our Skills Curriculum was carried out in what would have been free or elective time in the school schedule. Units were developed in the four areas of activity where we had agreed the children would need exposure in order to gain academic knowledge and skills required for life tasks—politics and government, business and economics, health and nutrition, and spiritual and leisure time or expressive activities—the arts, athletics, others.

I suspected that student involvement in such real-world or mock activities, carefully mediated by parents and teachers, could prepare them both to "get a job" and to protect and promote democracy, regardless of their prior or outside-of-school experiences. I had hoped that our SSCICC project would lead eventually to an early-childhood-through-college, or sixteen-year, preparatory experience. Toward this goal our SDP was and continues to be involved in a few prekindergarten programs (Comer-Zigler or CoZi) with Edward Zigler, the first Director of the Office of Child Development (now the Administration on Children, Youth and Families). While the outcomes were and are promising, our SDP did not have the financial support needed to give in-depth and continued attention to this work.[4] And we were not able to work beyond the high school level.

Staff and Parent Teams planned the units with our SDP social worker. It is of interest to note that after reporting on the outcome of this work, we received many requests for our Social Skills Curriculum. But we did not have a written curriculum. The content came out of parent and staff ideas about what students would need to prepare for adult functioning. The academic exercises were embedded in the activities. The power of this approach was in the parents and staff thinking about, planning, and assessing the activities together. They owned them, honed them, and passionately wanted them to work for the children. So they learned from each activity and worked to make the next more effective. Without these contextual conditions the activities could have been much less meaningful and beneficial. We followed the strategy we used in all our previous work—initial SDP staff involvement to help parents and staff make their first project efforts successful. When this is the case, people are more likely to try again or to "buy in" the second time around. As parents and staff gained skills, we were able to pull back and be available as constructive observers and friendly consultants.

Because a mayoral campaign was coming up, King School designed a fourth-grade Social Skills Curriculum unit in the area of politics and government. In their classroom social science period they discussed the local election as well as the purpose, organization, and function of government. The students all wrote letters inviting the three candidates for mayor to visit their school politics and government unit activity.

The mayor is an important person. Thus, the text, tone, spelling, and grammar of these letters required the students' best effort. In fact, if I am writing to the mayor, "I am important!" An activity like this also *helps to promote a sense of belonging, the right to participate and promote one's own interests, and the sense of responsibility related to doing so.* Many poor people lack such feelings. This sense of not belonging and not being valued is a barrier as powerful as a law barring participation. Remember the comment of the lady from my childhood: "We are poor people; you know he will never be a doctor!" Powerlessness is difficult to understand for many who are born into an empowering family and network milieu.

Parents hired buses to take the students, along with some staff and parents, on a tour of the city. They paid for the field trip with money earned from activities carried out as a part of the school social plan—the sale of school calendars, fashion show tickets, and so on. While on the tour they noted the conditions of the roads and buildings; identified government and other important buildings, policemen, shoppers, and other people and places; and talked about the role of government in their lives. Back in school the students wrote essays about their observations and thoughts.

The school was alive with practice and preparation for the program day. The students were taught how to raise tough questions with the candidates without being disrespectful—important academic and social skills. They practiced the dances, readings, and dramatic presentation they had planned for the candidates, their parents, teachers, and classmates. They were all taught the social skills needed to serve as hosts and how to behave in the social setting of the program day.

Some were selected to serve as visitor escorts during tours of the school, some as ushers, and two students were coached to serve as master of ceremonies. Teachers were assigned to provide back-up support just in case the students forgot their lines, became overly anxious, or whatever. The idea was to help the students experience success and then celebrate it, rather than the way it is usually done—not preparing them adequately, criticizing their failure or lack of ability, and punishing or holding low expectations of them. Incidentally, that is what we as a society have been doing to teachers and administrators in recent years.

In the culture of our pilot schools it was not appropriate for classmates to laugh at or ridicule anyone who was having performance difficulty. Parents, staff, and students were expected to help each other and could expect to receive help when they needed it. This was an ideal of course, just as my brothers and I were not supposed to fight each other. Kids try, but again, their emotions and impulses often override their controls.

Students had to be reminded over and over of these behavioral goals, and they had to remind each other of what was expected, especially on this special occasion. My favorite apocryphal story is that of a teacher saying sternly, "Johnny, did I not tell you not to run down the hall?" "Oops, Ms. Jones," he replies, "My head remembered but my feet forgot." If all of this sounds like home, and your mother, it should because the idea, again, was to provide the students with as many of the experiences and skills that mainstream children, more often middle and upper income, receive simply by growing up with their parents.

Prepared well, the kids put on a spectacular dance and drama program. The students listened intently during the presentations by the candidates. They raised excellent questions, even follow-up questions in response to answers they were given. The visitors were greatly impressed, and the parents were bursting with pride. The mayor, who was eventually re-elected, talked to the students about how what they learn in school, how they get along with others, and how they take care of their school building are all in preparation for participating in government and community life. When one student was asked by her teacher what she thought of the mayor's talk, she replied, "He respects me."

The teachers, already believers, were now blown away. One pointed out that a child in her class who appeared "just average" turned out to have great personal presence. His interactions with the mayor and the other visiting dignitaries were very impressive. All the students behaved and performed with an enthusiasm and vibrancy that suggested they had more ability than they had been displaying. We believe that this raised the expectations of the staff, which was conveyed back to the students, resulting in the first significant academic achievement jump.

I mentioned earlier that the voting booth in the school provided a clue as to why the test scores had not changed. The outcome of this exercise in politics and government, and others later, suggested that a major reason was marginalization. It appears that marginalization—not poverty—locks students and families and the people who interact with them in a powerful grip of hopelessness and powerlessness. Students, parents, and staff view themselves as "the bottom of the barrel." This leads to apathy, apprehension, and underperformance, withdrawal or harmful acting-out behavior, or all of the above. By creating conditions that allowed parents, staff, and students not only to participate in but to sponsor a mainstream activity, the grip of hopelessness and powerlessness was weakened. They could begin to hope and to view themselves as people who could be very successful. Students who had not made optimal investments in academic learning previously were turned on by the structure and context of the SSCICC learning activities. With well-thought-out, planned, and energizing learning experiences that gave a boost to the confidence and competence of staff, students, and parents alike, the test scores began to rise.

After the first SSCICC program year, I watched from my office window as Ms. Schraft walked through the parking lot with the nationally standardized test score results in her hand. By the time she reached the fifth floor I had aged ten years. When I read them I danced around the office in joy and relief. I knew the students were making gains, but I was not sure the scores would show it.

The scores indicated a nine-month gain over the previous year. Each subsequent class outdid the last for the next five years. By then, one school was almost two years above grade level in math and language arts achievement by the fourth grade, and the other was slightly behind. The schools were third- and fourth-highest-level academic achievers in the city. These schools were similar, indeed, one was the same school, to the schools that ranked thirty-second and thirty-third out of thirty-three schools eight years earlier when we began our program, and with no change in the social and economic makeup of the neighborhood. They were first in attendance in the city and there were no serious behavior problems. In fact, a citywide survey showed that our two pilot schools were the only ones that did not make a referral for very expensive residential treatment services.

These outcomes probably could not have occurred through the Social Skills program alone. They were due to improved overall school functioning as well as staff, parent, and student development. But I believe that the focus on the students' possible futures, in the context of a well-functioning, caring, and hopeful school setting, provided direction, success motivation, and achievement skills. These combined factors led to school success and the kind of experiences needed to move toward life success.

Of course, such experiences are not an inoculation or a success elixir. Continued good experiences all the way through school, and also at home and in the community, are needed for most children to achieve good outcomes. When the home and community cannot provide a positive environment, the school can to some degree.

Our assessment of the politics and government unit showed that most of the children knew the names and responsibilities of key local government officials. But they also knew the state and national government officials, as well as the location of all of the state capitals. The local experience appeared to stimulate their interest in politics and government in general and their desire to learn more about the world around them. Perhaps equally important if not more so, after the program *some of the parents registered and proudly voted for the first time.* Modeling matters, not only for the students but for their parents, and, in turn, it reinforces student participation and learning.

As mentioned, some of the parents went back to school and advanced their own education and job situations. More than the usual number of school staff people advanced their own training and now hold influential positions in education in many different places. The same is true of our CSC project staff. These outcomes are not because of SDP per se. But when a social context is created that is supportive, human beings, young and older, have a better chance to feel good about themselves and to express their full potential.

The other units had similar exciting outcomes. A student choir was organized around the spiritual and leisure time unit. They performed at school and in the community. The students, with thoughtful questions and suggestions from their teachers, decided on the program they would present, and they made travel and other arrangements connected to putting on a performance. Two-year-olds say, "I want to do it myself," and parents who are encouraging initiative and personal responsibility, when possible, will allow or help them to do so. Yet we often do not organize school activities for older children so that they provide the same opportunities.

The students organized and operated a school store as part of the business and economics unit. And a real-life school break-in, with theft of some of the store property, helped them get a deep understanding of the concept of insurance.

We began to disseminate our work and move it up to the middle school level in 1979. We began working in the Jackie Robinson Middle School in New Haven, using the basic nine-element model and the Social Skills Curriculum. Reginald Mayo was the principal at that time. He was one of the few people in the district actively seeking to implement the SDP model. He is now the superintendent of schools in New Haven.

The New York City Museum of Natural History was featuring a Jackie Robinson exhibition. It offered an opportunity to provide the students with meaningful exposure and learning—both academic and social—that would enhance their development. An in-school academic unit and a field trip to the museum were planned. The social science and language arts teachers collaborated to create a unit of study entitled "The Life and Times of Jackie Robinson." It explored racial, economic, and social conditions during the lifetime of Mr. Robinson as well as the impact his pioneering role in baseball had on the nation.

The students wrote essays, presented dramatic readings, engaged in role-playing, and other activities that gave them a real feel for the context of life in America during that period, how one life can help change institutions and history, and the impact of this historical event on their own lives. The young people prepared for their interaction with the people at the museum through role-playing. They were taught how to observe the exhibit, how to ask relevant questions, how to respond to curators and others. Mrs. Robinson, the widow of Jackie Robinson, was contacted and accepted the invitation of the students to be present at the time of their visit. The students were taught the social graces appropriate for interacting with Mrs. Robinson and the museum staff.

As a part of the field trip they would be stopping at a restaurant for lunch on the way back. Again, there was advance practice. They were taught all of the necessary social skills to handle themselves appropriately in the restaurant. They decided on games and activities for the bus ride, and appropriate behavior during the bus ride was discussed. Attention was given to compatible seating arrangements of students and staff, and thought was given to making the ride itself an educational experience—noting the sights of interest, historic areas, and so on.

Again, the young people were extraordinarily impressive. They raised very good questions and engaged in very thoughtful conversation with Mrs. Robinson and the curators. They received much praise for their thoughtfulness and their behavior. The same was true in response to their stop at the restaurant. The manager of the restaurant admitted privately that he was embarrassed by his initial reaction—"This could be my worst nightmare." He told the young people that they were some of the finest customers he had had. The bus driver made similar positive comments. The young people very much enjoyed the praise. They felt very good about themselves and their accomplishments. Questions about their visit and additional learning activities related to the field trip reverberated around the school for weeks after the event.

I will discuss our dissemination efforts more fully in later chapters, but I would like to describe an incident that occurred during the process that is relevant here. One of the first places our SDP model was implemented outside of Connecticut was in Benton Harbor, Michigan. During an orientation I talked with the staff of an elementary school about some of our ideas, and I described the Social Skills Curriculum. On my next visit one of the teachers, an African-American male, told me that he had not agreed with the idea of the staff teaching social skills when he heard it the first time. It raised questions in his mind about the school's right to impose values and ways of behaving that might be different from those of the students and their families. He went on to tell me the story of a recent experience that had caused him to change his mind.

His fifth-grade class had been "adopted" by a local community college, and they were invited to the college for a visit. It was a bucolic campus with a stream flowing down the middle; beautiful. Geese glided gracefully along, and numerous ducks, some with their ducklings in straight lines behind them, paddled peacefully. A reception committee of staff and students from the college stood on the bank on the other side of the stream, waiting to greet the young people as they crossed a short bridge.

Several of the boys, excited, jumped off the bus, grabbed rocks, and began to throw them at the ducks and geese. This caused loud squawking noises and a frenzied gathering of frightened ducklings, to the great delight of the boys. The hosts looked on horrified; the several adults from the school looked on in embarrassment. This was not a cause for zero tolerance discussions and punishments. This was a new experience for which the students did not have the needed personal development and social skills.

The teacher in charge stopped the show. He ordered the students back on the bus and took them back to their school. The teachers then taught them the needed skills. Later, when they returned to the college, the youngsters were able to elicit a positive response and to enjoy a beneficial growth and learning experience. This incident highlights the power and strategic position of the teacher. Neither the parents nor the hosts were in a position to provide the skills needed to establish a positive connection in the new relationship situation. Without the teacher connectors, the students would have been denied a positive learning experience.

Parents and teachers are important mediators of social interactions and learning; and when parents are not able to do this, for whatever reason, teachers must. Many school and community learning experiences are made meaningful by the mediator. This critical role is often not recognized.

An observation made by one of the teachers involved in our pilot project health and nutrition unit underscored the importance of teacher as mediator in the way young children learn. As part of the health unit activity, a doctor from the Yale pediatrics department gave a demonstration of a physical examination. The students appeared to be very interested, but their teacher pointed out later that they did not get a good understanding of what the doctor did and said. Their connection with him and the lesson was superficial; the best learning was in the follow-up discussion with their teacher. She raised questions about the activity that allowed her to assess their understanding and enabled her to clarify errors and misconceptions.

Questions raised by the students led to additional reading and research. I thought back to the questions I raised as a child after a visit to the museum, the zoo, and other places, on the way home in the car or the next day or days. My older sister, a teacher herself, would always send me to a book to search for answers myself and then inquire about what I found. The habits of analysis and reflection, searching for clarification, and using existing knowledge or understanding to gain new knowledge and deep understanding are encouraged in this way.

Most of the students who are not doing well in school probably have had the threshold level of care and stimulation needed to prepare their brains for reasonably high-level learning. We suspect that the underachievement problem is due to the absence of enough mediated interactions in a well-functioning, stimulating, supportive environment, not brain deficits.

Rarely now, but in the early days of our work I was sometimes asked whether what we were doing was a violation of the culture of the children and their families. I pointed out that an important purpose of education is to open up possibilities and to give students and their families options; in the case of our students this meant an opportunity to get an education, earn a living, and live as responsible citizens. How they elect to live is still their choice. Moreover, the activities were based on wishes of the parents for their children's futures.

Furthermore, it is probably not correct to call the life conditions and style of poor and marginalized people their culture. There is a vigorous academic debate going on about whether the concept of culture is still useful. Culture is what a group creates to enable it to survive and thrive. In complex societies, life conditions and styles that facilitate or limit such outcomes are created as much or more by powerful decision makers outside particular groups than by the group itself. Some conditions should be called cultures or outcomes of exclusion. The parents were calling for opportunities for mainstream participation. Our job was to try to provide them.

When we began to disseminate the School Development Program, we learned that new districts had difficulty managing the Social Skills Curriculum, even when they wanted to use the program. The newly trained facilitators from the districts did not have enough experience to provide the necessary support. We had to give up our pre-K to sixteen years preparation-for-life focus to concentrate on establishing our nine-element framework in enough elementary, middle, and high schools to give our approach reasonable visibility. I will describe how we did so in most of the following chapters.

It is difficult to explain how and why the process of the School Development Program works. Even after I have discussed the nine elements I am often asked how the process works. The question is really *why* does it work. A well-educated parent called me off to the side during a program celebrating outstanding achievement on the state test in the North Carolina elementary school that his son attended. He said, "They keep talking about the 'Comer Program,' but I thought this was the way schools were supposed to work." A reporter spent a week in one of the pilot schools and couldn't write a story. He noted that it was a very good school in the face of conditions that usually produce bad schools, but he didn't understand how this came about.

The explanation is in my previous discussion of human aggression and relationships: meaningful adults help children channel potentially harmful aggressive energy into the fuel of constructive development, learning, work, and play. Social organizations must do the same thing, particularly when the mission is as complex as that of a school. There is much about schooling, even under the best of circumstances, that is threatening, that holds the potential of bringing out the survival or aggressive energies of the stakeholders. Recall that the major cause of teachers leaving is a feeling that they cannot influence their school environments, do not receive enough administrator support, and were not prepared to do the job they are being asked to do. The SDP framework, when applied appropriately, allows the stakeholders to collaboratively channel their energy into improving conditions and outcomes for students rather than expressing it in harmful adult conflicts.

This enables individuals and the organization to create a process of continuous adult development, to get better and better with reasonable support. This promotes creativity, personal accountability, and satisfaction. Because this is rare in difficult situations, it is a cause for joy and celebration. Numerous observers comment on just this outcome in many SDP schools. The late and highly regarded sociologist James Coleman said to me with an expression of puzzlement, "Those schools using your model in Chicago sure are enthusiastic."

Coleman's work suggested that schools could not do much to help poor children because they lacked the social capital they should have acquired at home and in their communities.[5] The mechanisms, operations, and guidelines that undergird our SDP are powerful and synergistic, but silent. And yet a part of what they do is enable school staff and parents together to provide children with the social capital they need to be successful in school. The benefits to the adult school participants are almost palpable. I organized chapter 2, "Voices," in a way that the reader could feel the staff frustration, the movement toward successful management, and the satisfaction and joy of successful management and good outcomes. It is because the model is difficult to understand that we have written *The Field Guide to Comer Schools in Action*.[6]

All the activities described in this book are being done in one school or another across the country. In fact, I am often told about aspects of our SDP, "We did that." People working in poorly functioning schools often add, "But it didn't work." Often school environments are not well functioning, stimulating, and supportive of students, staff, and parents. The activities are not a part of a strategic plan to promote student development and learning goals. The building participants do not have a sense of ownership of the efforts. Without these conditions, the participants are less likely to experience progress toward specific goals and to be motivated to gain the knowledge and skills needed to bring about continuous change and growth.

I am often asked whether it is an approach for improving schools for poor students, minority schools, or all schools.

Several years ago I was asked to speak to the parents and supporters of a highly regarded private school in Pennsylvania. I asked the school head, "Why me? Most of my work has been in very difficult social environments." She pointed out that it was their belief that creating a context that supports adult and student development is what makes good education possible for all students. The purpose of my visit was to reinforce this point. I believe that good support for student development from birth to maturity is a universal need, and a central school responsibility. Good development and learning can protect and promote our democracy.

VIII
But Can It Fly?

The spirit of America that was generated first by the intensified civil rights movement of the 1960s and then by other movements was greatly diminished by the end of our SSCICC program support in 1980. Funding agencies—public and private—turned against social research and demonstration projects. Despite the dramatic improvement in the social and academic performance of our two pilot schools, and obvious promise, we could not get the funds needed to build on what we had learned.

We discontinued our direct involvement in the schools at the end of the SSCICC program in 1980. Fortunately, our SDP way of working had been internalized; our two pilot schools continued to function effectively, including carrying out the Social Skills Curriculum. Two years later, about twelve years after our initial work, the two schools had the third and fourth highest levels of achievement in the city on standardized tests in mathematics and language arts. They had the best attendance and no serious behavior problems. King School maintained high achievement levels for many years. Changes in leadership, teaching staff, and the housing project near the Brennan School, without staff development, eventually led to reduced performance there. Similar events led to a decline at King about seven or eight years after the 1983 high point.

After the SSCICC project support ended, we began to work with other inner-city New Haven schools without grant support. The Jackie Robinson Middle School, mentioned in chapter 7, was one of them. This made a natural experiment possible. A study by Ana Cauce found that students in this middle school drawn from one of our pilot schools performed at a statistically significant higher academic level than similar children who came from another school in the same neighborhood during the same years.[1] Several Jackie Robinson staff members noted that students from our pilot schools were more often student leaders.

The superintendent of schools, Gerald Tirrozi, began to explore ways to disseminate the SDP process model throughout the system. But the district as a whole was not prepared to try a new approach. The connection between improved climate and trust and improved social and academic school performance was less apparent twenty-five years ago than it is today. And although today there is growing interest in the possibility that development contributes to academic achievement, it remains a minority opinion. In the minds of most, school improvement can take place only through better instruction. For example, a principal who began using the model in 1979 described the warm feelings in his school on the day the male staff members prepared breakfast for the women teachers. He recalled that there were no fights or conflicts among the students that day, then added, "That's strange." He did not get it—how the climate influences behavior, both social and academic.

There were other issues that blocked local dissemination; some that did not surface. There were many local reasons for the lack of interest in our child development oriented model, but the absence of national pressure to improve outcomes was probably the main one.

Many claimed that our pilot project worked only because of the presence of the Yale Child Study Center team, and that it would not be possible to disseminate such a program outside a reasonable daily traveling distance for our team. Against our advice, another district in the state asked us to direct the program ourselves, rather than train their key staff to do so. To examine our assumption, we tried. It did not work, supporting my second-year observation that change had to come from within. With no financial support and no strong interest in our model, we faced the possibility of discontinuation of our work. And then opportunity struck—in a most unpredictable way.

A law clerk working for District Court Judge Douglas W. Hillman of Benton Harbor, Michigan, read about our work and called it to the judge's attention. Judge Hillman had been assigned to find a remedy for a school segregation case he had decided in the plaintiffs' favor ten years earlier. There had been fourteen years of litigation. Because school integration was not possible by then in this setting, he ordered the Benton Harbor, Michigan, school district to use our SDP model to try to compensate for the negative effects of deliberate race-based residential steering and the resultant school segregation.

This gave us an opportunity to field-test our model at a distant site without our day-to-day involvement. We were being asked to work at a significant distance from our home base when we had not had much success moving our project to other schools either in New Haven or within a reasonable traveling distance outside the city. The question we had to face: "But can it fly?"

Training the Benton Harbor school system staff to implement the model was a significant challenge. The situation was much like that of a person who did not want to do so being ordered to see a psychiatrist. There is often much resistance, and there was much resistance in that district. But James Hawkins, the superintendent at the time, was supportive. Despite his interest, the community was rife with strife that would eventually take its toll. But I was raised on "Nothing beats a failure but a try."

It was 1984, and just as there was no literature about intervention in 1968, there was none about dissemination of school reform models at this point; indeed, there may not have been another major school reform effort at the time. After visits and discussions in Benton Harbor, we agreed to train a change agent selected by the district. She was to work and study with us for a year, then return to her home district and facilitate change. Irma Mitchell, a special education specialist, was selected. This was a trainer-of-trainer model, but it soon had to be modified. We had forgotten one of the lessons learned from our previous work—the critical importance of relationships and trust that grow out of learning together and helps to make future collaboration possible.

When Ms. Mitchell returned to Benton Harbor the attitude of the people she attempted to work with was roughly, "You had that wonderful sabbatical year at Yale, now you do it." In short, "We dare you to try to change us!" The superintendent wanted the project to work. He came to New Haven and observed our two pilot schools that were continuing to function successfully even though we were no longer directly involved. He listened to our conceptual framework again. He and Ms. Mitchell suggested that we bring several teams to New

Haven for a three-day orientation experience—each team made up of parents, teachers, and administrators at building and district levels. So we did. The team members bonded and went back and worked together. The facilitator, with the sanction and support of those who received the orientation with her, trained others at home and brought about significant academic improvement in their project schools.

But the district had four superintendents in five years. The project schools continued to improve in spite of the community turmoil. Eventually however, local political and personal conflicts divided the system, and we were being drawn into the conflicts. Staff members trained and experienced in implementing the model were moved. A new school board terminated our project although it did not have the authority to do so. Many wanted us to fight to continue. Determined to stay out of conflict, we remained available if there was interest but essentially withdrew.

This experience made us fully aware of how policies and practices beyond the classroom and school have as much, or more, to do with the quality of education children receive as do the curriculum and instruction. The meaning of a test score in a chaotic community and school district tells you more about the context than the ability of the students, even the ability of the staff. Judging and punishing either group while ignoring the social context in which they work is unfair and not very helpful.

We learned much during our time in Benton Harbor. One experience in particular, though troublesome, provided an important insight. James Rutter, one of the superintendents with whom we worked, had been repeatedly told by staff that if he would just take that small group of children who are "impossible" out of the schools, they would be able to educate the others. He decided to create an academy for the "impossible" children. I did not like the idea, but we thought through the benefits and downsides. We discussed ways of carrying out the project that would avoid stigmatizing the young people selected. He handpicked a group of teachers who had been successful previously with similar children.

He called me back the next year to say that he had good news and bad news. The good news was that the "impossible" kids then in the academy had had an outstanding academic year with very few behavior problems. But back in their previous schools, they had been replaced by another group of "impossible" kids. It demonstrated what we believed in the first place. Conditions in many schools create a sense of inclusion and exclusion for various students. The most vulnerable kids experience a sense of exclusion that makes them "losers." The "losers" act up and act out in ways that interfere with their own education and the education of the other students. Our School Development Program works toward creating an environment in which all children feel a sense of belonging and are motivated to behave well and to learn. The intent is to create a win-win environment in which all participants are motivated to do their best.

I had forgotten just how much progress the students in Benton Harbor had made in three years of effective programming until I was drawn back into the case as a witness twenty years later. The case is still in litigation. I do not want to know how much money has been spent on lawyers and how much energy and emotion have gone into community struggles and legal wrangling rather than into educating the children. Again, there is nothing wrong with the children.

Our work in Benton Harbor suggested that even with discontinuity in the district office, and much community conflict, it was possible to train school people from distant sites and to achieve successful replication. But it was not possible to continue the Social Skills Curriculum. Schools must create and sustain a culture of collaboration, problem solving, and opportunity taking, and the associated skills and confidence, before they can carry out complex programs. In most cases, this requires good district-level support.

What we learned about the benefits of training together teams representative of all the adults was soon put to the test. In 1985 John Murphy, the new superintendent in Prince George's County, Maryland, invited us to work with his district. The district did not have the money to pay for a long training period or the time to do so. John was one of the first superintendents in the nation to disaggregate the achievement data of black and white students. He promised to close the gap. The community wanted immediate closure.

The facilitator selected by the district, Jan Stocklinski, came to New Haven for a month. She participated in all our regular program activities, and our SDP staff members worked with her individually. During her last week she was joined by a district team made up of parents, teachers, and administrators from the building and district levels. Together, they received an overview of how the process works and why it is needed, and a discussion of the skills and disposition needed to make it work. Back home they worked together to put the model in place.

During this same period we were able to field-test the model in about twelve school districts largely in the Southeast and Midwest—Lee County, Arkansas; Norfolk, Virginia; Topeka and Leavenworth, Kansas; and several other places. The outcomes were promising at all sites, but local funding problems and leadership changes led to the discontinuation of the project after several years in all but Topeka.

Most of the facilitators had only three weeks more training than their district teams. But they had been selected because of demonstrated skills that were likely to lead to success in this role—their facilitative leadership styles; their ability to relate well to parents, staff, and students; and particularly because of their interest in child development. The facilitators deepened their own understanding and increased "buy-in" in the district by periodically bringing new teams to New Haven for training. A few came for refresher sessions or new training modules. Some of the most successful new trainees were selected to become a part of a local facilitating team. In this way they were able to serve additional schools in their district.

We were successfully moving the SDP model during these field trials with orientations provided by me and only one or two others. Each school district facilitator and a group representative of the district stakeholders were trained through "chalk talk" discussions of child development and on how to create and use the model to meet student developmental needs. They also visited and observed our two initial pilot schools. The facilitator shadowed Yale staff who were trying to implement the model in several additional schools in New Haven. They were then expected to put the nine-element framework in place in their home districts. In all of the field-test districts we worked with a subset of schools, usually no fewer than four, but sometimes we worked with a single school. Even with this minimal preparation, we found that the principles of the model could be implemented at distant sites, but it required a greater presence of our Yale team than was possible or desired. Although the field-test schools made academic gains, our staff did not have the capacity to help them integrate pedagogy and developmental principles.

Our experience in Prince George's County deepened our understanding of the difficulties involved in real-world intervention and research. Social and behavioral science research very often glosses over or ignores the effects of unpredictable—

sometimes tragic, sometimes political, sometimes economic, and sometimes inexplicable—events at any given site. In Benton Harbor, political events dominated. In Prince George's County, if we did not see everything that could go wrong, we saw a lot of individual examples.

After outstanding improvement in eight, and reasonable improvement in four, of the fourteen Prince George's County pilot schools over a three-year period, the superintendent left the district. During that period, two very large budget cuts demoralized the entire school district staff. A very effective and much-loved facilitator died just after a random assignment research study was put in place. By chance, most of the schools that wanted to use the model were assigned to the comparison group, and those lukewarm or opposed were assigned to the experimental group. Some in the comparison group who were not supposed to receive training asked for, and got, it. A husband and wife, both principals, presented a leakage problem. He was in the treatment group and she was in the comparison group; unlike some married couples, they talked to each other. Researchers call it contamination.

For these and other reasons, the study showed no difference between the groups. Despite massive contamination, such a finding casts doubt. Fortunately, a later study of ten SDP schools in Chicago showed statistically significant academic, climate, and behavioral gains over randomly assigned comparison schools.[2] A report of the two studies was published at the same time, along with our challenge to the validity of the Maryland study findings.[3] As would be expected, those who do not want to believe that public schools can work point to the Maryland study; others who agree with our beliefs point to the outcomes in Chicago. A five-year follow-up study of the Chicago students showed that the academic lead has been sustained.

We were very fortunate that extraordinarily gifted and committed people were selected as facilitators in these first several districts. This still tends to be the case. When district leadership truly wants to address student development and academic needs, it finds people similarly inclined and able. Even now, but particularly in the early years, we do not have enough staff to support these districts adequately. Thus, good local facilitation is crucial. Despite our vulnerability, the subset of schools we worked with for more than a year in five districts during the field-test phase made statistically significant achievement gains over their districts as a whole. They also reported improved school climate and student behavior.

The description of me as training director, with my notes on a yellow legal pad, sketching explanatory diagrams on a chalk board is still a source of humor to SDP old-timers, myself included. I was beginning to feel that Mrs. Johnson's vision of me going all over the country to spread the gospel was indeed coming true. But that was not my job, nor was it a clear answer to the question "Can it fly?" I was still directly involved. We would not know whether we had a workable model until our staff, without my presence, could help local facilitators successfully use the approach.

In 1986 we received a research grant from the Carnegie Corporation of New York for a middle school project. At the time Ed Joyner, who has been the executive director of our SDP since 1994, was about to take a sabbatical year from the New Haven school system. John Dow, then the superintendent, knew that I was looking for someone to help with the Carnegie grant and referred him to me.

John Dow spent his adolescent years in East Chicago, Indiana, my hometown. Indeed, we lived a half block from each other. He often playfully mentioned that he grew up "hating" the Comer brothers, several years older than himself, because whenever his mother was displeased with his performance she would say, "Why can't you be like the Comer brothers?" His mother and my mother were mutual admirers. I digress to tell this story in order to again make the point that community relationships and modeling matter. John's interest in being helpful was not casual. Such networking is the norm in communities with well-functioning social networks yet almost impossible in communities with many fewer such networks.

Joyner joined our SDP team in 1986. He had been a vice principal at a high school in the city and a very successful principal at the Jackie Robinson Middle School. Without training and on his own, he had created components of the model—the School Planning and Management and the Mental Health teams—at Jackie Robinson. His interest in school change stemmed from his concern about racial problems and the dynamics of change. He had read my first book, *Beyond Black and White*, and appreciated the fact that it explored the roots of the problem rather than simply described it. His presence on our team gave us a chance to begin to create a training and implementation program that would minimize my direct involvement, making the model portable on a large scale.

The School Development Program, in education service delivery settings, was and is my action research laboratory. I was able to reflect on and write about my child psychiatry and public health practice in education based on activities in the laboratory, but I was not able to build robust clinical or basic science research programs. The magnitude of the service delivery challenge was just too great. And yet, clinical and basic science research is very important at a research university.

I was interested in finding someone to eventually lead the

clinical service, or SDP aspect, of my overall work. I had hoped to devote more time to clinical science research. Although the clinical service activity has intensified rather than let up, our goal is still to serve schools and students from what we can learn from basic and clinical science, particularly brain and neuroscience research. Also, I do not have formal training in education. I needed an education complement to my child and behavioral science knowledge base, a colleague with a background in education and an appreciation of the role of child and youth development and with particular knowledge and sensitivity to the learning challenges of poor and minority students.

In retrospect, because I did not have an education background, I had made a wrong assumption about the nature of the training that educators receive. It was reflected in the "teacher autonomy" approach to instruction that I supported in our early project years. I had assumed that school people knew that development and learning were inextricably linked, and that curriculum and instruction was based on this knowledge. Much of the public still believes that school people understand this link, or do not know that they should.

Joyner quickly took an interest in the need to marry child development and pedagogy. He also had an interest in organization theory and andragogy, or adult learning.[4] Equally important, he had a deep concern about the able students that were being left behind. His desire was to find a way to improve their chances. Also, like my own, many of his insights and understanding stemmed from his own background, which was both similar to and different from my own. Our mothers had been domestic workers. Our fathers had been laborers, mine in a northern steel mill, his mainly in southern agriculture. I have described my family as loving and functional; he describes his as loving but challenged.

His family's effort to provide him with a better education "up North" led him into brief gang activity in Boston and a lasting memory of the social and physical loss of talent of too many able young African-American males. He went into education with the hope of providing greater opportunity to such young people, but his experiences as a classroom teacher and school administrator led him to the opinion that the school, as it currently operates, cannot meet the needs of such students.

His concern was that the school treats students like thinking machines. Our colleague Jack Gillette calls it "brains on a stick." It ignores their feelings, relationship needs and capacities, dreams, and aspirations. His desire as a classroom teacher was to recognize and address these needs in a way that would "help turn stumbling blocks into stepping stones." He wanted to help the students see the beauty inside, even when it was camouflaged by the effects of poverty or marginalization, to nourish their potential.

He had hoped that as an administrator he could have a positive impact on a greater number of students. But he felt that as a classroom teacher and administrator he could not get emotionally close to enough students to have the sought-for effect. He was groping for a way that schools might work to address the full range of student developmental and learning needs. His use of the SDP components while he was the principal of Jackie Robinson, and before we ever met, was an effort to do so.

As a result of his background, perspectives, and experience, he hit the ground running during his sabbatical year. His interest and effectiveness led to a second sabbatical year and a service reimbursement arrangement through which he remained with the New Haven public school system, on assignment to the Yale Child Study Center. This arrangement eventually helped us work more closely with New Haven, while bringing his education and implementation skills and commitment to our growing SDP network of schools and other education activities.

University–public school projects often break down around "town-gown" or status, mission, and personality concerns and differences between the principle participants. These potential problems are not considered during planning, hiring, or reporting, but they often prevent success. Also, the magnitude of the task we set for ourselves—to find the spectrum of factors interfering with development and learning and to create action programs that point toward corrective measures—was great. The obstacles, as well as the solutions, are in family and community life, schools, districts, educator preparation programs, and policies; indeed, in all aspects of the education enterprise. Since going beyond our pilot schools in 1984, we have worked with more than one thousand schools in more than eighty school districts in twenty-six states.

At no time have we ever had more than eight professional people on our central staff. An outside evaluator commented that our SDP has given new meaning to the word "understaffed." And aside from the ten years of generous support from the Rockefeller Foundation, we have never had financial support that we could count on, nor support at the level needed. As a result our staff is stretched so thin that we are not able to reflect, plan, share, and map strategies as we should. This creates tension. But there is a powerful incentive that has enabled us to hold together.

Earlier I mentioned that my career direction change was prompted by the realization that the changed economy and the unchanged education system was going to leave too many students behind, and that this situation represented a threat to democracy. Joyner noted that the civil rights movement changed laws and opened doors, but it did not provide the preparation for education and citizenship that many needed to walk through the open doors or to widen and keep them open. Our work seeks to make the latter possible; it is a mission that bonds us.

And yet, human beings often think, feel, and behave like human beings. We have doubts, fears, jealousies, and frustrations that can interfere with relationships and productivity. Every now and then Joyner and I feel a need for what we call "leveling sessions," where we discuss what is "bugging" us, and we then go back to work. It is possible because we love and respect each other as people and because of our mutual interests. It is a spirit that permeates our entire SDP organization and eventually the leadership groups in the districts we work with. This enables a small number of people to gradually reduce the inertia inherent in all entrenched systems.

I have taken considerable time here to discuss our relationship, and the web of relationships involved, because trust and respect are critical issues in such human service activities as education, health care, police work, public welfare, and in social and behavioral science research. Indeed, the problems in police work and public welfare are more challenging because the motivation to achieve trust between the service providers and the consumers is not as great as in education and health care. The importance of relationships is often not discussed, and that is a major reason for the failure or modest outcomes in many programs, even with good intentions and high costs. It is the power and importance of these relationship issues, intangible and nonquantifiable, that troubles me about our society's over-reliance on numbers—quantitative research, survey data, test scores—to make important, life-affecting program, policy, and practice decisions in education and other human service areas.

Our SDP staff—I and one or two others—had been able to fuse governance and management with child development and relationship and behavioral science knowledge and skills in a way that brought about significant school improvement. We probably benefited from the selection of excellent district-level facilitators. But I knew that this would not be enough to make large-scale, facilitator-managed dissemination of the model possible. Our selection luck could not hold out. Large-scale dissemination—or flight—would require a sophisticated training program that integrated educational pedagogy and child development in the behavioral sciences.

By this time we were well aware that the classroom challenges of teachers and students came from all corners of the education enterprise. We suspected that it was not going to be possible to greatly impact the quality of education through school-by-school improvement. Thus, we needed an action research training and dissemination strategy that would enable us to use our nine-component basic program in schools and districts. It also had to empower local staff to operate with minimal presence of our Yale team. It had to use the principles of child and adolescent development, public health, and ecology to explore and address challenges beyond schools and districts.

Our dissemination opportunity was made possible by grants from the Rockefeller Foundation that began in 1990. They eventually equaled twenty million dollars over ten years. (That is generous in the context of traditional spending on education, but it is about the cost of three smart bombs.) The foundation noted that a huge amount of research money was being spent in education across the nation, and while generous, their funds would be a drop in the research-fund ocean, maybe two buckets. They were seeking a niche; to support an approach that might be critically important but that was not yet being addressed adequately.

After an extensive review of national programs led by Hugh Price, a vice president at the foundation, and numerous discussions with others and with us about our ideas and outcomes, they decided that our child- and adolescent-focused approach was the kind of program that met their criteria. Allow me one more word about networks and relationships. Hugh's father and his wife's mother were my teachers in medical school. One of his daughters was one of the few middle-income students to attend our project school, and she did so during the first, most difficult, and second, turn-around, years. It was one of the reasons he knew about the work. It was also the reason he sought so many opinions nationwide before he recommended our support. In fact, he assembled a national committee of experts before the foundation made the decision to grant us financial support.

In 1990 I asked Ed Joyner to develop a training program that would make it possible for our SDP model to fly—to be disseminated widely—without the regular presence of our Yale-based staff. The training program was expected to fully integrate organization and management, adult and child development, curriculum and instruction, and teaching and learning. Through a strong training program, SDP hoped to impact other parts of the education enterprise—schools of education, state departments of education, and local and national decision makers involved in education.

IX
Flight School

Throughout the first twenty-two years of our work we helped people think about how to support growth along the critical developmental pathways through the use of our nine-element framework. This approach remained at the core of our work as we moved forward. The training program we were developing was to bring about a better integration of educational pedagogy and developmental knowledge as we considered pathway growth. Edward Joyner, working with Norris Haynes, our director of research, began to bring greater specificity to our thinking and to better categorize and formalize our knowledge about development so that it could be taught in a more effective manner.

Joyner and Haynes reviewed the research on training and began to draw up plans for a training program. Joyner brought together a panel of experts to review and comment on this work. Two of the experts, Jack Gillette and Patrick Howley, eventually joined our staff.[1]

The training program would prepare trainees to use the SDP model or framework to turn sometimes poorly functioning schools into well-functioning social organizations through action research. Specifically, they would work with what we had learned about how to support growth along the six developmental pathways. They would be able to make modifications and create activities best suited for local situations. But to faithfully replicate the model, they would always use the basic nine elements or components. Finally, the trainees had to be able to promote trust and to engender fervor—perhaps energy and commitment—in their colleagues to enable them to move toward change.

The panel listed all the competencies needed to implement the program based on these criteria. Their discussions about what was needed and how to provide it shaped the content of the training sessions. We trained facilitators from participating schools and districts to carry out the SDP process in their home districts. The people who became facilitators included special education teachers, regular classroom teachers, social workers, and administrators. Eventually, university teaching faculties working with school districts in their geographic areas were trained as facilitators and coordinators. Representatives of all school participant groups have also been among the trainees. We worked with school districts alone, schools of education in collaboration with school districts, a youth service agency in collaboration with a school district, and some schools without much support from their districts. In a couple of instances, local foundations supported the schools and districts and maintained an interest in the implementation process and outcomes.

The trainee selected from a district to be primarily responsible for implementing the SDP at the local level is called a "facilitator." The person from our School Development Program responsible for a particular district is called the "district coordinator." The district coordinators provide the training at the Yale Child Study Center, and eventually through three regional centers as well. They teach the theories that undergird the model, the model itself, and empirical knowledge gained as they supervise and support implementation in the districts. Our colleagues from the partner institutions, such as the universities and child guidance groups that support the implementation at the district and school level, are also called "coordinators."

We have done orientation work with education policymakers in business and government at all levels. Our work with schools of education has been helpful to our SDP team and has enabled several of these schools to improve their child- and adolescent-rearing and development focus in the program they offer future teachers and administrators. We believe that university–school district–school of education collaborations hold promise as a way of bringing about school change and improvement on a large scale.

The training program is carried out largely through five Yale-based National Leadership Academies and, to a lesser extent, in the field. Remember that as this program has evolved, we have constantly been learning from our work in the field, and we have incorporated this new knowledge into our training in the academies and in the field. In this way our trainers and trainees are involved in teaching and learning. The facilitator trainees from a district are asked to work in this action research way and to train others to do so back in their districts. As a result, the building-level management teams, SPMTs, and the classroom teachers all begin to think in an action research way. This leads to a constant search for what will work in any given situation, as opposed to blaming the children for not being able to learn. When working in this way, the curriculum becomes an instructional guide rather than a prescription. Teachers and administrators become active in identifying obstacles to teaching and learning and in finding ways to remove them.

The *101 Academy* began as a two-week program. It was our first training academy and was designed to give participants a working knowledge of the nine components of the SDP, now commonly known as the Comer Process, so they could introduce the program in their district. Participants in this program learn about the six developmental pathways and consider strategies for promoting SDP and pathway growth in their own schools or districts. Also, they are taught how the SDP fits in with other initiatives in their schools and districts.

We quickly learned that two weeks was too long for school staffs to be away. It was disruptive to their schools and their personal lives. There was too much new information, more than they could digest, and it could not be immediately tested, modified, or otherwise managed based on real workplace experience. We changed the format to a one-week program followed by a year of practice with support from the district facilitator. (In some districts there are a group of facilitators.) Participants return the next year for a week in the *102 Academy*. When possible the same group that attended 101 returns for 102. In subsequent years, different staff teams attend, including some people who had not been trained previously, some new staff members, and some repeats.

In 102 they examine their implementation efforts—what went well, what did not—and then explore what is next. They think more about how they can apply child development knowledge in real-world situations. For example, how to understand and respond to the eight-year-old, unprepared to handle his school transfer, who kicked the teacher in the leg and ran out of the room, or the incidents of kicking and head butting mentioned by a principal in chapter 2. They think about how to apply their own ideas while using the nine basic components to faithfully replicate the model.

During 102 significant attention is given to child-centered planning in order to deepen knowledge of child development as a basis for teaching and learning. Participants work to strengthen their understanding of how the child-centered planning process integrates child development theory, assessment and modification, comprehensive school planning, staff development, and change theory. Participants consider group dynamics and work to improve their abilities to listen. Simultaneously, there is an emphasis on developing the interpersonal skill of giving and receiving feedback. All of this increases their skills in facilitating work among mixed teams of stakeholders.

The *Principals' Academy*—like Mary's little lamb—was sure to follow. The academies for staff introduced ideas that altered the way principals had to think and work. Several of them requested help in understanding the SDP and how they might work differently. The training in this academy focuses on the unique position of principals and the need and process of working collaboratively with staff and parents. We demonstrate how SDP governance components connect deeply with instructional issues. Principals work on providing clinical supervision to teachers and on understanding the impact of their leadership style on school improvement efforts. Often the challenge is to change a command mentality to a facilitative and collaborative mentality. The trade-off is that all of the stakeholders and the students become responsible for outcomes and not just the principal. The benefits are great and sometimes very interesting.

Once when I was at a national meeting, a stranger talking to a small group in the hall recognized me, stopped his conversation, and told me that I had saved his life. Always wary of hyperbole, I gave a wan smile, but he assured me that it was true. He told me that he had had a heart attack that was attributed to the stress of his job and his tendency to try to control everything. Once his school began to use the SDP and he began to work collaboratively, the stress was greatly reduced. It is unfortunate he could not advise a principal who recently attended a 101 meeting. This was his first time at one of our academies, and when I saw him he had stepped out of his session and was using his cell phone in the hallway, barking instructions to his staff, calling a student troublemaker to the phone to warn him to behave in advance of any misbehavior—the whole anxious, uptight, command approach and outcome.

The Principals' Academy helps administrators think about how to lead and to achieve goals with the input of all the participants, how to gain rather than lose their power and respect. This style greatly reduces administrator-staff conflict and does not tie the hands of the principal when administrative action needs to be taken. Principals who were once afraid to leave their buildings for fear that things would get out of control can now do so because should problems arise, their staff will be able and willing to manage. Some principals and superintendents cannot or will not work in a collaborative way, but most can.

Barbara Neufield, our first external program evaluator, noted that there was not enough child rearing and development content in our academies. Of the ten or twelve external evaluations done over the years, this is the only one that contained major negative comments. Once we stopped being defensive about the report, it helped us make significant improvement in our training. We had been making the point that schools of education were not paying adequate attention to child rearing and development, and we were doing the same thing. I have often told of asking my sibs and in-laws who were in education whether they had ever taken a child development course that helped them think about what developmental issues might be involved in a real-world problem, such as a playground fight. They had not, and they attended good schools of education. We were not doing any better in our training. Our reflections on this matter contributed to the creation of the Developmental Academy.

The *Developmental Academy* is designed primarily for teachers. It provides child development-based strategies for improving literacy and math skills, highlighting SDP's Essentials of Literacy and Balanced Curriculum processes described below. But it is open to all school staff and parents. All participants work together, focusing on development and learning. Again, children come into the world seeking and learning in an effort to meet their needs and in search of the skills needed to do so. The way much child rearing and schooling is carried out—pouring, even forcing, information into students' heads—creates a reaction to authority, to the point that too many students take the position, "I dare you to teach me," or, "You don't like me, I'm not going to learn your old work!"

Schooling that taps into where a child is developmentally—imitation, work or task completion, identity issues, and so on—can stimulate and facilitate self-interest learning. As students learn about themselves and opportunities in the environments around them, they will develop aspirations—developmental, academic, and social. These can be small and big, from the desire to please the teacher and get along with classmates to the little boy who said, "I want to be a doctor when I get to be a big man!" Parents and teachers can then structure the home and school environments to facilitate development and learning needed to meet student aspirations, general and specific. The academic requirements can be embedded in the student's personal thrust for desirable development. The motivation to learn will be greater.

The academy participants engage in systematic thinking and planning about what they can and need to do to help students promote their own growth along the six developmental pathways. They offer and blend their different perspectives in a way that enriches discussions and deepens understanding. Our *Kids' Academy,* founded in 1998 and headed by Valerie Maholmes, grew out of this thinking.[2] In addition to this three-and-a-half-day summer experience, held at the same time as the Principals' Academy, the students continue as school leaders throughout the year. Their leadership attitudes and behaviors positively impact their classmates and promote their own interests and development.

Fear of flying and large budget cuts in school districts led us to cancel the 2003 Principals' Academy. One district dropped its support of the Kids' Academy trip as well. The parents were as disappointed as their children, so they raised funds to send their children to the Kids' Academy without district support. Some contributed their own money, a significant sacrifice for low-income parents. This challenges the myth that low-income people do not care about their children or their education.

I wanted to understand why the parents highly valued the experience, so I paid particular attention to the 2003 Kids' Academy. There were ninety kids and forty-five attending adults. I spoke to a sea of orange T-shirts and enthusiastic, bright kids between the ages of eight and thirteen from five

school districts in the South, Midwest, and East. They studied
the brain, engaged in exciting learning games, and visited the
Peabody Museum of Natural History. They studied the principles of the SDP and the pathways and discussed how they
might use the knowledge to grow and to improve their schools.

They worked in groups of ten. The students, and the
adults independently, picked a person in each group that best
exemplified the principles of SDP, and these people were recognized at the first-ever dinner held in their honor. The excitement was electric, and yet the staff could still achieve order
in a short period of time by simply raising their right hands.
The fairness of the selection process appeared to limit bad feelings, and it emphasized the importance of performing in a way
that serves the self and the group well. The joy expressed by the
students and the adults was remarkable. I now know why the
parents wanted their children to have the experience.

Jan Stocklinski, now a member of our national faculty,
received a letter that gives some insight into the impact of the
academy.

> Dear Jan:
>
> I have a wonderful story to tell you about the
> effect the Comer Kids' Academy has had on one of
> the students . . . a ten-year-old boy.
>
> Many staff felt that his grades in social skills
> should prevent him from being selected. This stu-
> dent has been a straight A student in his academic
> subjects; however, he never received higher than a C
> in social skills, which has always kept him off of the
> Honor Roll. His behavior was often extreme, losing
> his temper with his classmates and his teachers. His
> interaction with adults could be very disrespectful.

At times he was unable to calm his emotions and he spent more than a few days in the office.

He showed many signs of brilliance. His ability to converse with adults and to think far ahead of his peers delighted many who knew him well. At times he simply seemed far brighter than those of us working with him. It was merely tact and humbleness that he lacked which got him into so much trouble.

At Yale, the student was awesome. He participated fully and his behavior was outstanding. One incident occurred when a girl from another district kept splashing him in the pool. He took it for a while and when it got too much for him he came and told me. I told him that some students might not know positive ways to make friends like he did and that I was sure this was a situation that he could handle appropriately. He returned to the pool and the incident caused him no more distress. Prior to this trip he would have retaliated and gotten into trouble.

The Kids' Academy seemed to be a turning point in the student's life. When he came back to school in August, he seemed like a new student. One incident occurred in September when someone called an Asian student a racial name. The student was a suspect because he sat near the Asian student. When accused by another student, he stood up and announced to the entire class, "I would never do something like that. I went to Yale this summer and I'm a role model now." In fact, he was the first to comfort the student.

November 26, students received their first
quarter report cards and he is now on the Honor
Roll for the first time. He received a B in social skills.
His goal is to make an A. [This is the kind of self-
motivation that grows out of experiences in the environment that schools can promote.]

The student says that being a Comer Kid Del-
egate taught him how to express himself in a positive way. I am sure of two things, the student is
going to do great things in this world, and he will
always see the Comer Kids' Leadership Academy as
an experience that helped him to greatness.

All the academies are designed to begin with ice-break-
ing, team-building exercises in the morning and an assessment
of the group's experience at the end of the day. Modules addressing the tasks listed above are presented by our staff, with
as much group participation as possible. Participants work in
small groups with people from other districts, and there is
time for the people from each district to plan together.

Because the benefits of our way of working are not immediately apparent to all, much attention is given to participant concerns. A superintendent was not happy with her workshop experiences. Two staff members took her to lunch and
clarified our methods and goals. She became a supporter. Her
district has been among the best in implementing SDP and has
had some of the greatest test score gains. A principal was still
doubtful on the last day. The elevator he was riding in stopped
at one floor, a student got on, shook his hand, and proudly
said, "I am a Comer Kid!" The principal concluded that if three
days could generate that much good feeling for the student, a
school designed to promote good feeling on an ongoing basis

had to be a good thing. Indeed, what has happened to the kids has been the selling point and the saving grace on a number of recent occasions as districts begin to examine the value of school reform approaches.

Implementation of the SDP, supported by the academies, co-ordinators, and facilitators, is expected to move through five stages over a five-years life cycle roll out, more or less sequentially and with some phase overlaps. The phases are: (1) planning and preparation; (2) foundation building; (3) transformation; (4) institutionalization; and (5) renewal. The coordinators, evaluators, and facilitators assess movement and adjust the implementation effort as indicated.

We implemented the SDP in many different places, with different kinds of arrangements, but we always encountered three major obstacles to teaching and learning. First, repeatedly we observed schools struggle with students who did not learn to read in spite of the school's best effort—to the detriment of the student's development and the school. Second, as the pressure to improve schools mounted, and high-stakes accountability became a reality, school staffs were overwhelmed by new standards, mandates, and tests—with no help in working differently. Indeed, the implication was that they were not working hard enough or, worse, were not smart enough. And third, even with help, often a community of self-help and continuous professional growth did not emerge.

Ed Joyner and our staff initiated three instructional programs to address these challenges. The three programs are not used uniformly throughout the SDP network, but aspects of all are a part of our training and implementation efforts. In districts able to carry them out, the fully elaborated programs have helped us better understand these challenges. They also point to the need for future research and work. With sufficient investment, we believe that all could be highly beneficial and should be widely used.

The three programs are: *Essentials of Literacy, Teachers Helping Teachers,* and *Balanced Curriculum.* The Learning, Teaching, and Development Unit (LT and D) of SDP helps districts carry out this work in the field and provides orientations in several of the academies. Intensive training in these programs occurs among several kinds of stakeholders in the school system: parents, teachers, and support staff; district and school administrators; community builders and volunteers; academics and student teachers; and policy makers.

Essentials of Literacy (EOL) is an intervention process that uses research-based components to improve the literacy skills of those students who have been identified by their teachers as "problem readers." There are six major essential elements— phonics, story sense, listening, guided reading, vocabulary, and writing. Trained adults, volunteers, and professionals help students achieve mastery in each area as they move through the six stations in Reading Rooms. The program was designed to be integrated into the school's language arts program, and it provides students with a safe, nurturing, highly stimulating, and rewarding environment in which to develop their literacy skills.

The EOL program relies on the daily practice of the three guiding principles of collaboration, consensus, and no-fault for effective implementation. It is undergirded by the adults' understanding of children's needs and their development along the six critical pathways. The program was introduced in 1991 at the Lincoln Bassett Elementary School in New Haven, Connecticut, with parents serving as aides under the leadership of its developer, Dr. Edward T. Murray.[3] Over the years, it was further developed by both Dr. Murray and Dr. Fay E.

Brown.[4] Dr. Brown now directs the program, and it is currently being implemented in twenty elementary schools in New Haven, twelve schools in New Jersey, and one school in Westbury, New York.

When it is implemented properly, students flourish. Some students achieve two grade levels in an academic year, and there is also growth and development along the language, social, ethical, and psychological pathways. Many nonreaders become serious behavior problems. Once they learn to read, the behavior problems, for the most part, go away. There have been many such stories. One of the most dramatic is Mauvin's story, told here by his Reading Room teacher, Mrs. Brantley.

> Mauvin was presented as difficult, stubborn, and disruptive. Children in his class did not like him. The enigma was even more apparent when one saw the handsome, articulate nine-year-old with the occasionally flashed smile. His defenses in quest for survival in the classroom masked his poor self-esteem.
>
> Because our school was already a "Comer School" and a large number of our staff had been trained in the School Development Program, it was easier to explain to the class that the three guiding principles of collaboration, consensus, and no-fault would also determine how our classroom operated. It was not long before Mauvin felt the challenge of the no-fault principle since his former way of handling conflict was to blame someone for his problem or get back at the person who had hurt him. We knew that we had to help several students, particularly Mauvin, in developing along the psy-

chological and social pathways before we could make progress with the cognitive pathway.

In one situation in which he was in conflict with a couple other students, we stopped the group and discussed how he and the other group members could better handle the situation. Mauvin did not feel isolated, but rather supported by his peers who helped him understand that his aggressive behavior was not acceptable and that they knew he could do better. Most important, Mauvin felt liked because everyone showed him respect.

In the Reading Room, his problems were never dismissed, his desire for attention was channeled into positive activities, and he was given an opportunity for his leadership skills to blossom. As the year progressed, I saw not only Mauvin's reading and comprehension improving, but also his ability to function appropriately in a group. The students had to collaborate on what action to demonstrate, come to consensus with the team, choose one action, and dramatically act out the word, guided by the no-fault principle. Mauvin was a star and a leader in this activity.

In June, the students were given a post-test on the KTEA [Kaufman Test of Educational Achievement] and an authors' tea was planned for students, parents, and other guests. Mauvin's test revealed a grade-level jump in his decoding and comprehension skills. His performance surpassed that of everyone else in the class of twenty students. During the "authors' tea," Mauvin had selected to read his favorite story. He stood tall and confident as he read to his grandmother, guests, and peers.

After hearing Mauvin's story and wiping away a few tears, his grandmother came and gave him a big hug. Mauvin's elusive smile returned. Mauvin came into the program aggressive and reading below grade level, but he exited as an assertive and responsible student and a confident reader.

Teachers Helping Teachers (THT) is designed to help teachers develop and use the best teaching practices to meet the learning needs of students. Using the THT process, teachers meet with a partner frequently throughout the year to help one another strengthen and develop teaching competencies and skills in the delivery of six basic instructional models. The program was first implemented in the Chicago schools during the summer of 1996 by Edward T. Joyner and Patrick Howley. More than forty schools have since initiated THT—in Chicago, Brooklyn, New York, Camden, Paterson, Trenton, Newark, Jersey City, and Westbury, Long Island. Howley provides ongoing leadership for this program. Based on the principles of child and adolescent development, the underlying premise of the program is that teaching will improve and student learning will be enhanced when teachers, in a climate of trust, take time together to reflect in depth on their teaching and on how children learn and develop. By combining the essence of the SDP, Richard Arend's description of six essential models of teaching, peer coaching strategies, and the feedback process outlined in the 102 training, Joyner and Howley developed a process for guiding teachers to do deeper reflection regarding their teaching.

Teachers are encouraged to open six "doorways" of reflection: (1) using the six developmental pathways they explore the developmental learning needs of children; (2) through observing each other, teachers explore classroom teaching; (3) by reading and analyzing models of teaching, teachers inquire into teaching theory; (4) through open dialogue, teachers explore the culture of the school and community; (5) by integrating THT with SDP's Balanced Curriculum process, teachers align and balance their curriculum and then support one another in implementation; and (6) by using the Myers-Briggs Type Indicator and Archetypes, teachers seek to gain an understanding of who they are as persons as well as professional teachers.

In the effort to quickly meet the demands for improving schools, reform efforts have overlooked the human factor—how people react to change. Teachers, for example, are not accustomed to having visitors in their classroom closely observing their teaching. Despite continuous reassurances that THT was not an evaluative process, teachers were fearful of being observed and rated. But as teachers learned that they were being paired with a colleague, that it was a confidential relationship without evaluation, that it was not peer coaching but instead something they were already doing to some degree or wanted to do more, they began to be less fearful and more open to the process. They slowly began to recognize the power of professional discussions with colleagues, especially when they were given helpful frameworks to guide them.

THT tries to honor the existing system, the culture of a school, and the concerns of teachers, yet at the same time it gently helps teachers to change. By creating a safe, supportive culture using consensus, collaboration, and no-fault, teachers are able to do reflective inquiry into what works in teaching and what does not. A transformation begins to take place.

One example of how powerful the need is for teachers to meet and talk comes from a school in Brooklyn that created a program called "Tea at Three." This was a time for teachers to meet and discuss how they felt about their work. "At first," they said, "it was sometimes a gripe session. Then as we met more often, trust developed. We opened up and talked about how we felt about kids, about our teaching, and finally, about ourselves and what we struggle with on a day-to-day basis."

A group of teachers in New Jersey began to call their Saturday morning THT meetings their "therapy group." "Yeah," one teacher said, "this is like teacher therapy because we talk about our work lives in the classroom and we listen to each other. Then we all feel less alone and isolated. And we give and get support from one another."

A principal in Brooklyn commented, "THT was easy to implement because it replicates the SDP process, only the focus is on teaching. We already had the trust in the building so it was a natural evolution for us to pair off and support each other in our teaching. The highlight of the year was when a group of us had dinner together one evening. The superintendent happened to come into the restaurant with some board members. The superintendent came over and asked us why we were meeting and we all shouted, 'THT!'"

The *Balanced Curriculum* process helps teachers and administrators systematically and collaboratively examine national, state, and local mandates, standards, and tests to determine what their students should know and be able to do. They then consider their students' current achievement levels, developmental abilities, and needs. Without teaching to the test, they balance or shape their curriculum and instruction activities so that these knowledge and need areas are adequately addressed.

There are two kinds of training offered: (1) in the districtwide option, SDP works with a district team to set objectives and design a staff development program, and (2) in the school-based option, a team of three to five staff members attends four training sessions during an eighteen-month period. This team plans, schedules, and conducts the Balanced Curriculum process with their colleagues in their school.

David Squires led the development of this process over the past eight years. This work is now led by Camille Cooper. It requires the staff to think, analyze, make good decisions, and use their own creativity. Staff development and consultation is provided to teachers to enable them to move from a "do your own thing" curriculum to this more systematic, analytical approach. Our Balanced Curriculum approach is currently being used in six or more schools in six districts in different parts of the country.

Three components of the curriculum are considered— courses, units, and significant tasks. The significant tasks are aligned with standards, textbooks, and high-stakes tests. Teachers/curriculum authors examine the results of the alignment and determine if the significant tasks are balanced. They ask whether each standard or assessment has appropriate balance within the structure of the significant tasks and then modify the significant tasks accordingly. Each piece of the curriculum must be in appropriate alignment with the other pieces— standards, textbooks, high-stakes assessments, student development and entering competencies—and teacher knowledge must be in balance.

Assessments are then developed. Teachers assess each student on each significant task, generating standards-based data by which all children's success can be judged. For each unit, students receive practice on high-stakes test formats. This allows students to demonstrate their knowledge and needs using the test formats. This also provides districts with data to use for further curricular improvement.

Grade-level or subject area meetings can then be used to support implementation of the significant tasks. Curriculum management, through teacher record keeping on the Web, allows administrators to determine whether teachers and students are making progress in teaching and learning the curriculum. Results of student assessment can also be captured to determine if students are, indeed, performing to high standards. Yearly revision captures teachers' learning in decisions about where tests and other assessments show need for improvement. To keep improving the curriculum, changing 20 percent of the significant tasks is necessary on a yearly basis. Experienced teacher/curriculum writers can revise a K-12 subject area curriculum in a few days of summer work. Student achievement has improved in all schools or districts that both developed and implemented the Balanced Curriculum process.

It is more difficult to prepare people to work in schools today than it was when we started. A facilitator from Chicago told me about a prekindergarten student who called his teacher a "mother-fuckin' bitch." Another SDP staff member told me that today some of the parents are gang members. We try to adjust our training to help address the new conditions.

But as I pointed out to the SDP staff, they are continuing to help school staffs improve academic achievement and behavior in some tough places. I asked them, "What are you doing differently?" The answer was that they are doing the same thing they have always done—creating a school social context that supports the development of students, staff, and parents. It is just much more difficult. The societal breakdown is greater than many will admit, and it can get out of hand.

X
Flight

L et me review our journey toward flight or national dissemination of the SDP model. We began working with two pilot schools in 1968. During the pilot phase we identified student underdevelopment and the lack of staff preparation to help them grow as the critical underlying problems in education. Using widely accepted principles of child and youth development, we created a framework to help the staff gain the capacity to create a social context that would promote student development and learning. The principles were organized through the concept of the developmental pathways, or growth from immaturity to maturity in all the areas needed for adult success.

Next we designed a Social Skills program to expose the students to the adult social environment and the skills they would need to live in such a world. The parents and staff helped students successfully manage these new situations. This program, embedded in the positive climate created by the basic framework, appeared to galvanize the school. This led to improved development and to significant academic and social success.

We field-tested the resultant model or framework in the New Haven area after 1980, and outside the area after 1984. The field-test districts had difficulty managing a complex program like the Social Skills Curriculum for Inner-City Children. After a couple of attempts, we proceeded using only our basic nine-element or component framework. We began a national training program in 1991 that made large-scale dissemination of this framework possible.

When we began national training, all the schools we had worked with previously participated along with new districts. The training program was our tool to marry development and pedagogy and to carry out large-scale dissemination of our model or, in other words, flight.

Through serendipity more than design, three distinctly different dissemination approaches were used. Our School Development Program team worked directly with some schools and districts. In Chicago we worked with a social service agency, Youth Guidance. A third approach grew out of the Rockefeller Foundation grant, which was designed so that we could work with schools of education. This enabled us to observe the relative effectiveness of the various approaches and their potential for promoting large-scale school reform.

Our nine-element framework was the centerpiece of our training program, and the focus on developmental pathways that we began with in our pilot project remained central. Although we had to drop the Social Skills Curriculum program, the idea remained dear. The principles were integrated into our work whenever possible, consciously and unconsciously.

There was a powerful reason the idea remained dear. Those of us in the school reform movement from low-income backgrounds know from experience that improved test scores alone will not be enough to prepare students from marginalized backgrounds to have a chance to be reasonably successful in life. Such young people need a level of development and related life-management skills that are gained through *meaningful interactions* with *meaningful caretakers* from birth through maturity.

For example, I was able to control my feelings and respond effectively when my high school literature teacher gave me a B while she gave two white students As, although our scores were only a point apart and well ahead of the class. This was the case not because I was capable of making an A, but because I had developed the personal controls and problem-solving skills through interactions and training in our family social network or culture. The brother of one of my three best friends, those friends who went on a downhill course, had the highest test scores in his advanced math class during his junior year. But because his family environment did not provide adequate preparation for life management, he had children too soon and eventually drank his way to an early death. He was never able to express his full potential despite his high intelligence and desire for success.

The need for good development is much greater today than it was in the past. Programs that do not help students develop adequately will leave most behind. They will do harm. In medicine it would be considered malpractice. Because we at the CSC have been so concerned about this matter, we have long wanted to return to a Social Skills-like curriculum and activities. Later on in this chapter I will discuss how we addressed these issues in classrooms through intentional teacher efforts.

When we began to field-test our model in 1984, there was little appetite for school reform. We had to be opportunistic. We went where a school staff person or leader had heard about us and expressed an interest in our model. Therefore, we placed few requirements on our hosts. We did not have the money or staff to spend time orienting the district or the community members who could either support or close down the project. Usually our SDP coordinator worked with district facilitator(s) who reported to someone at the district level, sometimes supportive and influential, sometimes not. Thus, we were very vulnerable to real-world conditions—staff turnover, low morale for reasons beyond our project schools, low priority for the program at the time of budget cuts, and more.

Leadership turnover at the top level, and often at the building level, was and is a major problem. On several occasions we worked in districts for five years and helped them achieve significantly improved social and academic outcomes. But a change in superintendent, a principal, or too many teachers at the same time could destroy the culture that made the gains possible in just a few months. Often new principals or superintendents wanted to put their own stamp on a district, even when they claimed a commitment to the program. The problem is exemplified in what I call the "tale of two districts."

A school in the Southeast, after using the model for three years, went from twenty-third to first in achievement in its city. There was a suspicion of cheating, with much attention from the media. The students had to retake the test just before summer vacation, this time with district-level administrators supervising. Several teachers told me they reminded the students that they were able to do well the first time, and so they expected them to do well the second time. I suspect that this admonition from people who cared about them protected them from the psychological effects of being called cheaters. The students did even better the second time they took the test, but media reports about the outcome were much less vigorous than they had been the first time around.

Thus, newspaper and television people stigmatized the parents, teachers, and students. They put them under a cloud of suspicion at a time when they should have been rejoicing in their achievement, adding to their ordinary social and psychological stress. When the accusers were proven wrong, they made no effort to make amends, and they made no effort to inquire about or try to understand how the schools achieved successes when they were not expected to do so. This is the point that the elementary school teacher from Detroit was making in the interview in chapter 2. Her suggestion that the news media are more interested in a story that sells papers than in providing helpful understanding appears valid here.

The superintendent moved the principal to a district-level position, ostensibly "to help other schools achieve in the same way." But no infrastructure work was done to make it possible. Staff turnover took place both for the usual personal reasons and also because the principal was removed. The school quickly returned to mediocre performance. I met a young science teacher from the school in an airport a year later. She was on her way to a job interview with a pharmaceutical company. She had been a strong supporter of our SDP model, and she very much wanted to be a teacher. But she was so disappointed by the recent chain of events that she was leaving the field.

When the superintendent moved the principal, he told a colleague, "We will now see whether it was the man [the principal] or the model." In addition to revealing bad will, the comments reflected flawed thinking. Certainly the skill and hard work of the leader play a big role, but the race is won by the horse and the jockey. The SDP model is not magic. The model without the growth and development of people cannot improve schools. It is a tool that makes teaching and learning more efficient and effective in the same way that a saw beats a hammer in cutting down a tree. And, Mr. Superintendent, what about the children?

In another city, this one on the East Coast, a school that had used the SDP model for several years went from thirty-fourth to first in achievement out of thirty-four schools. The principal was removed, but this time the staff did not sit still. They went to the district and requested a principal who supported the model. Their request was granted, and for the next four years the school remained at the top in achievement, rivaling neighboring suburban schools in mathematics at the eighth grade.

In our field-test work between 1985 and 1990, our primary focus was on building change. Our difficulties suggested a need to get more support for the model at the district level and in the communities around participating schools. There was an urgency about improving schools at that time, but many people still do not appreciate the difficulty and time it takes to do so. Some of the program planners felt we should work in as many schools as possible to create, as quickly as possible, a nucleus of successful schools, thinking this would encourage others to use the same method.

The problem was that there was and still is a lot of resistance to our approach. Change is slow even in the face of successful outcomes. Also, it is almost un-American for Americans to openly learn from others. There is a competition to be the first with the best, and this attitude and approach is rewarded.

Because of the desire for rapid change, we focused on schools, often on a cluster of schools, more than districts for the next five years. But again, because of talented and committed facilitators, with some central office support, we were able to get good outcomes that began to influence the entire system.

In 1992 the Fienberg/Fisher Elementary School principal, Grace Nebb, and her staff almost unanimously selected SDP from a menu of school improvement programs made available by the Miami–Dade County school district. She explained that the organizational framework we provided was what they needed to pull together the many innovations and activities in their school. The school was composed of poor immigrant families from all over the globe, mostly Hispanic but made up of forty-five different nationalities.

The school was in a heavy drug-dealing and other crime area, and it had a 54 percent rate of mobility and high absenteeism. Fifty percent of its students had limited language proficiency. And yet it was an environment where creativity, risk taking, respect, and development of students and adults emerged. The Florida Accountability System awarded the school a grade of A by the 1999–2000 academic year.

Our work with the district was through the director of intervention projects, Geneva Woodard. With her strong support, eleven Dade County elementary schools eventually adopted SDP. District facilitation was supported by our SDP coordinator. The results of a study done in 2000 indicated significant improvement in reading and math on the Florida CAT (Comprehensive Assessment Test). There was a marked decrease in student and staff mobility. And there was a significant decrease in suspensions, dropouts, and absences. Students in SDP schools outscored students in comparison schools at statistically significant levels in almost every category—more satisfaction and cohesiveness, less friction, difficulty, and disruptive competitiveness.

We began working in Chicago around the same time we initiated the national training program. I was very ambivalent about working in large school districts. We had already encountered numerous conditions that interfered with school functioning and learning in small- and middle-sized districts. I imagined that these problems would be compounded many times over in megadistricts. And then I met Vivian Loseth, a member of the staff of Youth Guidance, a social service organization.

In an Alabama drawl that she had retained despite many years of living in the North, she said, "You need to come to Chicago." I said, "No way." A year later we were working with Youth Guidance in one of the more challenging parts of Chicago, the West Side. Several Chicago foundations supported the team she had assembled, which consisted largely of social workers and educators. It was an opportunity to examine a social and behavioral science support team approach and to compare it with the effectiveness of education supported teams using the SDP in other places.

On one of my early visits to Chicago we met with Mayor Richard Daley, Paul Vallas, the CEO for education of the Chicago public school system, and other district leadership. They were more supportive than I had expected, but it was a different story in some of the schools. At one, an angry faculty member glared at me menacingly as a small group of us discussed the process. At another school, one of the parents had recently had a run-in with a local policeman. During our orientation session he expressed his anger toward all mainstream institutions. I received a tongue-lashing.

In the hallway afterwards one of the white teachers asked

me not to take it personally. She told me that I should try to understand that black men in that neighborhood had to put up with a lot; he was just getting it off his chest. I did understand. And I was impressed that she had empathy and understanding. Nonetheless, the tenor and tone of that first visit left me with the question about whether or not our program was going to work in this environment. I had experienced the same anger among some of the people sent to Yale for training in the early years. I was asking them to change, and change is difficult.

After the teams from the schools had participated in our academy, a facilitator was assigned full time in each of the ten schools using the SDP. These facilitators received additional training locally. They worked with the administrators, school staff, and parents to help put the basic elements of the model in place, and they helped those working in the schools live by the guidelines on an ongoing basis. Because of their social service orientation, they focused on helping the adults interact with the students in a way that promoted their development. Despite my bleak initial assessment, they were successful.

One of many reasons that the SDP was successful in Chicago was in the "small world" department. One principal whose school started off slowly worked very hard and made dramatic gains that inspired everyone. He was from my hometown, East Chicago, Indiana. One of his former and beloved teachers was my older sister, Louise. But overall, the combination of dedication and hard work by the Youth Guidance facilitators and the principals, in particular, led to significant improvement in Chicago.

In chapter 8 I mentioned that the random assignment study carried out over a four-year period by Tom Cook, a highly regarded researcher from Northwestern University, and his associates, indicated a statistically significant greater gain among students in schools using our program than in the nine comparison schools and the district as a whole, even when test scores were on the rise districtwide. Cook's follow-up study has shown that the students maintained the lead over the comparison group.

Cook wrote: "the data suggest that the Comer program caused positive changes in two socially important sets of outcomes: (1) standardized test scores and (2) beliefs, feelings, and behaviors relevant to disruptive and illegal behavior. It is rare for a single study to show changes in both of these domains, which are so central to current discussions of the need for school reform, particularly in the impacted inner-city areas."[1]

An interesting finding resulted from a troublesome situation. In 2000, due to funding problems, there was an 80 percent decrease in the level of facilitator support to schools from Youth Guidance. Schools that had been using the model less than three years showed a slight decline in academic performance. The schools that had been using the program for more than three years continued to gain in both math and reading. This suggests that the longer-duration schools had internalized the SDP way of working and as a result maintained their performance level. This was similar to the way our pilot schools carried on at a high level after we were no longer involved.

Chicago, along with Prince George's County and Detroit, now serve as regional training sites for school districts using the SDP model. They provide orientations to districts considering the program and some 101 sessions. We began our work in Chicago before we made a decision to work systemically or at the district level. And while the district has been generally supportive, we still do not have a systemic presence there.

Our work with Jerry Weast in North Carolina helped us fully appreciate the benefit of working systemically and moved us in that direction. In 1992, when he was a newly appointed superintendent, Weast expressed an interest in using SDP as a tool to pull together once separate urban, suburban, and rural districts into a single entity, the Guilford County, North Carolina, school district. The process brought together the key stakeholders in a way that decreased the tensions inherent in such mergers. In four years they had statistically significant test score gains at the elementary, middle, and high school levels, among the best in the state. They also significantly decreased the minority-majority test score gap.

Guilford County used the Paideia instructional model (largely Socratic inquiry with engagement of students' minds in higher order thinking through activities) developed by Terry Roberts. *The point here is that SDP can facilitate and enhance instructional models while simultaneously promoting desirable relationships and behavior.* This work influenced the approach used in Detroit two years later and moved us toward a districtwide rather than school-by-school approach.

In 1993 John Ziraldo of the Skillman Foundation contacted Ed Joyner about the possibility of using the School Development Program in Detroit. Again, there was concern about going into a large urban area, but it was an opportunity to establish the terms of engagement in a way that could provide us with support from all the major stakeholders. This would increase our chance for survival. The Detroit program also became the prototype for systemic work after 1995. Joyner and foundation staff discussed what would be needed and what kind of partnership might be created. In June 1993 a working group was convened of all the major stakeholders—teachers and administrator unions, the citywide school organization, school principals, various central offices in the district, each area office,

Eastern Michigan University (EMU), and the Skillman Foundation.

They met once a month for a year, with additional supplemental subcommittee meetings. They visited the Yale Child Study Center, other urban districts, and districts with university partners. The working group developed a partnership agreement that would bind all the parties to create the operational structure best suited for Detroit. This led to a partnership agreement in April 1994, and the Comer Schools and Families Initiative got off the ground.

Working with our SDP staff, a team from the Eastern Michigan University School of Education provided local support to the Detroit school district Comer schools. The Skillman Foundation provided a combined ten million dollars of financial support to the three partners over a ten-year period. Six schools began work in summer 1994 and six more in June 1995.

The first encounters between the community and EMU were difficult. But the willingness of Jerry Robbins, the dean, and Alison Harmon, a faculty member, to engage in orientation discussions on the community's turf created an important bond. Nora Martin, the current coordinator, is an EMU faculty member who has worked with the project from the beginning. Harmon was eventually recruited away to become a Skillman Foundation officer. Sherri Joseph, now with the Detroit school district, was the director of training for SDP at Yale. As members moved within the partnership network, they brought knowledge of the model to other partners, deepening understanding and improving trust and the capacity to work together collaboratively.

Our estimate—for most school clusters we work with, as of now—is that about a third of the schools will do very well, some remarkably so, about a third modestly well, and about a third will not move. An evaluation in Detroit by Abt Associates in 2000 reported implementation levels from high to low in line with this estimate. And very important, the schools that implemented the model best had the highest achievement levels and the most desirable behavior outcomes. Studies done at other sites by Christine Emmons, our staff director of evaluation, demonstrate the same result.[2] This rate of success is not likely to improve until school people are routinely trained to create conditions that facilitate student development, and are supported in doing so.

The positive impact of school improvement on suburban-dwelling students and staff is an important part of the Detroit story. I gave a talk at EMU describing the district-EMU-SDP collaboration. When I finished I asked for questions. Instead of asking questions, one after another, three young white women, born and bred in the suburbs, stood up and described how working in schools using SDP in Detroit had changed their lives, particularly the stereotypes they once carried. Student internships in education, nursing, psychology, and social work at EMU went from 0 to 90 to 180 and are still climbing. Some interns are remaining and are successful teachers.

My visit to the Gompers Elementary School in 1999 is a fond memory. The neighborhood was a disaster, but inside the school doors was a gem. The students were lively, spontaneous, and engaged in their work at appropriate times, yet quiet and attentive when they were supposed to be. They got along well with each other, and they were eager to demonstrate their abilities. The parents and staff members were very proud. This culture was created.

Every morning at a fifteen-minute assembly the students say the Pledge of Allegiance and their own school pledge. The latter contains the values, virtues, and goals they are expected to live by and strive for—a lot like what I received at my family dinner table. The custodian recognizes the "birthday boys and girls." The message here is that everybody is important and must be respected. Academic and other recognitions take place. During the announcements students can talk about challenging matters, for example, the sudden and premature death of a teacher or a disturbance outside the school. As poor as they are, they engage in activities to help others.

In 2000 the students in this school achieved the highest MEAP (Michigan Educational Assessment Program) test scores among elementary schools in their size category, around five hundred students. The governor visited and presented them with the Golden Apple Award for this achievement. It is of interest and concern that nobody, not the governor nor anybody in state government, ever asked how this was accomplished in the last place most would expect it. But at least they did not accuse them of cheating.

These achievements took place in the context of significant district-level tensions and turnovers. During the previous ten years there had been four general superintendents. There was a state takeover of the district just after we began our work. A state-appointed board was put in place, and this led to board-community tensions. The head of this board was Bill Beckham, Jr., an African-American who was determined to find a way to give the students the same chance he had had. He listened to the concept and visited an SDP school. He noted the excitement, energy, joy of the students, and he got it. He understood how a good culture creates the interactions that promote good development, teaching, and learning. Shortly after his visit he was appointed president of the Skillman Foundation. With his school board experience and new position, he was well positioned to help make a difference. The real world can be cruel: within a few months he died of a heart attack.

The fourth superintendent, Dr. Kenneth Burnley, was concerned about the many intervention projects and considered dropping them all. A visit to two schools that were successfully implementing the SDP model, and among the highest achieving in the state, suggested the value of the approach and won us another day. Recently, a celebration of the ten years of Skillman Foundation involvement took place. The excitement and joy among parents, students, and faculty had to be very close to what it is like after a Piston basketball team victory. The district has pledged to continue supporting the partnership.

It became clear that large-scale change would require a systemic or district-level focus. We had continued to encounter discontinuity problems related to turnover—buildings not receiving support for the change process from the district and so on. And while there continued to be problems in districts where there were agreements to work with partners, or to work with top-down, bottom-up (building-district level) collaboration, the existence of an agreement helped us face up to the problems and address them. We continued to work with individual schools, in part because government financial support encouraged this approach. Also, we had developed loyalties toward schools that were succeeding despite the absence of district support.

In 1995 we received support from the Rockefeller Foundation for districtwide or systemic work. With these funds three initial districtwide approaches were undertaken. Only one was highly successful, District 13 in New York City under the leadership of Lester Young, Jr. The other two locations were not yet prepared for districtwide work: turnover and other problems interfered with training and limited the effectiveness of these efforts.

A U.S. Department of Education grant in 1998 enabled us to use SDP districtwide in five new communities. With the systemic or districtwide approach, an effort is made to work with key stakeholders and opinion leaders in the district and the community—school board members, school union leaders, faith and business leaders, and others, as we had done in Detroit. Through exploratory discussions we describe the concept and implementation strategies and requirements, and the district participants describe their needs and expectations. When there is a match, a memorandum of understanding is signed.

A steering committee is established at the district level whose work parallels the function of the School Planning and Management Team at the building level. It brings together the key district stakeholders—curriculum and instruction, professional and nonprofessional support, representatives from partner institutions, and others—to collaboratively oversee the implementation of SDP in the district. This promotes ownership, coordination, and support for working with a child and adolescent development focus at the building, and now classroom, level.

And yet, because it is a new way of working, potential and latent resistance exists. Each district has a different history, personnel makeup, quality of past relationships, financial ability to support change, and the like. We generally begin with a subset of schools, including kindergarten–twelfth grade feeder patterns if possible. We work toward full "buy-in" and total district participation, with the district and SDP leadership making calculated decisions about how many schools to involve and how quickly to add additional schools, before and as we work.

Strong support often comes from converts. A very effective facilitator in Westbury, New York, told me that she initially volunteered to be a teacher representative on the first team sent for training from her district in order to learn as much as she could in order to go back and argue against adopting SDP. She recalls that she became a convert on about the third day of training; now she is a strong supporter and leader in the district.

Four of the five districts we began working with in 1998 reported significant elementary, middle, and high school gains in 2003. District 17 in New York City had the greatest gains in language arts in the city in 2002, and in the same year, District 13 had the greatest gains citywide in mathematics. Hertford County and Asheville, North Carolina, were among the top academic gainers in the state. Westbury was one of the top gainers in New York State: it moved past fifty-six school districts on Long Island in academic achievement.

Dr. Constance Clark, the Westbury superintendent, indicated that the SDP implementation process has facilitated a steady change in how the staff and administrators engage in systemic work. It is now based on the developmental pathways and collaborative decision making. Their apprehension and suspicion have turned into conversations about how they can serve the students differently and maximize the educational process in the schools.

By spring 2003, when SDP had been in full implementation for three years, Westbury exceeded the New York State English language arts performance index at the fourth-grade level, and the fourth-grade scores exceeded the state standard. The middle school was ranked number one in the state for having the highest gains in mathematics and was ranked sixteenth in the state for gains in English/language arts. Of the high school cohort, 75 percent passed the Regents examinations.

Many of the families in this district are poor, Haitian and Hispanic immigrants and native-born African-Americans, but they are located in a suburban community, sometimes further disadvantaged by this fact. As mentioned in the interview recorded in chapter 2, a third of the town, one of the wealthiest communities in New York, is located in the school district, but these children do not attend the schools. Outrageous enough to be mentioned again here, the law requires this poverty-packed and struggling district to pay the cost of busing rich and middle-income students to schools of choice outside the district.

The families whose children are bused, along with the elderly and others, regularly vote down district bond issues. The previous excuse was that the district performance was so bad that it did not deserve support. During the last state testing period available, 2002, the Westbury students made some of the greatest academic gains in the state. But the electorate again quietly voted down the next issue. Westbury often loses out on public and private grants because the district is thought of as well-off.

The SDP program in this community is in a university-district partnership arrangement between Westbury and C. W. Post University, similar to the arrangement between Detroit and Eastern Michigan University. The Westbury-Post partnership, however, is a part of our systemic or districtwide approach.

The superintendent, Connie Clark, had worked with us when she was an assistant superintendent in Washington, D.C. The previous superintendent, Robert Pinckney, and the dean of the C. W. Post School of Education, Jeffrey Kane, had met or had ties to Ed Joyner. Francis Roberts, a professor at the college and a strong supporter, had been in my class as a midcareer student at Yale. Again, I am drawing your attention to the importance of relationships and networks and the related trust and growth. If they do not exist naturally, they must be built in order for system change to take place.

As the School Development Program expanded we did not hire new staff for a long period. People who had a deep knowledge of the program and were very effective were hired as a part of our national faculty. Retaining expertise within the organization, keeping people who know and trust each other involved, and bringing new people into this network carefully also made trust and collaboration possible reasonably quickly. Problems were created when this was not done.

The rationale for working with schools of education was to provide support for school districts locally, and to enable the school of education partner to make its own programs more supportive of its students in real-world practice. The EMU students I mentioned earlier gave testimony to the change that took place in the schools and in their lives. Likewise, C. W. Post's work with Westbury contributed greatly to the academic achievement improvement of that district. Post (part of Long Island University) is now working toward creating an institute that uses child and youth development as the centerpiece of its teacher preparation program. There was a similar outcome with Drury University.

The partnership between Drury University and Springfield, Missouri, while not systemic, is unique in its service area and in outcomes for public school students, the university, and SDP. The partnership was seeded in 1995 when Jayne White, a Drury professor of education, spent some time at Yale University during her sabbatical. It has progressed—with the help of John Moore, the president of Drury and former assistant commissioner of education of Missouri, and Dan Beach, chair of the Department of Education at the university—to the creation of a School of Education and Child Development, the name reflecting the emphasis taken, in part, through our work together.

Drury first used SDP training and implementation to strengthen its ongoing relationship with two of the lowest achieving schools in Springfield, Missouri: Boyd/Berry Elementary and Pipkin Middle. After only two years, in 1998, the number of Boyd/Berry first graders writing at or above grade level had jumped from 11 to 64 percent. Kindergarteners reading at the desired level jumped from 6 to 62 percent. Standardized test scores more than doubled in three subsequent years and continue to go up.

About 35 percent of the children in Boyd/Berry are from the homeless shelter; most are white. The minority population of Springfield is about 6 percent, about 30 percent at this elementary school, about 20 percent at Pipkin, and about 15 percent at Central High School. All three schools were the lowest district performers. Pipkin began using SDP in 1998, Central in 1999. The test scores on the state test have not moved greatly, but the signs of movement are there—decreased suspensions, improved attendance, and increased parent participation.

After a year of working with SDP, the dropout rate at Central came down 50 percent and the attendance rate improved. They had the highest ACT (American College Test) scores in the city and in the state. Some of the good news is probably due to a free master's degree program that Drury provided for teachers working in the three schools. This program has decreased turnover and made the schools competitive recruiters. In these now-improved schools, many teachers experience success and satisfaction and want to stay. The SDP-Drury partnership has had a positive impact on important areas of the university's teacher education program. Courses have incorporated real-world experiences into preservice training. Theory and practice are connected for students by staff practicing in the field. In other university departments, both faculty and students have been able to work with the public schools through collaborative activities with the education school. The coordination this makes possible reduces fragmented efforts in the Springfield schools.

The EMU and Drury models, as well as several others not mentioned here, suggest that teacher preparation programs can promote large-scale school improvement. I will discuss this in chapter 12. The Youth Guidance work and direct work with some districts were very successful. Youth Guidance staff represent an important human development resource model, but university students and faculty are the resources we will need for nationwide school improvement.

Finally, our systemic work with former District 13 superintendent Lester Young in New York City has moved in a hopeful direction. SDP has worked with Dr. Young for more than a decade, first when he was at the New York State Department of Education and later at District 13. In May 2003 he was named senior executive for youth development and community services for the newly reorganized New York City school system. Dr. Young is one of the few school leaders I have encountered who, from the beginning, asserted that academic learning had to stand on good student development. It was because of his appreciation of the importance of development that we were first able to work in New York City.

District 13 has some of the most challenging social conditions in the city, yet its students have made significant social and academic achievement gains. But equally important, Young's leadership, and that of the parents, teachers, and community leaders, has called attention to the importance of helping children grow. Carmen Gonzalez's comments about her work in P.S. 46 in District 13 are found in chapter 2. In June Mayor Michael Bloomberg visited her school and observed the remarkable integration of social and instructional services responsible for student development and learning, in spite of challenging family and personal circumstances. He indicated that he wanted all the schools in the city to work like P.S. 46.

The effort to focus on youth development in New York City brings us back to the unfinished business of SDP. It was my hope in the 1970s that we would be able to develop a program from prekindergarten through college in which child and youth development would be the central and organizing theme. The very powerful positive impact that our pilot elementary school Social Skills Curriculum for Inner-City Children had on all involved suggested that we were on the right track. But we had to put that initiative on hold and create a critical and visible mass of schools where there was improvement, using our basic nine-element framework. Although the SDP had an impact on student development, it was indirect and not as powerful as it could be.

By the time enough schools were successfully implementing the basic model, in the late 1980s, I was the only one left on our staff who had experienced the power and excitement of the Social Skills Curriculum. The staff were deeply involved in training and dissemination of our basic framework.

They felt a need to better package the principles of the developmental pathways so they could be passed on to trainers who could then pass them on to local school staffs. But even as we worked on various ways to establish and utilize the basic model, we continued to work on ways to intensify our focus on child and youth development in schools.

For example, most child development people think of pathways in terms of the individual child. Our staff began to think about the classroom context and interactions that are involved in development. In other words, that the pathway is created by the child, the setting, and the interactions. As mentioned, Joyner and Haynes codified and formalized our developmental pathway work with the interactive aspect in mind. This enabled school people to begin to think about how to intentionally shape the environment or utilize all school activities—building and classroom—to help students grow, and to involve the students themselves in intentionally promoting their own growth. Every academic task, every behavioral problem—everything—provides a challenge and an opportunity to help children grow in the six critical areas, venues, or pathways.

I mentioned previously that from birth, throughout life, we are in a quest to acquire the skills and knowledge needed to cope, survive, thrive, and to find well-being and security, a quest to "make it" in the world. When I described my own childhood experiences, I was discussing my own growth along the six critical developmental pathways—physical, social-interactive, psychological-emotional, ethical, linguistic, and cognitive-intellectual—and how such growth prepares all of us to "make it." But I also did so to make the point that commonplace child-rearing activities promote development along all of the pathways.

In my description of how our school improvement framework emerged, I described many incidents in which school staff and parent interactions with students limited or prevented behavior problems and helped students grow along all the developmental pathways. Academic learning must be challenging in order to promote growth. Thus, every day all students face a potentially stressful challenge to their ability to cope socially and academically. The job of all adults around them should be to help them cope with social, behavioral, and academic challenges in a way that helps them grow. But this is often not the case.

For many years we have collected student comments about their experiences in school. The number one complaint is that teachers scream and punish too much. Again, children who receive positive, supportive comments from adults at home and in school do better in school than those who receive negative responses. Many low-income and marginalized students achieve at higher academic levels in schools that focus on promoting their development. Many more such students could do so. But again, we should not blame school people because they were not, and are not now, being prepared to understand underdevelopment and related student behavior or how to support good development.

Very little attention is given to preparing school staff to work in a way in which they can create and sustain a school context, or sense of community, that can simultaneously promote good student development and academic learning and continued parent and staff growth and development. Indeed, there is very little focus on child and adolescent development throughout the education enterprise—school, district, teacher preparation programs, state and national policy, and decision making. The need to do so is still not widely appreciated.

One of the reasons for the lag is the fact that most policy-makers, opinion leaders, professionals, and the general public disconnect their own success from their developmental experience. This is a cultural affect. One of our most cherished beliefs is that we make it on our own. This is a flattering myth that serves personal, political, economic, and social purposes. But we can no longer afford it. It denies adequate support in school for the underdeveloped and reduces appropriate learning opportunities for all.

Also, because of the disconnect, social and behavioral scientists often make child care and rearing sound unimportant and make child development sound autonomous and complicated. As a result, development is seen as some mysterious "scientific thing," the purview of mind and body doctors and social workers. Educators do not want to be seen as child rearers—"not professional enough," "the task of parents." "Teachers teach." And too many parents do not understand that the way they rear their children greatly influences development and learning. The way each simultaneously serves the other—care and rearing, development, teaching, learning; parents, teachers, other support professionals—is not fully appreciated or missed.

Our Developmental Academy was designed to help all the adults in schools think of themselves as child rearers, people who help children grow along the developmental pathways. And although some teachers began to use their new knowledge in the classroom, a pervasive focus on the pathways in classrooms was yet to come. The Developmental Academy was still an indirect method. And even though the Social Skills Curriculum for Inner-City Children provided students with exposure and experiences that would help them grow along the pathways, the support for development was often not conscious or intentional. It was provided by our SDP staff's indirect, even hidden, effort. The acceptance of a developmental focus was still not strong. The desire to raise consciousness and to be more intentional led to "Comer in the Classroom."

The thinking went something like this: since the SDP framework and process worked to change the culture of the school, and improved the performance of adults and students, might it not be even more effective in the classroom? Classroom teachers—the only adults with a continuous and emotionally large presence in the lives of children outside of the family and its network—are best positioned to help students develop, to draw them into an effort to become responsible for their own development. Would an intentional focus on the interactions involved in promoting growth along the developmental pathways provide a way for teachers to have an even greater impact on development and learning than the more general and indirect ways in which we had been working? Shouldn't such an approach prepare students for the social and academic challenges and thereby reduce anxiety? Shouldn't student reflection on their own development create a greater desire to observe and promote their own growth?

Maybe. Let's try. Indeed, some teachers were already working in this way. But the process was not yet systematic and was not open to study and review.

Teachers and administrators are asked to think of their students as people who have already developed a great deal from birth, but are still immature and therefore reasonably vulnerable, even if developing well. But some are underdeveloped for their age and stage or developing in a harmful way. Teachers are asked to think of themselves as people in positions to make a meaningful emotional connection to students in a way that

the library exercise. They lacked confidence and the social competence that adequate growth along the critical pathways could have made possible.

Many children fight because they do not have the social skills and the psychological-emotional and ethical development needed to negotiate and work things out in a way that protects and promotes their rights and needs without compromising those of others. Sometimes they do not know what is right and what is wrong; and sometimes they do, but their desires are greater than their inner controls. Some children fight because they lack the impulse control they need, often because their nervous system development is not adequate.

Without adequate development, they do not get along well with other children or work well in groups. Bigger or more aggressive children will bully or control others. Undesirable social behavior will lead to punishment or exclusion, often leading to deeper involvement with groups prone to problem behaviors, making matters worse. Some will withdraw, become loners, or fringe kids, further decreasing their ability to make progress and to experience a sense of belonging and well-being. Such kids often vandalize schools. In recent years some have gunned down their classmates and teachers. We are increasingly faced with destructive aggressive behavior and harmful expression of sexuality in schools and in communities. Religious, racial, gender, and other prejudices continue to plague us and threaten our well-being and our democracy.

The complexity, magnitude, and great threat such problems represent make it difficult to imagine that teachers can help. And while many other things must be done to fully address these problems, teachers can help. They can help by providing opportunities at an early age for students to learn healthy and effective ways to solve problems, relate to others, and generally cope with the challenges of school in preparation for coping with the challenges of life. The process of establishing healthy life patterns in school should continue through to maturity.

With such thoughts and concerns in mind, Fay Brown and Valerie Maholmes, with input from others on the SDP, developed a "Comer in the Classroom" implementation protocol. It is based on the nine SDP components, relationships, and developmental pathways used to change culture at the building level. Qualities and characteristics of each, and strategies for achieving each, modified for classroom use, were described. One example of modification is the shared decision making of the SPMT in the building taking the form of student participation in rule-setting in the classroom, or students, together, establishing consequences for breaking rules and rewards for keeping them.

The three guidelines of consensus, collaboration, and no-fault lend themselves particularly well to supporting teaching and learning in the classroom. Teachers encourage consensus decision making in the classroom, and students take ownership and responsibility for outcomes through the consensus process. They have some choice in instructional materials and classroom activities, but the staff does not abdicate its responsibility. The students learn to listen to the perspective of others and to tolerate views different from their own. They learn to negotiate, and in the process they develop respect for themselves and others.

Collaboration is expressed through teachers, students, and parents working together and getting along with one another. They often work in dyads and triads on cooperative learning projects. The principle of no-fault helps to make this possible.

No-fault is also modeled in the classroom. A positive tone is set from the first school day and is a goal for every day. Teachers explicitly teach students how to use nonjudgmental, descriptive language. They model the same, and new students are introduced to the expectation. In one school a substitute teacher was yelling at her students in an inappropriate way. An eight-year-old stood up and said, "We use no-fault in this school." The principal had to help the teacher understand the concept and quickly master the practice.

No-fault problem solving builds a sense of confidence in students and a belief that they can achieve. Again, the children who receive more praise in their families achieve at a higher academic level than others. The opposite of blame and fault-finding takes place—the celebration of anything and everything constructive that a student can do, and does. Again, their mere existence, particularly the birthday, and positive behavior of students is celebrated in school. How important is this?

A cynical newspaper reporter interviewing a hardened criminal with nothing to gain was surprised and saddened when he told her that the only good public and personal memory he had was his sixth-grade school play, with his mother and teachers in the audience applauding and beaming with pride. He then commented that maybe with a few more celebrations he might have gone another way. I am sure the determinants of his outcome were more complicated, but hope and celebration are a part of the success mix for all of us.

The SDP guiding principles help teachers promote mutual respect, trust, and high expectations in the classroom. These relationships enable teacher and students to work as collaborators toward goals they've established together. No longer are students declaring that they are not going to do that old teacher's work because they think the teacher does not like them. No-fault leads to teachers thinking about students' potentials and not their limitations, about how to build a bridge between what they know and what they will know.

In chapter 3 I discussed how mature caretakers must help children bring aggressive energy under their own control and use it constructively to achieve well-being. I have described how adults in social organizations must do the same so that the tasks of the organization can be successfully addressed. Here I am describing how teachers and school people in a well-functioning organization and classroom can help children and youth do the same. All of these outcomes are contingent on quality relationships.

With "Comer in the Classroom," developmental pathways are used as a framework for lesson planning. High expectations are evidenced in "words and deeds," and assessments are used to diagnose rather than to punish. Teachers explicitly helping students gain leadership and social skills is the classroom adaptation of building-level staff development. The building-level comprehensive school plan calls for classroom lesson plans in which the developmental pathways are being addressed and are serving as the organizer of teaching strategies and the promotion of a nurturing classroom environment.

Let me tell you about a North Carolina principal who used "Comer in the Classroom" embedded in the overall SDP. Carol Ray became the principal of the Hall-Fletcher Elementary School in Asheville, North Carolina, in 1999. The school began using the SDP in her first year. At the time the school had a 42 percent proficiency rating; just two-tenths of a percent above the "low performing" classification. The proficiency rating is based on the number of students at or above grade level on state tests in math, reading, and writing. The North

Carolina test is considered to be among the best and most challenging of state tests. The next year 69 percent passed all three tests, 72 percent in year three, and 78.6 percent in year four.

They began using "Comer in the Classroom" as an additional aspect of SDP after the third year. Ray said, "'Comer in the Classroom' made everything come alive at Hall-Fletcher." After the fourth year, Ray was moved to another school, and there was great concern about what would happen to the students' upward trend. She pointed out that SDP was a process and that they had internalized the model, that they would continue to do well. In the fifth year, the first with their new principal, Sam Listenbee, 97–98 percent passed all three tests. The achievement gap between black and white students is closing rapidly, now only 6 percent in reading and 0.6 percent in math.

There were no major changes in staff, parents, or students. The school serves nine federal housing projects. The families are 85 percent low income and about 70 percent African-American.

When they made gains during the first year, people told Ray that it had to be more than the Comer Process. Ray wrote, "I maintain it was *because* of the Comer Process: the process was the overarching framework through which we planned all of those strategies and nurtured all of those relationships—not just adult-to-adult, but adult-to-children and children-to-children—to really turn the school around."

As the model encourages, the creativity of the teachers was called on to find ways to integrate the focus on child development into the academic curriculum. A rich potpourri of activities followed. Incidentally, good teachers are very creative. Highly proscribed instruction does not tap into what they do best, what provides them with the greatest satisfaction, and what awakens the creativity of their students.

In the fourth and fifth grade, students kept pathway journals in which they made entries at least once a week. They described the progress and obstacles they were having along their own developmental pathways. Some thought about and discussed the problems they faced outside and in school, the way they interfered with their growth, and what they were doing to overcome them. Writing and reflecting promotes learning and often prevents impulsive, harmful action.

In a third-grade class, students formed groups based on the pathways, several to each group, and created collages. They cut out pictures and discussed among themselves whether they were appropriate for particular pathways or not. For example, did a picture of a doctor examining and talking to a little boy as his mother looked on belong in the physical or the receptive language (listening) pathway? The answer was less important than the structure and process—analysis, listening respectfully to the opinions of others, the appreciation of overlap and interaction, collaborative work, a hands-on activity.

The fourth and fifth graders wrote and produced a television news show using their closed circuit system. One news show feature was "The Comer Moment," with a guest host every day. A Shining Star Program recognized a student from each classroom every month, nominated by the teacher and the teaching assistant. The principal read what the nominating teacher and the assistant had written as the child sat proudly in the next chair. One said of the experience, "You read that in front of God and everybody!"

The basis for recognition was the expression of growth along any or all of the developmental pathways and all of the nine basic program components. Because academic achievement was already highly valued, it was not necessary to always base the recognition on such achievement. This allowed all students to have a chance to be successful without reducing anybody's commitment to doing his or her best in the academic area.

Again, some of what I have described is the same as what happens in many classrooms, but it is different in very important ways. Here it is not frills, doing nice, or entertainment. These efforts are very carefully designed to take into account performance standards, developmental objectives, strategies, and assessments, using a developmental framework to pull it all together in the classroom and building and to make it memorable and helpful to the growth of the child. When children are developing well, they learn well.

But equally important, "Comer in the Classroom" intentionally sets interaction and relationship standards for students and adults, and it recognizes and rewards the people that live by them. At an early age students begin to examine what is fair, right, and how to get along; they are allowed to raise questions about the inappropriate use of power and authority. This is an aspect of what it will take to provide the kind of education Thomas Jefferson had in mind—an education that will give students what they need to protect and promote democracy as adults. Indeed, the SDP guiding principles and performance expectations are essentially those needed to build and sustain a democracy.

Civic participation, particularly in the political process, is the foundation of an effective democracy. The SDP counterpart is representative governance with collaborative and full staff, parent, and student participation in social and academic activities in school. Expressing self-interest while being willing to listen to and be respectful of the views and needs of others are needed characteristics. Consensus-finding takes the place of actual voting in SDP. The vote and the rule of law could not be strong without reasonable consensus. The greatest weakness in our democracy is the time we spend placing blame for vote-getting purposes as opposed to fixing problems.

Everything a child needs to know to become a successful participant in, and promoter and protector of, our democracy can and should be learned in kindergarten and continued and practiced through to maturity. Athletics and the arts provide an intensity of relationships, purpose, and opportunity to support growth that cannot be matched. But they are being pushed aside for more academic learning time and whenever there is a budget problem. The fact that we do not adequately prepare school people to prepare students to be successful participants in our open democratic society is a costly, wasted opportunity.

This role of teachers—promoting development, learning, and democracy—reminds us of how special and critically important they are or could be. It is a big part of the reason why technology can support, but not replace, them. It is the major reason why just any warm body cannot be successful in the classroom, even when very smart, skilled, and committed. A very intelligent, highly respected medical colleague of mine tried his hand at teaching but turned back because of the classroom management problem.

Few traditionally prepared school people are intuitive and gifted enough to help create the context in which they can successfully engage students, parents, and colleagues and help promote growth among all. The curriculum, instruction, assessment, management, and infrastructure adjustments that have taken place do not go to the heart of the problem—the failure throughout the education enterprise to put child and adolescent development at the center, and to manage systems in a way that will support it and simultaneously support academic learning.

The challenge created by the higher level of development needed to function in this scientific and technological age, with weakened community and family support structures, is still not widely appreciated. Almost no attention is given to preparing school staff to work in a way in which they can create and sustain a school context, or sense of community, that can simultaneously promote good student development and academic learning and continued parent and staff growth and development. Ironically, but not surprisingly, elite private and public schools serving the affluent more often focus on the developmental needs of students, staff, and parents.

As I observe troublesome behaviors and tragedies in our country and around the world I am baffled at the fact that we spend so much time, money, and energy on raising test scores rather than preparing our students to participate in the workforce so they can meet life tasks, to get along with each other, and to be the kind of protectors of democracy Mr. Jefferson envisioned. There is a sense that modern behavioral problems are inevitable in the face of great change. I believe that with great attention to promoting desirable child and adolescent behavior, we could greatly reduce many of the problems we are all concerned about. We are paying a high price for not doing so.

XI
The Price We Pay

With a greater focus on child and adolescent development in school, most young people who are not developing well could be helped. They could be prepared for life success, and much problem behavior could be prevented. For the most part, we are missing this opportunity, even for young people from families that are not under economic and social stress. For this, our society is paying a high price. There is a financial, social, and psychological cost to the affected individuals, their families, and their social networks, as well as a financial and social cost to the society as a whole. Indeed, in time, the cost can weaken and even undermine our open, democratic way of life.

In chapter 3, I discussed how scientific and technological change has made education almost a prerequisite for acquiring living-wage work and thus the ability of families to function reasonably well. In chapter 7, I discussed how child and adolescent development is linked to democracy. Throughout this book I have been making the point that it is possible to educate all children, even most from difficult circumstances, in a way that will enable them to develop, succeed in school, and meet their adult tasks and responsibilities: to work, to provide for their families, and to become responsible, contributing members of the society.

The idea expressed by Thomas Jefferson that the ignorance and vice of untaught children will have a high future cost should not be lost on us today.[1] It reminds me of the slogan of a commercial advertising an inexpensive filter that can prevent expensive damage to a car's engine: "Pay now, or pay more later." To date, our society has elected to pay later and pay more.

All humans are born profoundly dependent and soon sense their vulnerability, with resultant insecurity. We are all in a quest for reasonable success and security. When we achieve these desires and needs, in a respected manner, we are more likely to behave in humane ways. When we are not able to manage the ongoing challenges of life, we are more likely to respond or act out in troublesome ways. These behaviors or patterns can become a part of our lifestyle, the way we manage under ordinary conditions. To learn to behave in an effective, humane, and responsible way as adults, children need considerable support for their development. Without it, and because of innate survival drives, they are likely to develop a pattern of harmful behavior—harmful to themselves and others.

Development is a lot like cultivating grass. To maintain an attractive lawn, we must continually tend it. If we stop for a few days, the weeds will come back. Children need support for development from before birth to maturity, and even with it, desirable behavior is not a guarantee, though it is more likely. When support is not continuous, or when it is inadequate, development will lag or take place in a way that leads to poor performance. With sustained difficult life conditions, the same thing can happen among adults and societies.

Most of the problem behaviors we are concerned about—school underachievement, difficulty in getting along with others, bullying, excessive passivity and eventually dependency, violence and crime, promiscuity, and other problem behaviors—usually occur when development is not adequate and continuous. School success, good social skills, a desire to meet life's tasks and responsibilities are more likely when children receive good support for development, when the garden is adequately tended.

Until the last half century, life success could be achieved without an education. Science- and technology-driven economic change has made this much more difficult. Peter Coy pointed out that in our society about 60 percent of children of poor families tend to be poor themselves as adults [2] This is unlike a generation ago when only about 30 percent remained poor.

I suspect that our society has not responded to this problem in part because of the still-pervasive notion that families and children who do not do well are just not trying hard enough. It is thought that their troublesome condition is their own fault. And the myth that the problem is race based persists. My almost illiterate mother often said: "They say our people ought to pull themselves up by their bootstraps. The problem is that colored people didn't get no boots." Once I realized that parents are thoughtful and intelligent, it occurred to me that she was on to something. African-Americans were denied access to the political, economic, educational, and social structures—their "boots"—that could provide access to adequate education and other mainstream opportunities (bootstraps). Because of past and current difficult social environment conditions, and the resultant generation-to-generation lifestyle transmission, African-Americans are disproportionately represented in most of the problem behaviors I will discuss here. There is a message behind this fact.

In 1965 Daniel Patrick Moynihan alerted the nation to the breakdown in two-parent families in the African-American community.[3] About twenty-five years later, white families were displaying breakdown at about the same level. Because of difficult historical experiences, emerging problems show up first and are more damaging in the most vulnerable communities. We often miss the "black marker" warning on the white field that is indicative of emerging danger for all because the behavior is attributed to race. For this reason, in part, we don't make the preventive adjustments soon enough.

In a similar way, children who are denied support for development—their "boots"—are overrepresented in all problem behavior areas. They are less able to meet their adult tasks and responsibilities. This is the case for all children. But poor, more often minority, children usually have fewer experiences that can prevent problem behaviors, less help after they engage in them, fewer "second chances," and harsher consequences. Prevention for such children is particularly important.

Changes wrought by a science- and technology-driven economy impact vulnerable communities—the poor, poorly functioning, and undereducated—first, including white communities. Without attention to the underdevelopment of children, and their resultant vulnerability in school and in life, a generation-by-generation increase of undereducated people who cannot function in the mainstream is inevitable. Yet it is unnecessary.

There is much to suggest that better development and education of all young people can lead to greater participation in the workforce, improved health practices, and fuller involvement in civic affairs. The Mortenson Research Seminar on Public Policy Analysis of Opportunity for Postsecondary Education identifies areas of people's lives that vary according to educational attainment. Consider the percentage of people who are not in the workforce by educational attainment: whereas only 14 percent of college graduates are not in the labor force, 32 percent of those with less than a high school degree are not in the labor force. Health practices: only 3 percent of female college graduates smoked cigarettes during pregnancy compared to 31 percent of those with less than a high school degree. Civic participation: 50 percent of college graduates wrote, telephoned, or signed a petition about an issue in contrast to 7 percent of those with less than a high school degree. Forty percent of college graduates attended a public meeting while only 13 percent of those with less than a high school degree did so. Ninety-one percent of college graduates voted in a national or state election while only 51 percent of those with less than a high school degree did so.[4]

The director of the National Center for Health Statistics of the Centers for Disease Control and Prevention made a presentation in October 1997 as part of a review of progress on Healthy People 2000 objectives. The presentation indicated that among mothers twenty years of age and older, use of prenatal care in the first trimester of pregnancy showed a clear educational gradient. In 1995, women with the most education (thirteen years or more) were 1.4 times as likely to receive early prenatal care as those with the least (less than twelve years). There is a pronounced correlation between lower educational attainment and low birth weight. And death rates show a strong inverse relationship with educational attainment. In 1995, age-adjusted death rates among people aged twenty-five to sixty-four with less than a high school education were more than twice those for people with more than a high school education.[5]

Catherine Ross and Chia-Ling Wu note in the *Journal of Health and Social Behavior* that "the well educated, have better health than the poorly educated, as indicated by high levels of self-reported health and physical functioning and low levels of morbidity, mortality, and disability." They indicate that the "gap in physical functioning among persons with different levels of education increases with age. . . . The higher the educational attainment is, the better the physical functioning. . . . Education significantly slows the decline in health over time." Income does not explain the effect of education on health. "Even adjusting for income and its interaction with age, education significantly affects age-based health."[6]

The Substance Abuse and Mental Health Services Administration (SAMHSA) of the Department of Health and Human Services obtains information on substance abuse. In a recent report SAMHSA notes, "Illicit drug use rates are generally correlated with educational status. Among adults aged 18 or older in 2001, college graduates had the lowest rate of current use (4.3 percent). The rate was 7.6 percent among those who had not completed high school."[7]

Civic participation is one way that the electorate can guide public policy relative to preventable problems. Thus it is disturbing to take a look at voter turnout rates. According to Election Nexus, in 2000, after deducting all those who were ineligible to vote, the turnout rate was 56.7 percent.[8] That is slightly more than half of the voting-eligible population. The young vote was at an alarmingly low rate. Youth voter turnout has declined since 1972 according to the Center for Information and Research on Civic Learning and Engagement (CIRCLE), which is based in the University of Maryland's School of Public Affairs. According to a report by CIRCLE's deputy director and research director, in 1972 the turnout per eligible citizens ages eighteen to twenty-four was 55 percent. In 1976 it was 48 percent. In 1996 it was 40 percent. In the most recent presidential election, only 42 percent of eligible citizens ages eighteen to twenty-four voted.[9]

Cost-benefit analyses are difficult and subject to methodological and other challenges. But the obstacles to mainstream participation and the negative consequences are too clear and massive to quibble about fine-tuning the methodolgy. As more and more young people reach adulthood unprepared, we approach a point of no peaceful or humane return. Recent reports suggest that the price of underdevelopment is dangerously high. We are missing low-cost opportunities to provide widespread support for child and adolescent development, and to protect and promote democracy.

In most cost-benefit analyses, there is a tendency to focus on the high cost of containment, control, and support for people who are not able to function adequately or appropriately—jail, welfare, and so on. Lost opportunity costs (what high negative contributors might have done, such as earn income, pay taxes, and so on) receive significant attention. The greatest lost opportunity is the chance to prevent problems by promoting more effective functioning of our formative institutions—home and school. These most effective, low-cost, high-benefit opportunities receive too little attention.

We act as if the police are the first line of defense. But the family and its social network is the first line of defense and offense —preventing undesirable and promoting desirable behavior. It has contributed to both throughout the ages. You do not need an expensive study to note that far too many parents are not doing a very good child-rearing job; you need only observe numerous troublesome parent-child interactions in the supermarket or restaurant.

Even though child rearing promotes child development, which is critically important for school learning and democracy, our society has done little to help parents gain the skills they need and, in my experience, desperately want. Recall the beleaguered parents working two jobs each who were leaning on the school for help in the interviews in chapter 2. Many parents have said to me, if a good beating is child abuse, what can I do? Although many middle- and upper-class parents have problems with their children, more often they have more resources to draw on. But only here and there have concerned mayors, governors, and state officials moved to help parents gain the skills and support needed to rear their children well—a low-cost opportunity lost.

Better-educated parents, already better prepared to support the kind of development needed for school success, often provide preschool preparation for their children. Government-supported programs have been doing so for poor children since Head Start was established in 1964. But as observed by the Center for Law and Social Policy, states served only 2.25 million children among 15.7 million children eligible for federal child care assistance (one out of seven children).[10] There is not enough outreach to those in greatest need, not enough places, or insufficient funding.

The National Institute for Early Education Research (NIEER) estimates the average benefits from a universally accessible program at ages three and four is at least $25,000 per child. The estimated cost per child is only $8,703 annually. These benefit estimates were derived from the Chicago Child-Parent Center study. The study found that at age twenty, the participants were more likely to have finished high school than children who were not in the program. They were also less likely to have been held back in school, less likely to have needed remedial help, and less likely to have been arrested. It's estimated for every dollar invested, the return is $7, based on the reduced costs of remedial education and justice system expenditures, and in the increased earnings and projected tax revenues for participants.[11] As Steven Barnett, director of NIEER, noted, "The national cost of failing to provide at least two years of quality early childhood care and education is extremely high, on the order of $100,000 for each child born into poverty, or $400 billion for all poor children under five today."[12]

We can give poor and marginalized children their "boots"—the developmental experience needed to participate more fully in society. We can do so in school at less cost than it takes to contain and control them because they were not prepared for school and life.

Help before school is generally available only for families that volunteer, because in our society nobody has the authority, nor should they, to intervene in families. But the public school has an opportunity to utilize child-rearing knowledge to support the development of all students. School people are the adults who are, or potentially are, emotionally close enough to help students develop well. *But to adequately support development, all the principles, practices, and outcomes of youth development discussed above must be integrally and intentionally incorporated into the classrooms throughout a school, throughout all schools.*

There are about 51.4 million children and youths in schools, during twelve to fourteen of their important developmental years. According to the U.S. Department of Education, enrollment in public schools grades 9–12 is 13,626,000, and the enrollment in public schools grades K–8 is 33,587,000. The U.S. Census Bureau notes that the total nursery school enrollment is 4,326,000.[13]

There are 3,111,000 teachers and administrators in schools, according to the U.S. Department of Education. National expenditures for public elementary and secondary education and other related programs totaled nearly $382 billion for the 1999–2000 school year, according to the National Center for Educational Statistics.[14] Most school people have not been adequately prepared or selected for their ability to promote child and youth development, and in only a very few places are schools geared to do so. Yet studies show that teachers who have taken one or more psychology courses have better student academic and behavior outcomes than those who have not.

School people are our second line of defense, and offense. Support for development is a win-win situation. Helping educators help children develop aids teaching and learning—the primary mission of schools. But in the vast majority of schools there is no focus on child and youth development. Not fully utilizing this precious resource is an enormous waste, *a colossal loss of a low-cost opportunity*—indeed, at a cost lower than it should be.

Often after-school programs, when such programming exists, focus on youth development. I cochaired, with Wilma Tisch, a national study of youth development and community organizations sponsored by the Carnegie Corporation of New York. The 1992 report, *A Matter of Time*, showed that there are numerous, often dedicated, and hard-working groups committed to supporting youth development. Such groups include faith, ethnic, police and fire, fraternal, and other organizations and better-known groups, such as Big Brothers Big Sisters, Teen Outreach Program, the After-School Corporation in New York, Boys and Girls Clubs of America, and Girl Scouts of America.[15] Supervised activities in such programs provide youth with chances to learn how to act in the world around them; to explore, express, earn, and sense belonging; and to constructively influence others. Studies show that young people who participate in these activities have more success in school and engage in fewer problem behaviors.[16]

The National Institute on Out-of-School Time reviewed studies of after-school programs. The studies found that children who attend high-quality programs have better peer relations, emotional adjustment, conflict resolution skills, grades, and conduct in school compared to their peers who are not in after-school programs. Children who attend programs spend more time in learning opportunities, academic activities, and enrichment activities and spend less time watching television than their peers. Students who spend one to four hours a week in such programs are 49 percent less likely to use drugs and 37 percent less likely to become teen parents than their peers.[17]

Public/Private Ventures made the point most relevant to this discussion. There are about 1,200 hours per year when youth need developmental supports and opportunities. They demonstrated the link between unstructured time and engagement in risky and problem behaviors. How much would it cost to provide 1,200 hours of youth development opportunities and supports to the 47 million youth ages six to seventeen years old in this country? They estimated that the cost would be $2.55 per hour, per youth ($3,060 per youth annually): $144 billion per year.[18]

Potential Return on Public Investment in a Youth

Investment

$3,060/yr. for 12 years of 1,200 hours of supports and opportunities (6–17 yrs. old)	$36,720
$6,564/yr. for 12 years of public education (grades 1–12)	$78,768
Total basic investment (12 years)	$115, 488

Minimum Expectation

Average annual salary (with high school diploma)	$22,895
Annual cost of living allowance	3%
Years of continuous employment	40
Total income (lifetime)	$1,726,312
Taxes (17% of total income)	$293,473
Consumption (60%)	$1,035,787
Personal savings without accrued interest (23%)	$397,052
Total contributions to society (taxes + consumption)	$1,329,260

Return on Investment

Return on investment (contributions to society − investment)	$1,213,772
For every dollar invested, society gains	$10.51

Source: Public/Private Ventures, "A Matter of Money: The Cost and Financing of Youth Development," in *Youth Development: Issues, Challenges and Directions* (PDF, p. 86; retrieved from http://www.ppv.org/content/reports/ydv_pdf.html).

Is it worth $144 billion to ensure that all youth have access to development supports and opportunities in their vacant hours? An investment of $2.55/hour for 1,200 hours per year to develop youth into economically and socially viable adults can result in a gain of $10.51 for every dollar invested. With more systematic organization and management of this entire enterprise, particularly staff training and support, the cost benefits could be much greater. Add better support for development at home and at school, and the cost benefits would be enormous.[19]

The prime time for violent juvenile crime is from 3:00 P.M. to 6:00 P.M., according to Fight Crime: Invest in Kids, a national anticrime organization made up of more than one thousand police chiefs, sheriffs, prosecutors, and heads of police organizations. In a national poll of its members about how to prevent youth violence, they picked "providing more after-school programs and educational child care" by a four-to-one margin over such alternatives as prosecuting more juveniles as adults and hiring more police officers, and by a seventy-to-one margin over installing metal detectors and cameras in schools.[20]

The strategies of after-school programs vary widely, however, and among some, what they do to support development is vague. Most programs are poorly supported. Staff salaries are low, lower than teachers on the whole, meaning they are very, very low. And too many are poorly trained. As a result, staff turnover is high and the chance for long-term continuity in relationships is low. And there are too few programs serving young people at greatest risk. The degree of coordination with school programs varies and is often not nearly as planful and collaborative as I have described in our SDP work. It all adds up to a lower level and quality of support for development from these precious and committed resources than is possible.

A sustained commitment is needed. State and federal initiatives are often short term and sometimes in response to high-visibility problems rather than part of an intentional and continuing effort to support youth development. Often the interest and funding disappear when the public is distracted by other issues. For example, in 1999 the federal government responded to high-visibility, mostly middle-class white school violence by creating a collaboration among the U.S. Departments of Education, Health and Human Services, and Justice that resulted in the Safe Schools/Healthy Students Initiative (SS/HS). The critical feature of the initiative was the linking and integration of existing and new services and activities into a comprehensive approach to violence prevention and healthy child and adolescent development. The theory of change here is that when schools, families, and community organizations collaborate more fully and positively with one another there will be more positive outcomes for youth.

Unfortunately, youth development is not always an intentional focus even in such programs. The embedded assumption here is that the implementation of integrated service systems involving schools, a home visitation program, after-school programs, and others—as opposed to the disconnected programs that now exist—would produce positive development and safe schools and communities. *Such programs are an important step forward, but they usually do not give enough attention to creating conditions that make possible emotionally powerful youth-adult attachments, interactions, continuity, and other factors needed to influence development. These issues are particularly important in the most difficult communities.* Again, the most difficult communities are greatly underserved.

To have a significant impact on the lives of young people, emotionally important and mature people must have a continuous presence in their lives. Three-year programs create situations where people jump in and out of children's lives. It took us seven years to turn around the two schools we began working with in 1968 (although many, many important changes happened a lot sooner). With our current knowledge base it takes much less time, but it still takes three to five years and requires careful selection of personnel, support, and continuity. It is difficult to create healthy student and staff relationships and a healthy school and collaborative organizational culture in a shorter time period, even with very experienced and competent change agents.

Given the complex citywide collaborations envisioned by the Safe Schools/Healthy Students Initiative, the first half of the three-year grant period could have been spent just on planning, hiring appropriate staff, and relationship-building among the adults. By the time the programs are up and running the adults have to turn their focus to figuring out how to sustain them beyond the grant period. Cities in a fiscal crisis find it difficult to impossible to support the programs on their own, and these are usually the communities that need these programs the most. As the third year commences, programs begin informing their staff that they cannot support them beyond the grant period. Seeing the handwriting on the wall, staff start to leave. Harm can be done to young people by "go and stop" relationships. It doesn't help with the empathy, identity, and trust issues young people are struggling with.

Programs like this are the kind of low-cost opportunities needed to promote development and prevent problem behaviors. But they must be well coordinated and integrated with schools, reasonably well funded, and provide a continuity of relationships between developing young people and mature adults. Our society is not making the most of the potential of these low-cost youth development organizations—another lost opportunity.

Let's look more closely at the cost of inadequate development and school failure. According to "Out of the School House, Into the Jailhouse," a report by the Coalition for Juvenile Justice: "Each year's class of dropouts drains the nation of more than $200 billion in lost earnings and taxes every year. Billions more are spent on welfare, health care and other social services." Approximately 35 percent of young adults who drop out of high school are unemployed. Poor school performance is "one of the strongest predictors of whether youth will drink, use weapons, attempt suicide, or have sex at a young age."[21] The Institute for Health Policy notes that alcohol and drug abuse alone costs the American economy $276 billion per year in lost productivity, health care expenditures, crime, motor vehicle accidents, and other conditions.[22]

Incarceration

The Department of Justice's Bureau of Justice Statistics (BJS) shows that at midyear 2002 the number of prisoners in the United States exceeded two million for the first time. The proportion of African-American men aged twenty to thirty-four who are incarcerated has never been higher: the figure, which has been rising in recent years, reached 12 percent in 2002 (as opposed to 1.6 percent among white men in the same age group). The BJS has estimated that black men have more than one chance in four of being incarcerated during their lifetimes.[23]

The "get tough" drug laws (without sound strategies and vigorous efforts to overcome the ill effects of marginalization, underdevelopment, and undereducation) have contributed greatly to this problem. The unintended consequences are formidable. Many of these men are felons who cannot work and cannot vote. They cannot support families, but they have children. These conditions will lead to similar situations in the next generation. In each generation, in a significant segment of the population, there are fewer males in a position to obtain an education, work, get married, and help create and live in well-functioning families and communities.

The problem has reached such a level that it contributes heavily to the shortage of black males who can pursue higher education and become attractive marriage partners. This is aggravated by an education system that cannot break the cycle of marginality; indeed, it leaves too many who received good support for development vulnerable to the powerful pull of a vibrant street culture. In turn, many of the best-educated black women will not find marriage partners and rear children. This situation is a quiet, ticking time bomb. There are now fewer white males in college than women. Similar forces are at play; blacks are simply more vulnerable.

There is little in place to break the cycle. Indeed, Tom Cook pointed out that the students in SDP schools in Chicago have just as many contacts with the legal system as in the comparison schools.[24] It is the environment, including the point the Chicago teacher made to me: it doesn't take much for a black male to make contact with the legal system. A white professor hired two black men to carry furniture up to his apartment. A passing policeman suspected them of robbery. The license of the nondriver had expired, and they were both arrested. A black male stopped and searched for drugs checked

out clean (no drugs, no previous record for anything). The policeman returned to the car and said, "What are you a faggot or
something?"

Harris notes that, "In Illinois, it costs the state each year
around $16,000 to keep an adult in prison (versus about $4,200
to keep one child in school." Moreover, he refers to studies that
show the close connection between crime and educational
problems. For example, he cites a study conducted by the Illinois Criminal Justice Authority that found that "72 percent of
the prisoners were high school dropouts, compared with an
average drop-out rate of 22 percent for all Illinois high school
age residents. Almost one quarter of the dropouts in prison left
school before tenth grade, and the average inmate had the educational skills of an eighth grader."[25]

Stephen Phillips notes, "In the United States, an estimated
70 percent of the more than two million-strong prison population lack the reading skills to navigate many everyday tasks
or hold down anything but a menial job." The average cost, nationwide, of incarceration is $25,327 annually per inmate, ac-
cording to the federal prison system. Moreover, Gainsborough
and Mauer point out that nearly $40 billion is spent annually
for prison housing and construction.[26]

Mental Health

Prevention, early intervention, and timely treatments of mental
disorders can promote healthful outcomes. Steven E. Hyman,
the director of the National Institute of Mental Health (NIMH),
stated at NIMH's June 19, 2000, Annual Research Roundtable
that research promises (and, indeed, already has shown) that
timely treatments of mental disorders and effective systems of
care can lay a necessary foundation for continued opportuni-

ties to develop and, for ever-increasing numbers of children, to recover from childhood disorders.

Child and adolescent research conducted at NIMH demonstrates that it is not inevitable that mild aggression among young children will escalate over the years into serious behavior problems and violence. An NIMH 2000 report indicates that successful early adjustment at home increases the likelihood that children will overcome such individual challenges and not become violent. Exposure to violent or aggressive behavior within a family or peer group, however, may influence a child in that direction.[27]

It is possible to nip problem behaviors in the bud. But a RAND study notes that "1 in 10 young people suffer from mental illness severe enough to cause some level of impairment. Yet fewer than 20 percent of these children receive needed treatment in any given year." It also notes that "The current cost of treating children and adolescents is estimated at nearly $12 billion, significantly more than expected on previous estimates. Despite these annual expenditures, nearly three-quarters of troubled youth do not get the care they need."[28]

Recall that our SDP pilot schools were not referring students for expensive mental health services, probably because general conditions and specific interventions nipped potential problems in the bud. Although we do not have follow-up studies, it is likely that the many interactions in which teachers in SDP schools enabled students to manage potentially harmful aggression prevented problem behaviors later in life.

Physical Health

"National Health Expenditures—Summary, 1960 to 1999, and Projections, 2000 to 2010" was issued by the Bureau of Census in 2001. The total public expenditures (federal, state, and local) for health services and supplies, medical research, and medical facilities construction, according to this report, will increase from $549 billion in 1999 to a projected $726 billion in 2003. However, we find that education attainment makes a difference in terms of health among people with low income.[29]

Unemployment and Welfare Dependency

The Employment Policy Foundation (EPF) is a nonprofit, nonpartisan public policy research and educational foundation based in Washington, D.C. In its 2001 report, "Building America's Workforce for the 21st Century," EPF indicated that employment demand for skilled professionals increased over the previous five years whereas the number of manual, service, and low-skilled occupations declined. If the trend continues, almost 45 percent of the jobs in the next thirty years may be in the high-skilled, highly paid occupations, nearly twice the proportion of thirty years ago. This shift has enormous implications for education and training, for family functioning, and for the future of democracy.[30]

In the future, we can expect even more job displacement as a result of changes in the structure of the economy (e.g., job loss in high import-competing industries). Lori Kletzer, in her testimony before the Committee on Finance, United States Senate, on July 20, 2001, observed that a person's educational attainment matters after job displacement. In her words, "Compared to high school dropouts, workers with a college degree (or higher) are 25 percentage points more likely to be reemployed, high school graduates 9.4 percentage points more likely, and workers with some college experience 11 percentage points more likely to be reemployed."[31]

For those who have been displaced or have been unable to obtain a job with a livable wage, dependency on welfare often results. And welfare is expensive. According to the 2002 Temporary Assistance for Needy Families (TANF) annual report to Congress, "TANF expenditures were $25.5 billion (combined Federal and State Maintenance of Effort [MOE] funds) for FY 2001."[32]

Domestic Violence

Michael Waldo cites research indicating that "although abusive men are not distinguished by a history of criminal arrests, over 80 percent of them witnessed or experienced abuse as children. This finding suggests that battering is a family pattern that is transmitted from one generation to the next." In 2003, an article in the *Journal of Interpersonal Violence* stated: "Childhood physical abuse increased the risk of victimization among women and the risk of perpetration by men more than 2-fold; childhood sexual abuse increased these risks 1.8-fold for both men and women; and witnessing domestic violence increased these risks approximately 2-fold for women and men. . . . These results suggest that as the number of violent experiences increases, the risks of victimization among women and perpetration by men also increase by about 60–70%."[33]

It is possible to prevent domestic violence from escalating by educating health care providers about this problem. Rachel Jewkes observes that most women welcome inquiries about domestic violence, but doctors and nurses rarely ask about it. When battered spouses do find the help that they need, family therapy could break the intergenerational pattern of domestic violence.[34]

The American Institute on Domestic Violence indicates that employers lose between $3 and $5 billion every year in absenteeism, lower productivity, higher turnover, and health and safety costs associated with battered workers. Businesses lose an additional $100 million in lost wages, sick leave, and absenteeism. More than 1,750,000 workdays are lost each year due to domestic violence. Domestic violence in the United States costs an estimated $67 billion annually. Interestingly, "66% of senior executives surveyed agreed that their company's financial performance would benefit from addressing the issue of domestic violence among its employees."[35]

Child Abuse and Neglect Services

Prevent Child Abuse America provides detailed statistical justification to show that the total annual direct cost of child abuse and neglect in the United States is $24,384,347,302. This figure includes hospitalization, chronic health problems, the mental health care system, the child welfare system, law enforcement, and the judicial system. The estimated annual indirect cost is $69,692,535,227. This figure includes special education, mental health and health care, juvenile delinquency, lost productivity to society, and adult criminality.[36]

Montgomery and Rossi reviewed research studies that show that "although many severely abused children become remarkably well adjusted adults, battering places children at increased risk of lifelong emotional/behavioral problems, impaired intellectual functioning, and permanent physical or neurological damage." Moreover, child and adolescent violence research conducted at NIMH in 2000 reveals that "the mental health outcomes of child abuse and neglect has demonstrated that childhood victimization places children at increased risk for delinquency, adult criminality, and violent criminal behavior."

Child abuse and neglect is not inevitable. This is a preventable problem. The Montgomery and Rossi's NIMH report goes on, "An inverse relationship of family income and parental education with antisocial behavior has been found in many population-based studies." This means that as parents' income and educational attainment increases, the likelihood that they would abuse or neglect their children decreases.[37]

On the flip side, there is an added economic value of a high school diploma or college degree. According to a special 2002 study by the U.S. Census Bureau, for adults ages twenty-five to sixty-four who worked at any time during 1997, 1998, and 1999, "average earnings ranged from $18,900 for high school dropouts to $25,900 for high school graduates, $45,400 for college graduates, and $99,300 for workers with professional degrees." Moreover, "Over a work-life, individuals who have a bachelor's degree would earn on average $2.1 million—about one-third more than workers who did not finish college, and nearly twice as much as workers with only a high school diploma."[38] The better educated have the best chance of creating well functioning families and preparing their children for success in school and in life.

Oregon and Vermont: Two Very Different Approaches

Oregon was in the news a great deal in 2003 because of the debates in its legislature about ending the the school year early due to the state's budget crisis. Interestingly, since 1980 Oregon increased the amount of general tax revenue spent on prisons by 282 percent. The portion for postsecondary education increased

by only 21 percent. The average cost per day per student in 2001–
2002 was $18.45. The average cost per day per inmate was $62.24
in state prisons and $79.25 in county jails. More than 70 percent
of Oregon prisoners have math and reading deficiencies.[39]

Vermont realized that it could either continue to build
more prisons or prevent the need for them. That state invested
almost $40 million in state and federal funds for crisis preven-
tion. This shift in policy is paying off slowly but surely. By
helping families at risk function better, the state has improved
infant mortality and reduced low birthweight rates; decreased school dropout rates; and lowered the rates of child
abuse, teenage pregnancy, childhood poverty, and welfare
caseloads.[40]

Our society as a whole already spends a great deal of
money on prevention. There are approximately sixty federal
funding streams available to support early childhood programs
and services. There are more than one hundred federal funding streams that support program and services for school children and their families. In addition, there are local and state
support structures. But these many programs are fragmented,
overlapping, and often not organized and focused on helping
adults support the development of children across the developmental pathways needed for school and life success. As a result we don't get the proverbial "bang for the buck" we need.

The focus on prevention in Vermont has led to collaboration among state agencies, local and regional service agencies, and individual citizens. Together they have worked to
break down the bureaucratic walls and more cooperatively
help families avoid parenting, financial, and health crises.

The fiscal cost pales in comparison to the emotional pain that
is created by our failure to prevent problem behaviors through
effective development, education, and preparation for living in

an open but complex democratic society. Stories in the daily media of pain and suffering—battered and abused, murdered children and adults—appear to grow more horrific every day. The hospital emergency rooms are crammed with the victims of what most call "senseless violence." The violence may be senseless, but it is not unexpected given the poor job we do in helping our children grow up.

As a child psychiatrist I have seen firsthand the emotional and developmental costs for children related to problems among their caretakers. The child who fired the Wiffle ball at me as hard as he could when I pointed out that it must be hard for him to see his father on the street corner drunk was in pain. He was a behavior problem in school, and his academic achievement level was low.

I saw a hint of what was possible in one of our pilot schools thirty-five years ago. The school's top "bad boy," a fifth grader, had been responding well to the nurturing environment. His academic achievement had improved greatly. But just before Christmas he got into fights on three straight days. As the staff stopped the last fight, in the hallway, and speculated about what was going on, he went into his classroom, knocked over his desk, and stood in angry, actually painful, defiance. His teacher walked in and said, "Johnny, what is the matter? What is going on?" He paused, dropped his head, and began to cry.

He explained that his father was scheduled for a release from prison for Christmas but something had happened and he would not be coming home. The teacher told him that she understood how much that must hurt him. She went on to explain that by getting in fights with others he was only making matters worse for himself. She helped him write a letter to his father expressing his own disappointment and what must be his father's disappointment, wishing him the best under the circumstances, and telling him how much he looked forward to the day when he could visit. The youngster was no longer a powerless, acting-out victim. He learned something about how to handle his feelings. Indeed, it was also a language arts lesson. And the stature of and emotional attachment to his teacher grew enormously. After that she had only to look at him to limit troublesome behavior.

Throughout this book I have cited incidents, projects and programs, and research findings that demonstrate that support for good development can prevent the high social, emotional, and financial costs of problem behaviors, even among students from very difficult circumstances. It is also very clear that we are not making the most of low-cost opportunities. We must do a better job in rearing all our children well in all our formative institutions, in preparing them to meet adult responsibilities in this complex age. Neither the farm nor the factory is available to save them as in past eras. Even the military that once saved many now needs well-educated people. Down the road we will pay the ultimate price—loss of our open and democratic society—unless we pay now to better prepare families, schools, and other resources to support the development of all our children, to leave no child behind.

XII
To Leave No Child Behind

When I was a young psychiatrist just beginning to confirm Mrs. Johnson's vision of my future, I would stop by home when I had a trip in the Chicago area. My mother was always a little uncertain about "this psychiatry business." She had sacrificed so that I could become a "real doctor." She wanted to know what I was doing in schools. As I explained, she listened, and listened, and listened for more, and finally said, "Is that all? It sounds a lot like common sense to me." She thought a moment more and said, "And they pay you for that?!!"

My mother had less than two years of formal education, but she understood that children behave and perform best when their caretakers provide them with good preparatory experiences. She felt that everybody must know that. Our work has focused on providing such support in schools. I recently described our SDP framework to the president of a prestigious university. His response: "It's so obvious. Why is it not being done?"

It is common sense and an obvious need. There is an enormous body of scientific literature, now buttressed by brain research, that suggests that child and youth development should be the foundation for academic learning. Throughout this book I have been discussing how such knowledge can be applied to improve schools, by those serving the most marginalized students as well as those serving the most privileged. The price of not using low-cost opportunities to prevent the high-cost problems that result from not adequately supporting child and youth development should interest policymakers and taxpayers alike. But the inertia and resistance to doing what is needed is great.

In an earlier chapter I described the inertia and resistance our SDP team encountered at the individual school level largely because of tradition and fear of change. We eventually realized that the same is true in other *secondary* or service networks and in the *tertiary* or policy networks, as well as in the *primary* family networks. Behaviors that influence education outcomes take place in all three. Keeping things the way they are is a widespread way of trying to deal with the threat of the unknown involved in change. This tendency creates more problems than it solves or prevents in this age of rapid change.

The political, economic, and social forces operating to maintain the status quo are even more powerful than the psychological forces. It often takes courage to protect the little ones or to provide opportunity for the less powerful. A superintendent told me that he just had to "bite the bullet" and fire two teacher assistants who were repeatedly abusive of children, even though one was a relative and the other a close friend of one of his board members who was pushing for their retention. In the 1930s a white school board member and his family in Mississippi left town under the threat of death because he suggested that the disparity between funds for the white schools and the black be dropped from 90 percent to 80 percent.

And which computers should we buy anyway? There are a multitude of purchasing and employment decisions that can be affected by changes in school and district leadership, programs, and ways of working. In most places there is no fire wall between the delivery of education services and local politics. The needs and changes in local political leadership impact education policy for better and for worse. Bureaucracy is often cited as a huge problem, and it is a major source of inertia. But it is the way people function and relate that makes it a problem.

Unfortunately, even when poor and marginalized people get a voice, their knowledge base often limits their ability to do what is in the best interest of their children. In our early pilot project years, and until a collaborative and success-oriented culture emerged, members of our Yale team sometimes found themselves tactfully protecting the best interest of the children in opposition to the demands of parent leaders—like using project money to hire full-time doctors and nurses. Given the lack of clarity about the mission of schools and how to measure success, this is often true of affluent, well-educated people as well. Making decisions about how to improve complex systems like schools is a challenging process for all.

While there are many kinds and sources of inertia, there are two that carry unmatched power. They are the platform on which many other difficult issues stand and grow. The first is the point made by the retired superintendent of schools and implied by others in the interviews in chapter 2, the inequitable way that we fund our education system—particularly property taxes and the failure to make adjustments for low tax base, high-need areas. The second is our focus on curriculum, instruction, and testing or assessment without providing adequate support for development.

Both produce outcomes that make it possible to use very powerful myths and rationalizations to obfuscate the real causes of underachievement and problem behaviors. Indeed, the resistance to a developmental perspective is rooted in the most powerful and widespread of many myths—that school learning is a product of genetically determined intelligence and will only. Thus, "'They' are not able, are not responsible, are not interested, will take our jobs, and more." Usually left unsaid is a belief that it is not cost-effective to invest more in the education of poor and marginalized students. Reactions to these myths lead to conflict and struggle rather than problem solving.

For these, and for many other reasons that benefit various groups of mainstream adults, school improvement approaches that would obviously help all students are not taken, even when the approaches are supported by research-based evidence. In order to effectively push for change, we must greatly weaken these rationalizations and myths. From the beginning of our SDP work we have felt that helping to achieve success where it is not expected is the best way to weaken resistance and to promote support for large-scale school improvement for all students. I have not forgotten that the town of Westbury voted against a school bond issue even after the district made extraordinary gains, but continued and more widespread school success among students from difficult backgrounds cannot be ignored indefinitely.

To speed up the process, the dots—high cost of inadequate education when known ways to improve it exist—must be connected for parents, community leaders, and others. Also, we have not done enough to call attention to public school successes and how the numbers can be increased by addressing student underdevelopment and staff underpreparation. More must be done to point out the danger of not preparing students from all backgrounds and of all achievement levels to promote and protect our democratic way of life. Providing evidence (existing successful schools and districts), and exposing the many myths and rationalizations, should begin to help many more people see their own best interest in the improved education and adult functioning of all children, to enable many more to understand, as did the building principals in our pilot schools, that by thinking and working differently we can create a win-win situation.

To leave no child behind we need a *change strategy* in which we use proven knowledge and skills that reduce inertia and resistance in schools and districts, that will create a present and future educator workforce capable of using proven approaches, and that will help decision makers in all networks create policies that will enable education practitioners to create school programs that will support good student development, instruction, and learning. Although this is a daunting task, it is possible because just as we found in our pilot schools in 1968, today most people—not all—want good public schools.

When it becomes apparent that such schools can be created regularly, at lower short- and long-term costs than inadequate schooling, it will be possible to mobilize the level of political pressure needed to strongly promote improved education as social justice, the bedrock of American democracy. The appeal to our essence as a nation—and making the economic benefits apparent—will override existing inertia and resistance. This is the way American democracy has worked since the soldiers who fought in the War of the Revolution wrestled reasonable opportunities from the landed aristocracy through to the modern civil rights and women's movements.

The political pressure is growing, and it will increase as parents, educators, and employers call for real solutions. But traditional curriculum-, instruction-, and assessment-oriented approaches, even with recent reforms, will not be enough. Until we adequately focus on the underlying problem of under-development, and the underpreparation of caretakers at home and at school, we will not have a viable alternative ready when a strong commitment to good public school education is made. My concern is that we will be like a friend of mine who partici-pated in the North Carolina drugstore sit-ins against racial segregation. When they finally agreed to serve him, he did not have a dime for a cup of coffee.

Several programs, past and present, suggest ways, with impor-tant changes, that we can simultaneously overcome resistance and provide all students with the kind of education that will enable them to be successful adults and to protect our democ-racy, even in an increasingly complex age. The situation we are in today is similar to that at the turn of the twentieth century when the nation was moving from an agricultural to an indus-trial economy. Farmers were working in traditional ways when far more productive techniques were known. Research and demonstration programs at universities and other organiza-tions had better outcomes and were organized in ways to study and do research that would provide knowledge that would bring still better outcomes. But there was no way to bring knowledge to practice, and there was resistance to change.

To overcome the obstacles to improved farming, the Agricultural Extension Service evolved from several existing programs. The service systematically brought improved methods to farmers, informed resisters of the benefits in working differently, provided financial incentives, and its success overcame the remaining inertia and resistance. It also made America the breadbasket of the world. This helped the country take a lead in industrial development, and eventually in science and technology. Good education for all is the key to continued American economic leadership and support for democracy in the world. An Educational Extension Service (EES) can address the obstacles to improving education at this early stage of the twenty-first century.

There is new and better curriculum, instruction, school management, and adult and student development knowledge available, but it is being resisted or being utilized in less than optimally effective ways primarily because we all but ignore child and adolescent development issues. This is largely because the professional identity of *teacher as instructor,* rather than as a *child and youth developer in the service of teaching and learning,* is established first in schools of education and then reinforced in practice with colleagues who were similarly prepared. Thus, taking a developmental perspective is not something that comes naturally or easily in practice situations in which few hold it as a part of their identity.

This is the reason that it takes significant time and energy to promote and to sustain a focus on student development in schools. And it often goes away when the training, key supporters, or other facilitating factors are removed. But if doing so is part of what it means to be a teacher or school leader, there would be little, if any, resistance. (Education agencies within schools of education would also be well positioned to help teachers and administrators already in practice incorporate new ways of working.) But the best chance to balance, perhaps fuse, the emphasis on curriculum, instruction, and assessment with that of child and youth development is during the initial professional development of educators—before they begin to teach or become school leaders.

Many view schools of education as a major source of inertia and resistance; I feel they are a major, well-connected, and strategically located resource. It was with this in mind that we looked to several schools of education to help us to disseminate our SDP model. When this approach proved successful, it occurred to me that this model could evolve into a mini-model of an Education Extension Service.

I envisioned a unit within schools of education serving as an extension service agency that could help primary and secondary schools and districts in their region apply child and youth development knowledge and skills to all aspects of their work—organization and management, the creation of a school culture that supports development, and the utilization of knowledge about development to structure and guide curricular activities and instruction. This would involve some of their senior faculty in real-world or field work. It would enable their students to work in schools under the supervision of faculty-district teacher collaborations. It would allow students and faculty to provide feedback that would, in turn, enable the university to modify their preservice programs to better prepare future educators to work in the real world, to better support student development and learning.

Such an arrangement would also enable the arts and sciences, physical education, liberal arts, medicine, and other schools and departments within a university to work with local schools and districts in a planned and coordinated way. This approach, along with many other adjustments in how support services are provided to schools, could begin to address the problems of fragmentation, duplication, inefficiency, ineffectiveness, and waste involved in the underplanned, uncoordinated, poorly integrated way that services are now often provided.

It would also allow relationships to be established that would enable people and products, and other resources from outside a particular school, to be delivered in a more personal and emotionally meaningful way. Recall the pizza store owner's relationship to the school I discussed in chapter 2. He was a meaningful part of the school's and the students' community. As such he and others were in a position to interact with and motivate the students in a deeper, more meaningful way. Without these emotional ties, professional and nonprofessional school helpers provide services that sometimes look good but are quite superficial and not very useful. I will discuss this again below when we consider how schools can and must work with community organizations.

Our SDP program has had alliances with about ten schools of education. As described previously, units headed by senior staff from these schools have helped districts implement SDP without our Yale team's presence on an ongoing basis. All the dissemination arrangements—youth service, education departments, school district units—have had numerous successes, but because schools of education can prepare large numbers of future teachers and administrators, they have the highest potential for promoting large-scale change. On the other hand, the collaboration with Youth Guidance, which had impressive outcomes using social workers, underscores the need to prepare professional support staff in a way that they can help other professionals create school cultures that help staff and parents function well and help students grow.

Our experience with the partnerships between Eastern Michigan University and Detroit, C. W. Post University and

Westbury, New York, and Drury University and Springfield, Missouri, suggests that full-blown model education extension agencies could be developed. In all three of these instances child and adolescent development-focused changes have taken place in university-based preservice curricula and teaching, in the in-service internships of students under senior faculty supervision, and in in-service support of their school district partners.

At Drury, in particular, other departments have served the school district through collaborations with the school of education. All our university partners have made some internal changes. A master's program based on the SDP was created at the University of Illinois, Chicago. A free master's program for teachers working in schools using the SDP was created at Drury. It attracted new teachers, improved retention, and improved teaching and achievement outcomes. This incentive suggests a way to promote a focus on child and youth development.

In addition to the agency component that I have described, our EES mini-model included a provision for an *interdisciplinary council* at the Yale Child Study Center, a *summer policy institute,* and an instructional program that evolved from our original Social Skills Curriculum Program and deepened our effort to integrate development and instruction. This is the Comer in the Classroom approach that I described previously (see chapter 10). Our intent is to create *a school curriculum that integrates developmental and academic teaching and learning from pre-K to maturity, perhaps through college.*

The purpose of the interdisciplinary council component is to expand the knowledge base of education by involving basic and clinical researchers with practitioners in mutually beneficial ways. Our colleagues at the Yale Child Study Center represent the mix we had in mind—geneticists, neurochemists, epidemiologists, others. We are particularly interested in the implications of modern brain research for teaching and learning. Indeed, one of the reasons that education is often a second-class citizen in the academy, and a football in the political arena, is that it is not strongly rooted in its natural basic science—child development. I suspect that if this were the case, most of what I have discussed in this book would already be widespread education practice.

The absence of basic science anchoring and of arts and science connections contributes to the charge that educators are intellectually narrow, or worse. It is a bum rap. The tiny bit of research I have seen does not support this claim. But if there is a problem, I suspect that we will do more to broaden the interests and perspectives of educators by bringing these university-based disciplines into education than by sending future educators into classrooms to hear lectures devoid of real-world school context and knowledge application, courses that will be too superficial to provide the disciplinary components that make the knowledge useful in practice. This is more possible where a part of a school of education is serving as a component of an EES.

We realized early in our work that, like most educators, policy makers, business and opinion leaders, and the general public know very little about child development, its relevance to school learning, or how to promote it. This has serious negative consequences for education. The intent of our EES-like summer institute was to create an opportunity for policy-makers and practitioners to talk to each other, to promote mutual understanding and improved relationships. An experience I had at EMU suggests both interest and possibilities.

The chair of the Education Leadership Department arranged for me to address school board members in a small, rural county of Michigan. During the discussion, and as a response to my appeal for attention to child development, a board member stood, agreed with the need, and suggested to the chair that the university create a child development-related course for school board members. That is exactly what the agricultural agents did one hundred years ago to help overcome the inertia and resistance to improvements in farming.

We have held three summer institutes, one in New York City and two in Washington, D.C. The second included a session on Capitol Hill sponsored by Congresswoman Sheila Jackson Lee, then the chairperson of the Children's Caucus in the House of Representatives. In the two years about twenty members of Congress have shared their perspectives with us. Participants have heard from representatives of parents; students; teacher and administrator unions; boards of education; businesses; foundations; and local, state, and federal policymakers.

Dr. Valerie Maholmes provided leadership for this work and is currently doing an assessment of the effectiveness during the 2003–2004 academic year. Our early reflections on our EES-like work suggest that it can be an effective way to address the several critical obstacles blocking large-scale school improvement, and it supports our notion that schools of education should provide the central ingredient—the education agency.

Again, why schools of education? Willie Sutton robbed banks because "that's where the money is." Schools of education must play the key role in an EES approach because most of the nation's three million teachers and administrators, and many of the professional support people that make up the only reasonably reliable resource we have to continue the development of students, passed through them, and will continue to do so. Also, they are connected to other child knowledge bases, with private and public oversight arrangements, in a way that other preparatory programs are not. These connections and conditions are particularly important at a time when biotechnological discoveries about the brain and mind, with implications for teaching and learning, are rapidly taking place.

Our EES mini-model is not grandiosity, I hope. Successful ideas hatched and incubated in mini-models have a chance of growing to the point that they inform large-scale change.

Most schools of education will need to make significant adjustments in order to be effective as education agencies; indeed, simply to be effective schools of education. Over the past fifteen years or so there has been much good thinking among educators about how to improve curriculum, instruction, and assessment, including the use of *technology in the service of these activities*. I emphasize this point because too often technology is put forth, by educators and politicians alike, as the magic button or sign of enlightenment that will save education rather than as a facilitation tool, which it really is.

There has been much, much less thought about child and youth development beyond developmentally appropriate teaching. The thinking that has been done is usually limited to interactions between teacher and child, sometimes about interactions with other children and behaviors in the classroom. Very rarely does it extend to how every aspect of school functioning can be used to promote child and youth development. Instructional communities and communities that promote development and learning are not the same thing. The latter is more likely to help many more students to enjoy an experience in school that will enable them to meet their adult tasks and responsibilities.

A brief review of the changes and the challenges in the nature of community and society, and the lack of change in the needs of children and youth for support of their development, should be helpful here. The support for development once naturally embedded in less complex communities, and the safety valve of earning a living without a good education, have been greatly diminished. None of our institutions have created systems of support that will adequately meet this basic and irrepressible need of the young.

Our Yale Child Study Center team approached these challenges by asking what is it that children and youth are "brain wired" to do and what conditions will lead to constructive outcomes. In chapter 3 I pointed out that children are born exploring their environment in the service of survival. While learning is rooted in this powerful, basic human need and impulse, academic learning is not. Academic learning can, however, become an important tool for survival, for successfully addressing life's tasks, and for finding meaning and purpose in life. This occurs best when caretakers and institutions respect and facilitate the child's need and impulse to grow or develop along all the pathways that contribute to successful functioning in the world—physical, social-interactive, psychological-emotional, ethical, linguistic, and cognitive-interactive.

Our education system focuses first on instruction, with or without adequate development. I have heard school people say they wished that the students were as enthusiastic about their studies as they are about their time with their friends, their fads, their appearances, and more. That enthusiasm stems from the fact that they are engaged in growth activities that are the essence of being human. They are in the process of growing up and away from dependency and vulnerability. And just as most, with the help of caretakers, begin to manage their bodies and their environment reasonably well, their bodies and often their environment begin to change rapidly, and they need to modify their relationship with their families to continue to grow. Making it in the world is more clearly becoming their responsibility. These are anxiety-provoking, threatening situations.

As they use their not-yet-well-socialized and channeled aggressive or survival energy to deal with all of this, a great deal of confusion, uncertainty, noise, anger, sometimes fights, frustration, disappointment, and the like take place. This is often mixed with joy, exuberance, a desire to challenge and to be challenged. All of this is grist for the academic learning mill, but we treat it as a bother. By doing so we forfeit our opportunity to establish pupil-staff-parent relationships that will enable school people and parents to become meaningful in positive ways because we help them *grow and learn* rather than force them to *learn without adequate growth*. When school staffs understand the struggle to grow that is going on with students, and the power and potential this represents, they can tap into this ferment to make academic learning meaningful and exciting.

This was the focus of the Social Skills Curriculum. The prime developmental impulse of elementary school age children is to work and achieve things, to be like adults around them.[1] The content and methods of this project were consistent with adult life participation, including the consideration and practice of appropriate behaviors, self and situation management skills, rights, responsibilities, and much more. The staff, the parents, and the students together provided the engine that pulled the curriculum, instruction, and learning. This approach often brought the community into the school and took the school into the community; it engaged all in the support of growth along important developmental pathways. In traditional schools curriculum and instruction are expected to pull the students along.

As important as academic learning is, it must be remembered that it is a tool and an aspect of development. It is important to remember that development is the primary need and the precursor, when not the prerequisite, for academic learning. In the case of many children who have inadequate preparatory experiences, academic instruction is like trying to hang out clothes to dry without a clothesline or clothes pins. A teacher friend added "on a windy day" to this analogy. There is too little overall development to utilize the information being poured in; perhaps "laid on" makes the point better here. The healthy child will turn away, withdraw, or act out rather than fail.

Throughout this book I have mentioned good education practice in highly successful schools serving marginalized students who were not expected to achieve at a high level. On several occasions teachers mentioned successes with individual children because they were using SDP, or development-oriented, principles (1) in particular activities, for example, the Essentials of Literacy teacher-student discussion about best choices; (2) in the management of classes as described in Comer in the Classroom (see chapter 10); and (3) in the management of the school. In short, the effects of a developmental perspective on behavior and learning are influenced at several levels, and they are cumulative. Recall that student academic success often followed staff helping them manage relationship and performance challenges. And academic, relationship, and behavior problems were often prevented by adequately preparing students to manage challenges in their environment before engaging in activities that would promote excessive threat.

Students are most open to help with their growth when there is a reasonable degree of continuity of relationships with key and caring caretakers. They need reasonably safe places where they can express themselves, where they can engage in activities that begin to help them figure out who they are, what skills they have, where they want to go, what it takes on their part to get there, how to begin to take responsibility for themselves, and generally, what it takes to be a good human being, liked and respected by others. The school, like the home, is a venue in which young people attend to their primary challenge—developing in these ways and growing up and away from dependency and vulnerability. I want to make this point again and finally: students who are developing well will learn well. I acknowledge differences in aptitude, potential, talents, traits, and more. But the task of public and private education systems is to promote optimal growth and preparation for adult life among all. This requires adequate support for development of all.

The case I have made here suggests that all teachers, administrators, and professional support staff should be prepared, both in preservice and in-service, to create a school context, community, or culture that enables them to explore student development and use it to make academic work meaningful and useful to students in promoting their own full development. The obvious implication here is that schools of education must prepare their students to help support development at the several levels and points of influence in and out of school. The less obvious implication is the need to change a deep-seated education culture obstacle.

Education reformers often look to medicine and law for models that will guide improvement in their own professional practice. Because making a diagnosis is often difficult, and there is variance in the response to treatment, a culture of consultation emerged in medicine. As a physician and an outsider, I have always been struck by the absence of a culture of consultation in education. In most schools there is no time built in for colleagues to plan, to reflect on their practice and its outcomes with each other, to share insights and understandings. Indeed, the individual teacher is supposed to have a knowledge base that is applicable to all students, all the time. But students are not inanimate objects. Each is different in the way they think, learn, and behave.

Actually, teaching is more like psychotherapy. The relationship with the teacher, like that with the therapist, is a part of "the treatment." The cause of "dis-ease" often stems from dysfunctions that are more amorphous than those in the more biology-based medicine, the treatments are less definitive, and the outcomes are less easily observed and measured than with largely biology-based problems. Trying to understand the challenge facing students and how to address it is at least as difficult as making a diagnosis in medicine. Good teaching, like good child rearing, requires an ongoing action research approach, with professional colleagues sharing and learning how to best meet student needs.

Indeed, this is the best model for student learning. Shared thinking, problem assessment; thinking about how children think; thinking about how to help them think about the way they think, how to use thought to explore the world around them, and more, leads to deep understanding and an interest in thinking as a tool for academic learning and for general learning and expression. A school staff working in this way provides a useful model for student thinking and growth.

Teachers, for the most part, are isolated practitioners. Recall the joy of the "Teachers Helping Teachers" group because this approach enabled the staff to examine their practice, something all professionals should do. Many schools of education do not prepare students to work in this way. A veteran teacher who recently participated in our SDP 102 training session, a year after she attended 101, asked, "Where is Dr. Comer? I don't even know the man, but I want to give him a big hug! This is what we should have learned in college!" She did, and she's right. *All the money we spend on research, training, equipment, instructional programs, and the like will give us too small a return on our investment until we help the adults working together in a building learn to create a culture in which they can collaborate with each other in a way that will support the development of students.*

For students, their family life, kin, network of friends, organizations to which they feel a sense of belonging, and community-based health, recreation, housing, and other services impact their ability to develop and learn just as much, if not more so, as what they learn in the classroom. The effects of these experiences outside the classroom are cumulative, as are what happens in school. In chapter 11, in particular, I discussed how we are not getting the "bang for the buck" that we should from these services because they are fragmented, do not promote a continuity of relationships, and, very important, particularly in health, housing, and welfare services, are often impersonal and demeaning rather than supportive of good family functioning and child and youth development.

It is not possible to save every child or to fix every ill in the world. People must help themselves and not count on government or philanthropy to do so. And most people want to help themselves to the extent possible. Our sense of adequacy depends on it. The problem is that services that were once available from emotionally meaningful people in most primary social networks now reside in the more impersonal secondary social networks of schools, workplace, health care provider locations, and other places. Too often there are barriers between those in need of service and the providers. Not enough attention has been given to how people can access these services in ways that are not demeaning.

For many, simply needing help is demeaning, and the status, attitude, and behavior of the helper is often perceived as a part of the problem until the helper-client interaction proves otherwise. Powerful issues, such as positive identity, self-respect, self-confidence, fear of failure, a sense of adequacy, trust, and much more, are at play when a human being, groups, or nations seek to help one another, particularly when social marginalization, past dominance, or exclusion has been a factor. It is human nature. What does the two-year-old say? I'll do it myself! Affected by the same concerns, leaders in third-world or underdeveloped countries have sometimes wanted to place outside helpers in their best-functioning communities rather than in those with the greatest need. A black student was performing at a very low level on a test given by a white psychologist until they took a break. During the break he observed his tester's black colleague warmly embrace her, and his performance improved dramatically when the testing resumed. A black physician working to help dysfunctional families was challenged by one participant who said, "What right do you have to tell me how to live?" Many years ago the three Comer brothers, all college students, tried to encourage a relative still in high school who had demonstrated outstanding academic ability but had no family support and was drifting toward trouble. While he didn't say what was said to the doctor, on reflection his nonverbal behavior and demeanor conveyed the same message.

But a continued lack of success on the part of the two-year-old, and anybody else, can lead to defeat, hopelessness, dependency, and worse. Because many young people will not have a chance to experience reasonable success without adequate supportive relationships and services, we must give great attention to how we can provide them in an empowering way.

What enables the two-year-old to accept help when the task is too great? It is a relationship in which the caretaker demonstrates genuine respect and commitment to full growth and opportunity for the child. A similar relationship is needed when working with underdeveloped or marginalized individuals or groups of all ages. Help must be provided—beginning in the home, continued through school, into the community and the larger society—in a way that promotes a level of self-respect and confidence that can lead to successful independent and responsible interdependent mainstream functioning.

The school can collaborate with community services to provide continuous, integrated, personalized support for development in a way that no other service provider standing alone really can. It is the social organization best positioned to link home and community in a reasonably harmonious fashion and simultaneously serve its own interest—help students develop and learn in a way that serves individual interests and protects democracy. When the school can "connect," the school is family. Recall the youngster who ran away after an incident with his mother and was found by his teacher in the cold, in the dark, huddled against his closed school house door.

Another example of the kind of relationships that are helpful is provided by Joy Dryfoos, who described a school-based health clinic founded by Aaron Shirley, a local physician and civil rights activist in Jackson, Mississippi, in her book *Full Service Schools:* "Aaron Shirley and his staff knew the name of every baby in the child-care center. They demonstrated a strong commitment to pregnancy prevention with individual follow-up of every sexually active student who obtained contraceptives from the school clinic."[2]

This school health clinic is a good example of the way services once based in communities and with no relation to schools can be integrated or fused with the work of the schools in support of the overall development of children. The positive attitude and disposition of the providers makes the services respectful, and therefore potentially growth-producing. The services—whether health, the arts, athletics, job preparation, preparation for participation in government, indeed, for all aspects of life—can be integrated into the curriculum and instruction activities of schools. The service providers are also additional teaching resources. In short, the essential elements of community that existed in a natural way before the effects of the application of science and technology to all aspects of life can be systematically restored through well-integrated community-based programs in schools.

Our Social Skills Curriculum in the 1970s and 1980s demonstrated that this approach can enliven schools and improve performance among parents, schools, and students across race, income, education, and other differences that could be barriers. Schools working with community services, with supportive dispositions, can promote behaviors and skills needed for mainstream participation, needed to prepare young people to protect and promote democracy as adults. The ill effects of marginalization reflected in the troublesome behaviors I described in chapter 11 can be reduced.

Some municipalities are trying to put in place similar relationship sensitive, yet powerful, supports and services. Mayors in particular, but also other community leaders, recognize that they must try to bring together human services in a way that will promote inclusion, that will support desirable family functioning and a quality of child rearing that prepares children to elicit the support they need for school success and responsible adult functioning rather than continue marginality. The challenge is to find a positive way to seamlessly integrate the available inside and outside resources to help school and other service provider staffs overcome negative outside-of-school effects when necessary, to help all students develop adequately.

The mayors are on the front line. The high cost of poor education hurts them first and most. I suspect they are going to be the greatest force for realistic problem solving; that is the way it is supposed to work in a democracy. An initiative undertaken in 2001 by the Institute of Youth, Education, and Families of the National League of Cities (NLC), supported by a grant from the Carnegie Corporation of New York, is a model of the kind of structures and relationships that can be useful. The NLC, the 49 state municipal leagues it works with, and the elected leaders of the 1,700 member cities and 18,000 state league cities have the potential of getting the nation to focus on how family and child functioning can shape our national future.

Five cities received a Municipal Leadership in Education grant to bring together community leaders to find ways to work toward providing quality public education. New Haven, Connecticut, was one of the cities selected, along with Charleston, South Carolina; Fort Lauderdale, Florida; Lansing, Michigan; and Portland Oregon. I serve on the New Haven committee. The committee is cochaired by Eleanor Osborne, the assistant superintendent of schools for curriculum/instruction, and Sheila Allen Bell, community services administrator for the city of New Haven.

The mayor, John DeStefano, Jr., who gave us the charge

has retained a keen interest in this project. He has since become the president of the National League of Cities.[3] When I first met him a decade ago he talked about the need to provide better child care, early childhood development, and youth development programs as a way to improve education and to prevent problem behaviors. I was impressed because there were not many public officials who had made that connection, and if they had, they were not talking about it.

About twenty-five people serve on the New Haven committee. They represent almost every segment of the community: parents, teacher union, faith community, business, community college, teachers college, alderman, police, public library, and others. After reviewing the school district's mission and current effort and the resources in the community, we agreed that there was a need to find a way to integrate community services and resources with the school program in a way that would make the help available in a coordinated, emotionally meaningful, and seamless way, and make it continuously available where possible. Otherwise, the go-and-stop help and helpers, mentioned in the previous chapter, can be a part of the problem.

This project dovetailed nicely with the New Haven school district's Accountability Plan. Dr. Reginald Mayo, the superintendent, and I had cochaired the committee that developed the plan over a two-year period. One of our conclusions was that everybody is responsible for the education of a community's children, and we recommended activities and goals for in-school and out-of-school groups. We also asked for measures of success that included, but went beyond, test scores. *We hope to measure behaviors and performances that are more directly related to school and adult success, to encourage instructional activities that are true precursors of life success.*

The New York City Department of Education, Office of Youth Development and School-Community Services, headed by senior executive Lester Young, Jr., has put together a project entitled Youth Placed at Promise Network. The initiative is in collaboration with the Harlem's Children Zone, Bedford-Stuyvesant Restoration Corporation (BSRC), and the Partnership for After School Education.

Importantly, BSRC, well known for its housing and physical community development over the past thirty years, has made a commitment to people development as the way to revitalize communities. While attention must be given to both, as a nation, we have had a "bricks and mortar" mentality. *The higher level of development needed today requires that we also acquire a people development mentality, that we put in place an infrastructure that makes good child and youth development and learning possible on a large scale.* What is most promising about this project is that dedicated, highly skilled people deeply embedded in the life of the communities involved want to make it happen. The schools and the community-based organizations *will have a positive relationship status* with nonmainstream families, which should enable them to address sensitive child-rearing issues related to child development and academic learning.

The target communities are Central Harlem in Manhattan and Bedford-Stuyvesant in Brooklyn, communities where 75 and 66 percent of the children, respectively, are born into poverty or marginalized conditions relative to the political, economic, and social mainstream. With children in school at the center of the design, appropriate academic, social, human, and medical services are to be delivered in a way that promotes improved student development, learning, and preparation for successful adult life. The School Development Program framework will help guide the thinking, structuring, and processes involved in implementing this work. An effort will be made, through training and field supports, to promote good developmental practices through seamless home-, school-, and community-based organizations and agency activities. Federal, state, and local government and foundation, public and private financial support is now involved, and collaboration with other community organizations will be sought as the project evolves. The goal is to give these young people an opportunity to experience the American dream like most other Americans.

These fragile efforts are being launched in a swirling, changing tide of political, economic, and social issues. Similar projects that attempted to promote improved social environments have come and gone. And these may not get off the ground. The effort to focus very directly on child and adult development in these projects probably makes them even more vulnerable. Critics call such efforts "soft and fuzzy"; charge that the effects cannot be measured; and some question whether people development is a proper role of government, or the appropriate use of taxpayer money.

The critics have a linear and sequential causality conceptual mind-set that does not adequately take the interactivity of individuals with their environments or the interactivity of institutions in the environment into account; does not take feelings and emotions and their relation to development and performance into account. As to the proper role of government, Adam Smith, widely considered the founder of modern economics, suggested three. The third is relevant here: first, to protect from outside military attack; second, protecting every member of the society from the injustice or oppression of every other member; third, erecting and maintaining public works and institutions that are advantageous to a great society but are not profitable to any individual or small number of individuals.[4] A high level of people development and education, particularly of the lower-income working class and poor, is not profitable when done fairly and appropriately, and a great society cannot exist without these conditions.

On the other hand, the concerns expressed about such interventions are not without some merit. Social interventions often proceed without a clear theory of change, without appropriate assessment efforts, without mechanisms for change or methods to sustain desirable outcomes. This is what contributes to a "fuzzy," directionless, start-and-stop sense about many such programs. An Education Extension Service—with development, learning, and preparation of students for adult life as a central focus—could provide the kind of framework and infrastructure needed, first, to bring school and community together in a strong collaborative and cohesive way, and then, to guide, support, monitor and study, and modify as indicated, individual and social environment change efforts. This would give such programs a focused sense of purpose and direction and make them more efficient, effective, and cost-effective; thus more sustainable.

Policy makers often talk about creating large-scale change programs based on successful project models. But even with a strong focus on promoting development, what works in one place with a particular group of people may not work in the next. What is needed is a framework like an EES that systematically generates knowledge and transmits best practice principles to designated groups but allows participants in particular places to modify practices when justified to meet particular local needs. Without an EES-like framework that makes development possible in many ways and in many places simultaneously, in little boutiques of effort, such as our SDP, we will keep discovering what we already know, what my unlettered mother knew years ago: children perform well when caretakers provide them with a good experience.

The human service departments most involved in people development—social work, clinical psychology, nursing, and others—already exist in many schools of education or in their universities. As mentioned previously, the arts and sciences can strengthen the knowledge base of existing and preservice educators and human service providers. Research programs at colleges and universities can give focused attention to more appropriate ways of understanding the effects of individual and institutional interactivity and feelings on social environment or context, and on individual and group behavior and performance. This will require public health, human ecology, and clinical perspectives and methods similar to what we used to bring about school culture or context changes in our School Development Program.

People development leads to the kind of social and political action needed to promote investment in personnel and appropriate training, to bring about a fair system of funding public education. Again, the needs of children performing well, desirous of a fair chance, and backed by increasingly powerful forces cannot be ignored indefinitely. Most Americans want to provide all children with a fair chance, but not by adding to their already strained budgets.

An Education Extension Service approach, combined with school- and community-based and agency alliances, and with political action, constitutes the kind of change strategy that could make a great positive difference—reduce the forces of resistance; create a present and future education workforce capable of using proven approaches to connect with families and community-based organizations in a way that enables them to collectively support the development and learning of all students; and promote fair and coherent education policy. This would give many more students an opportunity to experience the American dream, to have the stake in it needed to make it worth protecting, and to reduce the high cost of preventable problem behaviors. Although much of our SDP work has been in low-income and minority communities, some of it has been in middle-income communities; the difference in needs is only a matter of degree and time.

Great teams fail to win the play-off game when they abandon the strategies that got them there. Today America is a better democracy and a superpower in large part because of policies and practices that enabled an ever-increasing number of people to benefit from the rule of law and reasonable access to the economic and educational conditions that made personal, family, and community well-being possible. Great civilizations can begin to decline when they stop doing what got them there. We can and must preserve desired conditions for most, and we must provide opportunity for the children and families left behind. We will leave no child behind when we close the gap between the support for development and learning that today's children need to perform well in today's and tomorrow's world and what they are actually receiving.

Notes

Chapter One. Right Church, Wrong Pew

1. For further discussion on the topic, see John D. Bransford, Ann L. Brown, and Rodney R. Cocking, eds., *How People Learn: Brain, Mind, Experience, and School* (Washington D.C.: National Academy Press, 2002); Robert J. Sternberg, "The Concept of Intelligence and Its Role in Lifelong Learning and Success," *American Psychologist* 52:10 (October 1997): 1030–37; Howard Gardner, *Multiple Intelligences: The Theory in Practice* (New York: Basic Books, 1993); and Committee on Integrating the Science of Early Childhood Development, Board on Children, Youth, and Families of the National Research Council and Institute of Medicine, *Neurons to Neighborhoods: The Science of Early Childhood Development*, ed. Jack P. Shonkoff and Deborah Phillips (Washington, D.C.: National Academies Press, 2000).

2. For further discussion on the topic, see Linda Darling-Hammond, *The Right to Learn: A Blueprint for Creating Schools That Work* (San Francisco: Jossey-Bass, 1997); Chip Wood, *Yardsticks: Children in the Classroom Ages 4–14* (Greenfield, Mass.: Northeast Foundation for Children, 1997).

3. For further discussion on the topic, see James P. Comer, Edward T. Joyner, and Michael Ben-Avie, eds., *The Field Guide to Comer Schools in Action: When Children Develop Well, They Learn Well* (Thousand Oaks, Calif.: Corwin Press, 2004).

4. For further discussion on the topic, see James P. Connell and the Institute for Research and Reform in Education, "First Things First: A Frame-

work of Successful School Reform," *A White Paper Prepared for the Ewing Marion Kauffman Foundation* (rev. January 2003).

5. For further discussion on the topic, see Lorrie A. Shepard, "The Role of Classroom Assessment in Teaching and Learning," *Center for the Study of Evaluation,* Report 517 (February 2000).

6. For further discussion on the topic, see David C. Berliner, "Averages That Hide the True Extremes," *Washington Post,* Outlook Section (January 28, 2001); David C. Berliner and Bruce J. Biddle, *The Manufactured Crisis: Myths, Fraud, and the Attack on America's Public Schools* (New York: Addison-Wesley, 1995); and Edmund W. Gordon, *Education and Justice: A View from the Back of the Bus* (New York: Teachers College Press, 1999).

7. For further discussion on the topic, see Eric Schaps, "Creating a School Community," *Educational Leadership* 60:6 (March 2003): 31–33.

8. For further discussion on the topic, see Maurice J. Elias and Robert P. Weissberg, "Primary Prevention: Education Approaches to Enhance Social and Emotional Learning," *Journal of School Health* 70:5 (May 2000): 186–90.

9. For further discussion on the topic, see Geoffrey Canada, *Fist Stick Knife Gun: A Personal History of Violence in America* (Boston: Beacon Press, 1996).

10. For further discussion on the topic, see James A. Banks and Cherry A. McGee Banks, eds., *Handbook of Research on Multicultural Education* (San Francisco: Jossey-Bass, 2001); Committee on Increasing High School Students' Engagement and Motivation to Learn, National Research Council and Institute of Medicine of the National Academies, *Engaging Schools: Fostering High School Students' Motivation to Learn* (Washington, D.C.: National Academies Press, 2004); and James P. Comer, "Black Children and Child Psychiatry," *Journal of American Academy of Child and Adolescent Psychiatry* 24:2 (March 1985): 129–33.

11. For further discussion on the topic, see Lee S. Shulman and Pat Hutchings, "The Scholarship of Teaching: New Elaborations, New Developments," *Change* 31:5 (September/October 1999): 10–15; Darling-Hammond, *Right to Learn;* Mariale M. Hardiman, *Connecting Brain Research with Effective Teaching: The Brain-Targeted Teaching Model* (Lanham, Md.: Scarecrow Press, 2003); Jane M. Healy, *Your Child's Growing Mind: Brain Development and Learning from Birth to Adolescence* (New York: Broadway Books, 2004); and Eric Jenson, *Teaching with the Brain in Mind* (Alexandria, Va.: Association for Supervision and Curriculum Development, 1998).

12. Geoffrey D. Borman, Gina M. Hewes, Laura T. Overman, and Shelly Brown, "Comprehensive School Reform and Student Achievement: A Meta-Analysis," Center for Research on the Education of Students Placed

at Risk (CRESPAR), 59, November 2002 (retrieved from http://www.csos .jhu.edu).

13. For further discussion on the topic, see Abt Associates Inc., *Evaluation of Detroit's Comer Schools and Families Initiative* (April 17, 2000); George W. Noblit, William W. Malloy, and Carol E. Malloy, *The Kids Got Smarter: Case Studies of Successful Comer Schools* (Cresskill, N.J.: Hampton Press, 2001).

Chapter Three. Change and Challenges

1. For further discussion on the topic, see James P. Comer, *Maggie's American Dream: The Life and Times of a Black Family* (New York: New American Library, 1988); James P. Comer and Alvin F. Poussaint, *Raising Black Children* (New York: Plume, 1992).

2. For further discussion on the topic, see Claude M. Steele, "Thin Ice: 'Stereotype Threat' and Black College Students," *Atlantic Monthly* (August 1999) (retrieved from http://www.theatlantic.com/issues/99aug/9908stereotype).

3. For further discussion on the topic, see Carol D. Lee, Margaret Beale Spencer, and Vinay Harpalani, "'Every Shut Eye Ain't Sleep': Studying How People Live Culturally," *Educational Researcher* 32:5 (June/July 2003): 6–13.

4. Betty Hart and Todd R. Risley, "The Early Catastrophe: The 30 Million Word Gap by Age 3," *American Educator* (spring 2003): 8.

5. For further discussion on the topic, see James P. Comer, "The Social Power of the Negro," *Scientific American* 216:4 (April 1967): 21–24.

6. Frank Hobbs and Nicole Stoops, "Demographic Trends in the Twentieth Century," *Census 2000 Special Report* (PDF, p. 32; retrieved from http://www.census.gov/prod/2002pubs/censr-4.pdf).

Chapter Four. The New World

1. For further discussion on the topic, see William Julius Wilson, *When Work Disappears* (New York: Random House, 1997).

2. For further discussion on the topic, see Commission on Children at Risk, *Hardwired to Connect: The New Scientific Case for Authoritative Communities* (New York: Institute for American Values, 2003).

3. For further discussion on the topic, see James P. Comer, *Waiting for a Miracle: Why Schools Can't Solve Our Problems and How We Can* (New York: Plume, 1998).

4. U.S. Bureau of the Census, "Married Couples by Labor Force Status of Spouses: 1986 to Present," 2001 (retrieved from http://www.census.gov/population/socdemo/hh-fam/tabMC-1.txt); U.S. Bureau of the Census, "Historical Living Arrangements of Children," 2001 (retrieved from http://www.census.gov/population/www/socdemo/hh-fam.html).

Chapter Five. Living In and Learning About Schools

1. For further discussion on the topic, see James P. Comer, *School Power: Implications of an Intervention Project* (New York: Free Press, 1993).

Chapter Six. The Framework

1. For further discussion on the topic, see James P. Comer, *School Power: Implications of an Intervention Project* (New York: Free Press, 1980).

2. For further discussion on the topic, see National Commission on Teaching and America's Future, *No Dream Denied: A Pledge to America's Children* (January 2003).

3. For further discussion on the topic, see James P. Comer, "Educating Poor Minority Children," *Scientific American* 256:11 (November 1988): 42–48.

4. For further work by Edward T. Joyner, see Edward T. Joyner, "Large Scale Change: The School Development Program Perspective," *International Handbook of School Change, Part Two,* ed. A. Hargreaves, A. Lieberman, M. Fullan, and D. Hopkins (Boston: Kluwer Academic Publishers, 1998).

Chapter Seven. Development, Learning, and Democracy

1. For further discussion on the topic, see Marvin W. Berkowitz, "The Education of the Complete Moral Person" (retrieved from http://tigger.uic.edu/~lnucci/MoralEd/aotm/article3.html).

2. Paul Leicester Ford, ed., *The Writings of Thomas Jefferson,* 10 vols. (New York: G. P. Putnam's Sons, 1892–99), 4:480, 10:99.

3. For further discussion on the topic, see John I. Goodlad, "Common Schools for the Common Weal: Reconciling Self-Interest with the Common Good," *Access to Knowledge: An Agenda for Our Nation's Schools* (New York: College Entrance Exam Board, 1990), 1–22; John I. Goodlad, *A Place Called School: Prospects for the Future* (New York: McGraw-Hill, 1984); and Deborah Meier, "So What Does It Take to Build a School for Democracy?" *Phi Delta Kappan* 85:1 (September 2003): 15–21.

4. For further discussion on the topic, see James P. Comer, Edward F. Zigler, and Barbara M. Stern, "Supporting Today's Families in the Elementary School: The CoZi Initiative," *Reaching Today's Youth* 1:3 (spring 1997): 37–43.

5. For further discussion on the topic, see James S. Coleman, *Equality and Achievement in Education* (Boulder, Colo.: Westview Press, 1990).

6. For further discussion on the topic, see James P. Comer, Edward T. Joyner, and Michael Ben-Aie, eds., *The Field Guide to Comer Schools in Action: When Children Develop Well, They Learn Well* (Thousand Oaks, Calif.: Corwin Press, 2004).

Chapter Eight. But Can It Fly?

1. For further discussion on the topic, see Ana M. Cauce, James P. Comer, and D. Schwartz, "Long-Term Effects of a Systems-Oriented School Prevention Project," *American Journal of Orthopsychiatry* 57 (January 1987): 127–31.

2. For further discussion on the topic, see Thomas D. Cook and Robert F. Murphy, "Comer's School Development Program in Chicago: A Theory-Based Evaluation," *American Educational Research Journal* 37:2 (summer 2000): 589.

3. For further discussion on the topic, see James P. Comer and Norris M. Haynes, "The Dynamics of School Change: Response to the Article, 'Comer's School Development Program in Prince George's County, Maryland: A Theory-Based Evaluation,' by Thomas D. Cook et al.," *American Educational Research Journal* 36:3 (fall 1999): 599–607.

4. "Andragogy Is the Art and Science of Helping Adults Learn." Malcolm S. Knowles, *The Modern Practice of Adult Education: Andragogy versus Pedagogy* (New York: Association, 1970).

Chapter Nine. Flight School

1. The panel included Bob Kranyik, the dean of the University of Bridgeport School of Education; Frank Smith, the chairperson of the Department of Education Leadership at Teachers College Columbia; Jack Gillette, an expert in organization leadership; Patrick Howley, a teacher training specialist and former counselor; Norris Haynes, our director of research; and James Boger, a member of our implementation team.

2. For further work by Valerie Maholmes, see Valerie Maholmes, "What School Is All About," *Education Week* (October 23, 2002).

3. For further work by Edward T. Murray, see Fay E. Brown, Valerie Maholmes, Edward T. Murray, and Lola Nathan, "Davis Street Magnet School: Linking Child Development with Literacy," *Journal of Education for Students Placed at Risk* 3:1 (1998): 23–38.

4. For further work by Fay E. Brown, see Fay E. Brown and Darren W. Woodruff, "Getting the Most from Students: Effort and the Student-Teacher Relationship," in *Child by Child: The Comer Process for Change in Education,* ed. James P. Comer, Michael Ben-Avie, Norris M. Haynes, and Edward T. Joyner (New York: Teachers College Press, 1999).

Chapter Ten. Flight

1. Thomas D. Cook and Robert F. Murphy, "Comer's School Development Program in Chicago: A Theory-Based Evaluation," *American Educational Research Journal* 37:2 (summer 2000): 589.

2. For further work by Christine L. Emmons, see Christine L. Emmons, James P. Comer, and Norris M. Haynes, "Translating Theory into Practice: Comer's Theory of School Reform," in *Rallying The Whole Village: The Comer Process for Reforming Education,* ed. James P. Comer, Norris M. Haynes, Edward T. Joyner, and Michael Ben-Avie (New York: Teachers College Press, 1996).

Chapter Eleven. The Price We Pay

1. Paul Leicester Ford, ed., *The Writings of Thomas Jefferson,* 10 vols. (New York: G. P. Putnam's Sons, 1892–99), 4:480, 10:99.

2. Peter Coy, "Less Chance to Rise in Life," *Business Week* 3808 (November 18, 2002): 28.

3. U.S. Department of Labor, Office of Policy Planning and Research, "The Negro Family: The Case for National Action" (retrieved from http://www.dol.gov/asp/programs/history/webid-meynihan.htm).

4. The Mortenson Research Seminar on Public Policy Analysis of Opportunity for Postsecondary Education, "Private Correlates of Educational Attainment" (PDF, p. 3; retrieved from http://www.postsecondary.org/home/default.asp), 9, 18.

5. Healthy People 2010, "People with Low Income" (retrieved from http://www.healthypeople.gov/Data/PROGRVW/LowIncome/).

6. Catherine E. Ross and Chia-Ling Wu, "Education, Age, and the Cumulative Advantage in Health," *Journal of Health and Social Behavior* 37:1 (March 1996): 104, 110, 113, 117.

7. U.S. Department of Health and Human Services, Office of Applied Studies, "Illicit Drug Use" (retrieved from http://www.samhsa.gov/oas/NHSDA/2kNHSDA/chapter2.htm).

8. Election Nexus, "Turnout Rates for Voting-Age Population and Eligible Population" (retrieved from http://elections.gmu.edu/turnout_rates _graph.htm).

9. Peter Levine and Mark Hugo Lopez, "Youth Voter Turnout Has Declined, by Any Measure" (PDF, p. 9; retrieved from http://www.civicyouth .org/research/products/fact_sheets_outside.htm).

10. Jennifer Mezey, Mark Greenberg, and Rachel Schumacher, "The Vast Majority of Federally Eligible Children Did Not Receive Child Care Assistance in FY 2000" (PDF, p. 2; retrieved from http://www.clasp.org/DMS/ Documents/1024427382.81).

11. National Institute for Early Education Research, "Economic Benefits of Quality Preschool Education to America's 3- and 4-Year Olds" (retrieved from http://nieer.org/resources/facts/index.php).

12. Steven W. Barnett, "Long-Term Effects of Early Childhood Programs on Cognitive and School Outcomes," *Future of Children* 5:3 (winter 1995): 45.

13. National Center for Educational Statistics, "Enrollment in Educational Institutions, by Level and Control of Institution: Fall 1980 to Fall 2005, Table 2" (retrieved from http://nces.ed.gov//pubs2002/digest2001/list_tables .asp); U.S. Census Bureau, "Preprimary School Enrollment—Summary: 1970 to 2000, No. 218" (PDF, p. 144; retrieved from http://www.census.gov/ prod/www/statistical-abstract-02.html).

14. National Center for Education Statistics, "Teachers in Elementary and Secondary Schools, and Senior Instructional Staff in Degree-Granting Institutions, by Control of Institution: Fall 1970 to Fall 2011, Table 4" (retrieved from http://nces.ed.gov//pubs2002/digest2001/list_tables.asp); National Center for Education Statistics, "Total Expenditures for Public Elementary and Secondary Education and Other Related Programs, by State: School Year 1999–2000" (retrieved from http://nces.ed.gov/quicktables/ Detail.asp).

15. Carnegie Council on Adolescent Development, *A Matter of Time: Risk and Opportunity in the Non-School Hours* (New York: Carnegie Corporation of New York, 1992), 11.

16. Public/Private Ventures, "A Matter of Money: The Cost and Financing of Youth Development," in *Youth Development: Issues, Challenges and Directions* (PDF, p. 86; retrieved from http://www.ppv.org/content/ reports/ydv_pdf.html).

17. National Institute on Out-of-School Time, "Making the Case: A Fact Sheet on Children and Youth in Out-of-School Time" (PDF, p. 2; retrieved from http://www.niost.org); For further discussion on the topic, see

Nellie Mae Foundation Out-of-School Initiative at http://www.nmefdn.org/initiatives/outofschooltime/index.htm?i=5.

18. Public/Private Ventures, "Matter of Money."

19. Ibid., 94, 95, 96.

20. Fight Crime: Invest in Kids, "Investments in Children Prevent Crime and Save Money" (retrieved from http://www.fightcrime.org).

21. Coalition for Juvenile Justice, "Out of the School House, Into the Jail House" (retrieved from http://www.juvjustice.org/publications/jjmonitor/0001.html).

22. Institute for Health Policy, Brandeis University, "Substance Abuse: The Nation's Number One Health Problem" (retrieved from http://www.ncadd.org/facts/numberoneprob.html).

23. U.S. Department of Justice, "Prison and Jail Inmates at Midyear 2002" (PDF, p. 1; retrieved from http://www.ojp.usdoj.gov/bjs/abstract/pjim02.htm).

24. Thomas D. Cook and Robert F. Murphy, "Comer's School Development Program in Chicago: A Theory-Based Evaluation," *American Educational Research Journal* 37:2 (summer 2000).

25. Irving B. Harris, *Children in Jeopardy: Can We Break the Cycle of Poverty?* (New Haven: Yale University Press, 1996), 106.

26. Stephen Phillips, "Literacy: A Global Problem—Jail Breakers" (retrieved from http://portal.unesco.org/en/ev.php@URL_ID=10552&URL_DO=DO_TOPIC&URL_SECTION=201.html); U.S. Department of Justice, "Federal Prison System—Cost Per Inmate for Fiscal Years 1975 thru 2003" (PDF, p. 117; retrieved from http://www.usdoj.gov/jmd/budgetsummary/btd/1975_2002/2002/pdf/page117–119.pdf); Jenni Gainsborough and Marc Mauer, "Diminishing Returns: Crime and Incarceration in the 1990s" (PDF, p. 3; retrieved from http://www.sentencingproject.org/pdfs/9039.pdf).

27. Steven E. Hyman, "Fourth Annual Research Roundtable—Opening Remarks on Children and Adolescents" (retrieved from http://www.nimh.nih.gov/research/roundtable.cfm); National Institute for Mental Health, "Child and Adolescent Violence Research at the NIMH" (PDF, p. 2; retrieved from http://www.nimh.nih.gov/publicat/violenceresfact.pdf).

28. RAND Corporation, "Mental Health Care for Youth: Who Gets It? How Much Does It Cost? Who Pays? Where Does the Money Go?" (retrieved from http://www.rand.org/publications/RB/RB4541/).

29. U.S. Census Bureau, "National Health Expenditures—Summary, 1960 to 1999, and Projections, 2000 to 2010" (PDF, p. 91; retrieved from http://www.census.gov/prod/www/statistical-abstract-01.html).

30. Employment Policy Foundation, "Building America's Workforce

for the 21st Century" (PDF, p. 6; retrieved from http://www.epf.org/labor01/index.asp).

31. Lori G. Kletzer, "Measuring the Costs of Trade-Related Job Loss" (retrieved from http://www.iie.com/publications/papers/kletzer0701.htm).

32. Temporary Assistance for Needy Families, "Introduction and Executive Summary," *2002 TANF Annual Report to Congress* (PDF, p. 1; retrieved from http://www.acf.dhhs.gov/programs/opre/ar2001/indexar.htm).

33. Michael Waldo, "Also Victims: Understanding and Treating Men Arrested for Spouse Abuse," *Journal of Counseling and Development* 65 (March 1987): 385; Charles Whitfield, Robert F. Anda, Shanta R. Dube, and Vincent J. Felitti, "Violent Childhood Experiences and the Risk of Intimate Partner Violence in Adults," *Journal of Interpersonal Violence* 18:2 (February 2003): 176.

34. Rachel Jewkes, "Preventing Domestic Violence," *British Medical Journal* 324:7332 (February 2, 2002).

35. American Institute on Domestic Violence, "The Corporate Costs of Domestic Violence" (retrieved from http://www.aidv-usa.com/Statistics.htm).

36. Suzette Fromm, "Total Estimated Cost of Child Abuse and Neglect in the United States" (retrieved from http://www.pcain.org/Services_Programs/cost_analysis.pdf).

37. A. F. Montgomery and R. J. Rossi, "Becoming at Risk of Failure in America's Schools," *Schools and Students at Risk: Context and Framework for Positive Change* (New York: Teachers College Press, 1994), 5, 4.

38. Jennifer Cheeseman Day and Eric C. Newburger, "The Big Payoff: Educational Attainment and Synthetic Estimates of Work-Life Earnings," *Current Population Reports* (PDF, p. 2; retrieved from http://www.census.gov/prod/www/abs/popula.html); ibid., p. 4.

39. Julie Suchanek, "Education Not Incarceration Report" (April 13, 2002): 20, 25, 21. Available from Oregon Student Association, Portland, Ore.

40. *Burlington (Vt.) Free Press,* "Prevention Paying Off" (retrieved from http://www.ahs.state.vt.us/608frpre.htm).

Chapter 12. To Leave No Child Behind

1. For further discussion on the topic, see Theodore R. Sizer, "No Two Are Quite Alike," *Educational Leadership* 57:1 (September 1999): 6–11 (retrieved from http://www.ascd.org/publications/ed_lead/199909/sizer.html); Theodore R. Sizer, *Horace's Hope: What Works for the American High School* (New York: Houghton Mifflin, 1996).

2. Joy G. Dryfoos, *Full-Service Schools: A Revolution in Health and So-*

cial Services for Children, Youth, and Families (San Francisco: Jossey-Bass, 1998).

3. Today, the unique partnership among NLC, the 49 state municipal leagues, and the elected leaders of the 1,700 member cities and 18,000 state league cities provides a powerful network for information sharing and for speaking on behalf of America's cities in Washington, D.C., and all state capitals. The NLC staff is organized into an executive office that oversees organizational operations, five centers that provide services to members, and six offices that provide internal administrative support and special programming. The Institute for Youth, Education, and Families was established early in 2000 as a special entity within NLC to help municipal leaders take action on behalf of the children, youth, and families in their communities. Responsive to municipal officials on a wide range of issues, the institute focuses on five core program areas: education, youth development, child care and early childhood development, the safety of children and youth, and family economic security.

4. Adam Smith, *An Inquiry into the Nature and Causes of the Wealth of Nations*, ed. Edwin Cannan (London: Methuen, 1904) (retrieved from http://www.econlib.org/library/Smith/smWN1.html).

Bibliography

American Institute on Domestic Violence. "The Corporate Costs of Domestic Violence." 2001. (Retrieved from http://www.aidv-usa.com/Statistics.htm.)

Barnett, Steven W. "Long-Term Effects of Early Childhood Programs on Cognitive and School Outcomes." *Future of Children* 5:3 (winter 1995): 25–50. (PDF, pp. 25–50; retrieved from http://www.futureofchildren.org.)

Borman, Geoffrey D., Gina M. Hewes, Laura T. Overman, and Shelley Brown. "Comprehensive School Reform and Student Achievement: A Meta-Analysis." Center for Research on the Education of Students Placed at Risk (CRESPAR) 59 (November 2002): 1–45. (Retrieved from http://www.csos.jhu.edu.)

Carnegie Council on Adolescent Development. "A Matter of Time: Risk and Opportunity in the Non-School Hours." *Report of the Task Force on Youth Development and Community Programs.* New York: Carnegie Corporation of New York, December 1992, 1–52.

Coalition for Juvenile Justice. "Out of the School House, Into the Jail House." *Juvenile Justice Monitor Online* 5:6 (November-December 2001). (Retrieved from http://www.juvjustice.org/publications/jjmonitor/0001.html.)

Comer, James P. "Black Children and Child Psychiatry." *Journal of American Academy of Child and Adolescent Psychiatry* 24:2 (March 1985): 129–33.

Commission on Children at Risk. *Hardwired to Connect: The New Scientific Case for Authoritative Communities.* New York: Institute of American Values, 2003.

Committee on Increasing High School Students' Engagement and Motivation to Learn, National Research Council and Institute of Medicine of the National Academies. *Engaging Schools: Fostering High School Students' Motivation to Learn.* Washington, D.C.: National Academies Press, 2004.

Committee on Integrating the Science of Early Childhood Development, Board on Children, Youth, and Families of the National Research Council and Institute of Medicine. *Neurons to Neighborhoods: The Science of Early Childhood Development,* ed. Jack P. Shonkoff and Deborah Phillips. Washington, D.C.: National Academies Press, 2000.

Cook, Thomas D., and Robert F. Murphy. "Comer's School Development Program in Chicago: A Theory-Based Evaluation." *American Educational Research Journal* 37:2 (summer 2000): 535–97.

Coy, Peter. "Less Chance to Rise in Life." *Business Week* 3808 (November 18, 2002): 28.

Day, Jennifer Cheeseman, and Eric C. Newburger. "The Big Payoff: Educational Attainment and Synthetic Estimates of Work-Life Earnings." *Current Population Reports.* Washington, D.C.: U.S. Census Bureau, July 2002. Pages 1–13. (PDF, pp. 1–13; retrieved from http://www.census.gov/prod/www/abs/popula.html.)

Election Nexus. "Turnout Rates for Voting-Age Population and Eligible Population." U.S. electoral system maintained by Dr. Michael McDonald, Department of Public and International Affairs, George Mason University, Fairfax, Va. (Retrieved from http://elections.gmu.edu/turnout_rates_graph.htm.)

Employment Policy Foundation. "Building America's Workforce for the Twenty-first Century." Washington, D.C., 2001. Pages 1–58. (PDF, pp. 1–58; retrieved from http://www.epf.org/labor01/index.asp.)

Fight Crime: Invest in Kids. "Investments in Children Prevent Crime and Save Money." (Retrieved from http://www.fightcrime.org.)

Ford, Paul Leicester, ed. *The Writings of Thomas Jefferson,* 10 vols. New York: G. P. Putnam's Sons, 1892–99.

Fromm, Suzette. "Total Estimated Cost of Child Abuse and Neglect in the United States." Prevent Child Abuse America. 2001. (Retrieved from http://www.pcain.org/Services_Programs/cost_analysis.pdf.)

Gainsborough, Jenni, and Marc Mauer. "Diminishing Returns: Crime and Incarceration in the 1990s." Washington, D.C.: The Sentencing Project, September 2000. Pages 1–31. (PDF, pp. 1–31; retrieved from http://www.sentencingproject.org/pdfs/9039.pdf.)

Hardiman, Mariale M. *Connecting Brain Research with Effective Teaching: The Brain-Targeted Teaching Model.* Lanham, Md.: Scarecrow Press, 2003.

Harris, Irving B. *Children in Jeopardy: Can We Break the Cycle of Poverty?* New Haven: Yale University Press, 1996.

Hart, Betty, and Todd R. Risley. "The Early Catastrophe: The 30 Million Word Gap by Age 3." *American Educator* (spring 2003): 4–9.

Healthy People 2010. "People with Low Income." *Healthy People Progress Review* (October 30, 1997). (Retrieved from http://www.healthypeople.gov/Data/PROGRVW/LowIncome/.)

Healy, Jane M. *Your Child's Growing Mind: Brain Development and Learning from Birth to Adolescence.* New York: Broadway Books, 2004.

Hobbs, Frank, and Nicole Stoops. "Demographic Trends in the Twentieth Century." *Census 2000 Special Report* (November 2002): 1–222. (PDF, pp. 1–222; retrieved from http://www.census.gov/prod/2002pubs/censr-4.pdf.)

Hyman, Steven E. "NIMH Fourth Annual Research Roundtable—Opening Remarks on Children and Adolescents." Washington, D.C., June 19, 2000. (Retrieved from http://www.nimh.nih.gov/research/roundtable.cfm.)

Institute for Health Policy, Brandeis University. "Substance Abuse: The Nation's Number One Health Problem." 1993. (Retrieved from http://www.ncadd.org/facts/numberoneprob.html.)

Jenson, Eric. *Teaching with the Brain in Mind.* Alexandria, Va.: Association for Supervision and Curriculum Development, 1998.

Jewkes, Rachel. "Preventing Domestic Violence." *British Medical Journal* 324:7332 (February 2, 2002): 253–54.

Kletzer, Lori G. "Measuring the Costs of Trade-Related Job Loss." Testimony prepared for the Committee on Finance, United States Senate, Washington, D.C., July 20, 2001. (Retrieved from http://www.iie.com/publications/papers/kletzer0701.htm.)

Levine, Peter, and Mark Hugo Lopez. "Youth Voter Turnout Has Declined, by Any Measure." CIRCLE (The Center for Information and Research on Civic Learning and Engagement), School of Public Affairs, University of Maryland, September 2002. Pages 1–11. (PDF, pp. 1–11; retrieved from http://www.civicyouth.org/research/products/fact_sheets_outside.htm.)

Meier, Deborah. "So What Does It Take to Build a School for Democracy?" *Phi Delta Kappan* 85:1 (September 2003): 15–21.

Mezey, Jennifer, Mark Greenberg, and Rachel Schumacher. "The Vast Majority of Federally Eligible Children Did Not Receive Child Care Assistance in FY 2000." Washington, D.C.: Center for Law and Social Policy, October 2, 2002. Pages 1–12. (PDF, pp. 1–12; retrieved from http://www.clasp.org/DMS/Documents/1024427382.81.)

Montgomery, A. F., and R. J. Rossi. "Becoming at Risk of Failure in America's

Schools." *Schools and Students at Risk: Context and Framework for Positive Change.* Robert J. Rossi, ed. New York: Teachers College Press, 1994.

Mortenson Research Seminar on Public Policy Analysis of Opportunity for Postsecondary Education. "Private Correlates of Educational Attainment." March 28, 1999. Pages 1–20. (PDF, pp. 1–20; retrieved from http://www.postsecondary.org/home/default.asp.)

National Center for Educational Statistics. "Enrollment in Educational Institutions, by Level and Control of Institution: Fall 1980 to Fall 2005, Table 2." *Digest of Education Statistics, 2001.* (Retrieved from http://nces.ed.gov//pubs2002/digest2001/list_tables.asp.)

———. "Teachers in Elementary and Secondary Schools, and Senior Instructional Staff in Degree-Granting Institutions, by Control of Institution: Fall 1970 to Fall 2011, Table 4." *Digest of Education Statistics, 2001.* (Retrieved from http://nces.ed.gov//pubs2002/digest2001/list_tables.asp.)

———. "Total Expenditures for Public Elementary and Secondary Education and Other Related Programs, by State: School Year 1999–2000." *Quick Tables and Figures.* (Retrieved from http://nces.ed.gov/quicktables/Detail.asp.)

National Institute for Early Education Research. "Economic Benefits of Quality Preschool Education to America's 3- and 4-year olds." *Fast Facts.* (Retrieved from http://nieer.org/resources/facts/index.php.)

National Institute for Mental Health. "Child and Adolescent Violence Research at the NIMH." Bethesda, Md.: National Institute for Mental Health, April 2000. Pages 1–11. (PDF, pp. 1–11; retrieved from http://www.nimh.nih.gov/publicat/violenceresfact.pdf.)

National Institute on Out-of-School Time. "Making the Case: A Fact Sheet on Children and Youth in Out-of-School Time." Center for Research on Women, Wellesley College, January 2003. Pages 1–6. (PDF, pp. 1–6; retrieved from http://www.niost.org.)

Phillips, Stephen. "Literacy: A Global Problem—Jail Breakers." *New Courier* 2, UNESCO. April 2003. (Retrieved from http://portal.unesco.org/en/ev.php@URL_ID=10552&URL_DO=DO_TOPIC&URL_SECTION=201.html.)

"Prevention Paying Off." Staff editorial, *Burlington (Vt.) Free Press,* June 8, 1996. (Retrieved from http://www.ahs.state.vt.us/608frpre.htm.)

Public/Private Ventures. "A Matter of Money: The Cost and Financing of Youth Development." *Youth Development: Issues, Challenges and Directions.* Philadelphia, Pa., fall 2000. Pages 81–124. (PDF, pp. 81–124; retrieved from http://www.ppv.org/content/publications.html.)

RAND Corporation. "Mental Health Care for Youth: Who Gets It? How

Much Does It Cost? Who Pays? Where Does the Money Go?" *RAND Health Research Highlights*. 2001. (Retrieved from http://www.rand.org/publications/RB/RB4541/.)

Ross, Catherine E., and Chia-Ling Wu. "Education, Age, and the Cumulative Advantage in Health." *Journal of Health and Social Behavior* 37:1 (March 1996): 104–20.

Suchanek, Julie. "Education Not Incarceration Report." Oregon Student Association Board of Directors, Portland, Ore. April 13, 2002. Pages 1–32.

Temporary Assistance for Needy Families. "Introduction and Executive Summary." *2002 TANF Annual Report to Congress*. Pages 1–4. (PDF, pp. 1–4; retrieved from http://www.acf.dhhs.gov/programs/opre/ar2001/indexar.htm.)

U.S. Bureau of the Census. "Historical Living Arrangements of Children." 2001. (Retrieved from http://www.census.gov/population/www/socdemo/hh-fam.html.)

———. "Married Couples by Labor Force Status of Spouses: 1986 to Present." 2001. (Retrieved from http://www.census.gov/population/socdemo/hh-fam/tabMC-1.txt.)

———. "National Health Expenditures-Summary, 1960 to 1999, and Projections, 2000 to 2010." *Statistical Abstract of the United States: 2001*. Pages 89–130. (PDF, pp. 89–130; retrieved from http://www.census.gov/prod/www/statistical-abstract-01.html.)

———. "Preprimary School Enrollment-Summary: 1970 to 2000, No. 218." *Statistical Abstract of the United States: 2002*. Pages 131–78. (PDF, pp. 131–78; retrieved from http://www.census.gov/prod/www/statistical-abstract-02.html.)

U.S. Department of Health and Human Services, Office of Applied Studies. "Illicit Drug Use." *2001 Summary of Findings, National Household Survey on Drug Abuse*. (Retrieved from http://www.samhsa.gov/oas/NHSDA/2kNHSDA/chapter2.htm.)

U.S. Department of Justice. "Federal Prison System—Cost Per Inmate for Fiscal Years 1975 thru 2003." *Budget Trend Data, 1975–2003*. Pages 117–19. (PDF, pp. 117–19; retrieved from http://www.usdoj.gov/jmd/budgetsummary/btd/1975_2002/2002/pdf/page117-19.pdf.)

———. "Prison and Jail Inmates at Midyear 2002." *Bureau of Justice Statistics Bulletin* NCJ 1988877 (April 2003): 1–14. (PDF, pp. 1–14; retrieved from http://www.ojp.usdoj.gov/bjs/abstract/pjim02.htm.)

U.S. Department of Labor, Office of Policy Planning and Research. "The Negro Family: The Case for National Action." March 1965. (Retrieved from http://www.dol.gov/asp/programs/history/webid-meynihan.htm.)

Waldo, Michael. "Also Victims: Understanding and Treating Men Arrested for Spouse Abuse." *Journal of Counseling and Development* 65 (March 1987): 385–88.

Whitfield, Charles L., Robert F. Anda, Shanta R. Dube, and Vincent J. Felitti. "Violent Childhood Experiences and the Risk of Intimate Partner Violence in Adults." *Journal of Interpersonal Violence* 18:2 (February 2003): 166–85.

Index